Approaches to Teaching the Works of Anton Chekhov

Approaches to Teaching World Literature

For a complete listing of titles, see the last pages of this book.

Approaches to Teaching the Works of Anton Chekhov

Edited by

Michael C. Finke

and

Michael Holquist

The Modern Language Association of America

New York 2016

Printed in the United States of America

Library of Congress Cataloging-in-Publication Data
Approaches to teaching the works of Anton P. Chekhov / edited by
Michael C. Finke and Michael Holquist.
pages cm. — (Approaches to teaching world literature ; 141)
Summary: "Offers pedagogical techniques for teaching Anton P. Chekhov's plays and short
stories in the college classroom in relation to creative writing, translation, adaptation,
stage history, film, performance, *Facebook*, postmodernity, and Tennessee Williams.
Includes information on editions, reference works, biographies, and online resources.
Gives syllabus suggestions for undergraduate and graduate courses"—
Provided by publisher. Includes bibliographical references and index.
ISBN 978-1-60329-267-2 (hardback) — ISBN 978-1-60329-268-9 (paper) —
ISBN 978-1-60329-269-6 (EPUB) — ISBN 978-1-60329-267-2 (Kindle)
1. Chekhov, Anton Pavlovich, 1860–1904—Study and teaching. 2. Chekhov, Anton Pavlovich,
1860–1904—Criticism and interpretation. I. Finke, Michael C., 1957– editor.
II. Holquist, Michael, 1935– editor.
PG3458.Z8A67 2016
891.72'3—dc23 2015033662

Approaches to Teaching World Literature 141
ISSN 1059-1133

Cover illustration of the paperback edition: Nikolay Petrovich Bogdanov-Belsky, *Sunday Reading at Country School*, c. 1895. Oil on canvas. State Russian Museum, St. Petersburg

Published by The Modern Language Association of America
85 Broad Street, 5th floor, New York, NY 10004-2408
www.mla.org

CONTENTS

A NOTE ON TRANSLITERATION, CITATIONS, AND DATES

Scholars writing in American English about Russian literature and culture must choose, or find a compromise, among several standard transliteration options. The situation can become very complicated when you cite sources from languages other than English or Russian or when you use materials where no consistent transliteration method has been employed. Add to this the fundamental difference between approaching transliterated Russian names and terms with a knowledge of the language and without it: for those who do not know Russian, transliterated terms are often no easier to pronounce than the Cyrillic original.

Also, until the Russian Revolution, the Julian calendar was in use in Russia. It lagged our Gregorian calendar by twelve days in the nineteenth century and by thirteen days in the twentieth.

In order to make sure that none of our readers will be misdirected or confused, we have adopted the following conventions in this volume:

All dates will be Old Style, per the Julian calendar, unless otherwise indicated. This usage follows the standard practice in Russian scholarship.

When Russian text is cited or a Russian term discussed, especially where the sound shape or etymology of the original is relevant, we provide the Cyrillic; transliteration using J. Thomas Shaw's system 2, which in essence is the Library of Congress method minus diacritics; and an English translation. Note that in the transliteration, the Russian soft sign (ь), in the middle or at the end of a word, is transliterated as ', not as ’. Although we follow Shaw's system 2, common place-names and names of persons are rendered in ways conventional, familiar, and pronounceable for English-speaking readers. Citations always respect the originals from which they are taken. Therefore there will be inconsistencies in spelling: it is "Chekhov" as a rule, but "Chekov," "Tchekoff," "Tchekhov," "Čehov," and "Čexov" may also occur.

When a Russian work is named in Russian, we provide the title in this format: transliteration (Cyrillic; "translation"). When the title is in italics, both transliteration and Cyrillic are italicized. In parenthetical references, only the transliteration is given.

All references to Chekhov's Russian originals are keyed to the thirty-volume scholarly edition *Polnoe sobranie sochinenii i pisem* (*Полное собрание сочинений и писем*; "Complete Collection of Works and Letters"). In the parenthetical references, *Sochineniia* refers to the eighteen volumes of his works, and *Pis'ma* refers to the twelve volumes of his letters.

Citations from Chekhov's letters may be keyed to the scholarly edition or, if from a translated source, to that source. The date (unless there is no date) and addressee of the letter will be provided in every case, so as to facilitate the letter's location by all users of this volume.

Because translators vary in their renderings of Chekhov's titles, we have appended a concordance of titles.

Because Chekhov has been so widely translated over the past century, and because an instructor's choice of translation will vary in accordance with pedagogic purposes—which may also involve comparing translations, as some of our author-teachers advocate—we could not insist that all contributors to this volume employ the same sources.

Part One

MATERIALS

A daunting array of choices faces instructors teaching Chekhov in English. New renderings of his texts, including the letters and other nonfictional writings, continue to see publication, old and out-of-copyright translations abound in cheap print editions or can be read free on the Internet, and there is an ever-growing list of titles in visual media: filmed theater productions of his plays, adaptations of the plays and stories scripted for film, and amateur performances—especially of the one-act plays—that can be found on such venues as *YouTube*. Biographical approaches to Chekhov vary dramatically, with significant revisions to prior understandings gaining wide acceptance in the past twenty-five years. Meanwhile the unsophisticated researcher is vulnerable to discredited, misinformed, and factually incorrect material that remains on library shelves or, more likely, appears high on the list of Internet search results. Like most great authors, Chekhov has attracted many nonacademic commentators, biographers, and critics who, even when they are insightful, lack the language skills and research training and discipline to make their publications reliable sources. (A recent example of this unreliability is the program notes published with the BBC Video *Anton Chekhov Collection*, which have Chekhov writing *Cherry Orchard* "on the *island* of Yalta" [Program Notes].)

Instructors will want to make deliberate choices and also convey the rationale behind them—this can be a teaching moment. It has become extremely difficult to ensure that all participants in a classroom are working with identical materials or, for that matter, platforms for reading them. A strategic choice must be made: either one insists on the use of one text by all, so that all will be quite literally on the same page in a lesson in close reading, or the instructor exploits differences among the translations in use or between a translation and the original. In my courses there is always a heritage or native speaker or two who prefer to read in the original and who can often help foreground questions of translation in class discussion. (Caution is advised, however: heritage speakers may have limited linguistic skills.)[1]

What follows are selective recommendations rather than a comprehensive overview, and these recommendations are not always followed by the volume's various contributors. The editors could not insist that all the college and university instructors writing about their teaching of Chekhov refer to the same translations of his works. Chekhov has been very widely translated, but no single translator has translated his entire oeuvre. Some titles are quite difficult to find in good translations; others have been repeatedly translated, sometimes very well. The range of works treated here—though still a small percentage of Chekhov's total output—is broad, and the volume's contributions represent quite varying pedagogic missions. Readers should not be surprised to find, expressed in this volume, preferences that do not match the editors' own.

Chekhov's Biography: Outline, Useful Resources, and Notes on Biography as an Object of Study

Anton Chekhov was born on 17 January 1860 in the city of Taganrog, the third son of Pavel and Evgeniia Chekhov. His paternal grandfather had been a serf who bought his family's freedom when Chekhov's father was a teenager and managed a large estate; eventually he set Chekhov's father up as the owner of a small general store in the then prosperous port city of Taganrog, where Chekhov and his older brothers worked long hours as schoolchildren. A petty tyrant who enforced a rote and pedantic religiosity on his children, Chekhov's father went bankrupt and fled to Moscow in order to escape debtors' prison. Soon the rest of the family joined him there, except for Chekhov and one of his two younger brothers, Ivan, who continued their secondary education in Taganrog. Ivan lived with relatives while Chekhov was left to fend for himself as a tutor and boarder in what had been his family home. In spring 1877, he began sending some of his earnings to his parents and siblings, thus initiating a lifelong pattern of assuming responsibility for them.

In 1879, Chekhov enrolled in the faculty of medicine at Moscow University with a town scholarship from Taganrog. January 1880 saw his first known publication: "A Letter from the Don Landowner Stepan Vladimirovich N. to His Learned Neighbor Dr. Fridrikh" ("Письмо донского помещика Степана Владимировича N к ученому соседу д-ру Фридриху"; "Pis'mo donskogo pomeshchika Stepan Vladimirovich N k uchenomu sosedu d-ru Fridrikhu"), under the signature ". . . v" (*Sochineniia* 1: 11–16). Soon he was pseudonymously publishing anecdotes, stylized letters, dialogues, spoofs on popular authors, and cartoon captions, in the journal *Dragonfly* (*Стрекоза*; *Strekoza*) and other journals of the so-called small press.

In 1882, Chekhov was invited to publish in the St. Petersburg humor magazine *Fragments* (*Осколки*; *Oskolki*). Some stories from 1883 are generally recognized as comic masterpieces, such as "Death of a Clerk" ("Смерть чиновника"; "Smert' chinovnika"), "Daughter of Albion" ("Дочь Албиона"; "Doch' Albiona"), "Fat and Thin" ("Толстый и тонкий"; "Tolstyi i tonkii").

In 1885, Chekhov began publishing in *Petersburg Gazette* (*Петербургскаиа газета*; *Peterburgskaia gazeta*), and he soon progressed to even more profitable and culturally weighty venues, in particular with the February 1886 publication of "Requiem" ("Панихида"; "Panikhida") in *New Times* (*Новое время*; *Novoe vremia*). Whereas, with few exceptions, he had previously published only pseudonymously, he used his own name to sign "Requiem," a practice that soon became his norm.

Chekhov's 1887 trip to his home town and the southern landscapes of his childhood provided material for "The Steppe" ("Степь"; "Step'"), his first serious long narrative, which was published in a prestigious "thick journal" in 1888. In fall 1887, Chekhov began his career as a playwright of note with the quickly written *Ivanov* (*Иванов*), staged in the Korsh Theater in Moscow. The play was subsequently revised and staged in St. Petersburg (1889) with spectacular success. In October 1888 Chekhov was awarded the Pushkin Prize by the Division of Russian Language and Letters of the Imperial Academy of Sciences for his volume of stories *In the Twilight* (*В сумерках*; *V sumerkakh*).

In spring 1889, Chekhov cared for his older brother, Nikolai, who was dying of typhoid fever, tuberculosis, and alcoholism. At the same time, Chekhov was writing his next major play, *Wood Demon* (*Леший*; *Leshii*), which would be revised as *Uncle Vanya* (*Дядя Ваня*; *Diadia Vania*). After Nikolai's death, Chekhov wrote the bleak "Boring Story" ("Скучная история"; "Skuchnaia istoriia") and started contemplating a journey to the far eastern prison island of Sakhalin. He left Moscow for Sakhalin in April 1890 and returned in December; the round trip, which preceded the construction of the Trans-Siberian Railway and included truly perilous moments, covered roughly ten thousand miles. The study of the prison colony that he published afterward, *Sakhalin Island* (*Остров Сахалин*; *Ostrov Sakhalin*)—an idiosyncratic mix of travel writing, geography, agronomy, and medical sociology, perhaps best categorized as a work of medical geography (Valencius, "Chekhov's *Sakhalin Island*")—had a major influence on penology in Russia.

In February 1892, Chekhov bought a somewhat dilapidated, 575-acre estate south of Moscow and moved there with his extended family. That summer he served as an unpaid public health physician and took on very tiring duties in combating a cholera epidemic. He loved gardening and had a long-range perspective on improving the lives and the lands around him—he had planted trees at the little hospital in Voskresensk during a short stint there, regularly treated area peasants for free at his home, established and equipped school libraries, and built three schools and a church (see the essay in this volume by Jane Costlow on Chekhov's environmentalist sensibilities).

In fall 1895, Chekhov wrote *The Seagull* (*Чайка*; *Chaika*). The St. Petersburg premiere of that play in October 1896 became one of the most famous fiascos in Russian theatrical history (see the essay in this volume by Olga Levitan). Fortunately, Chekhov did not keep his oath to never again write for the theater. *Seagull* would succeed sensationally when handled by the new Moscow Art Theater of Vladimir Nemirovich-Danchenko and Konstantin Stanislavsky in late 1898. It was the first of what are commonly considered Chekhov's four mature dramatic masterpieces, followed by *Uncle Vanya* (1898), *The Three Sisters* (*Три сестры*; *Tri sestry* [1901]), and *The Cherry Orchard* (*Вишнёвыи сад*; *Vishnevyi sad* [1904]).

With the controversial story "Peasants" ("Мужики"; "Muzhiki"), Chekhov felt he had exhausted the literary value of his life as a landowner; moreover, just a few days after finishing the story, in March 1897, he suffered a major lung hemorrhage, and his life would have to change. His first bout of blood spitting dated back to 1884, but he had since avoided medical care and denied his illness. Now he became something of an invalid, traveling for stays in supposedly therapeutic locations and eventually settling in Yalta.

In January 1899, Chekhov signed an unfavorable contract with the publisher Adolf Marks that provided a lump-sum payment in exchange for the rights to all writings, past and future, which were to be published in a full collection of his works. His production of new works, which had slowed because of illness, declined further as he gathered, reread, and edited (or in some cases rejected) for republication everything he had published since the start of his career.

Chekhov's work with the Moscow Art Theater introduced him to Olga Knipper, an actress with whom he became close in 1899 and would marry in 1901. At the beginning of 1900, he was selected as a member of the Imperial Academy of Sciences, Division of Russian Language and Literature, but in 1902 he resigned from the academy to protest the annulment of Maxim Gorky's selection for political reasons. In his last years Chekhov was something of a patron and adviser to Gorky, as well as to other young and aspiring authors.

Chekhov's health continued to deteriorate. Although Chekhov had been wintering in the south and in the warmer months visiting Moscow primarily but also Petersburg and other places, his Moscow specialist advised him to spend the winter of 1903–04 in Moscow. There Chekhov attended the premiere of *Cherry Orchard*, during which the theater organized a celebration of his twenty-five years of literary activity. In February 1904, he left for Yalta; he returned to Moscow in May quite ill and was ordered abroad for his health. He departed Russia in early June, settling in the Black Forest resort town of Badenweiler. Whereas in April he had talked about traveling to the Far East to volunteer as a physician in Russia's conflict with Japan, on the eve of his departure to the West he reportedly stated to a friend that he was leaving Russia to die. In the early morning hours of 2 July 1904, a physician was summoned to his room. When the doctor ordered a glass of champagne for the patient, Chekhov famously uttered, in German, "Ich sterbe . . ." ("I am dying"). His last conscious words were "It's a long time since I drank champagne," and he died at three a.m. The return of his corpse for burial in Moscow involved incongruities often remarked in his biographies, because they are so reminiscent of his humor: his body arrived in a refrigerated railroad car labeled "For Fresh Oysters," and his funeral procession was confused with that of a general being buried at the same time.

It will be the rare undergraduate course that can afford to make space for and expect students to actually read, from cover to cover, one of the interesting and reliable biographies of Chekhov available in English. But instructors may wish to assign sections of a biography that pertain to what is being read, screened, viewed, or staged and biographies might be placed on reserve for reference or ordered as optional. Donald Rayfield's revisionary 1997 *Anton Chekhov: A Life* best immerses us in Chekhov's personal life and is available in an affordable paperback edition, but it is probably too long to be read in most undergraduate courses. Ronald Hingley's shorter *A New Life of Anton Chekhov* (1976) includes a useful appendix outlining Chekhov's publishing career, but it suffers from lack of access to the full spectrum of materials that became available to Rayfield and, in my view, from opinionated, unreliable assessments of many of Chekhov's works. Ernest Simmons's lengthy but out-of-print *Chekhov: A Biography* (1962) still serves. Very fine insights into Chekhov the person, and the opportunity to work with the epistolary genre that he practiced abundantly and artfully, are available through the selection of his letters translated by Michael Henry Heim and commented on by Simon Karlinsky in *Anton Chekhov's Life and Thought* (1973), which is still in print. Last, there are translations of some of the memoirs of Chekhov's friends, family, and colleagues, of which instructors should be cognizant. A few examples that are still in print are *Anton Chekhov and His Times*, compiled by Andrei Turkov, which includes reminiscences and some of Chekhov's letters; Ivan Bunin's unfinished memoir, translated by Thomas Marullo; and the memoir of Chekhov's brother Mikhail, *Vokrug Chekhova* (*Вокруг Чехова*; "Around Chekhov"), translated by Eugene Alper under the title *Anton Chekhov: A Brother's Memoir*. (Others are available in old and long-out-of-print translations.) Courses with a focus on the late Chekhov, and especially those involving the plays performed by the Moscow Art Theater, may be interested enough in the actress who became his wife to look at the letters, as translated and edited by Jean Benedetti (*Dear Writer*), or the biography of her by Harvey Pitcher (*Chekhov's Leading Lady*).

For most users of this volume, the best way of incorporating Chekhov's biography in an undergraduate course may be to have students read an encyclopedia article, such as my own in *Dictionary of Literary Biography* ("Anton Pavlovich Chekhov").[2]

To find visual images of the author and his places, friends, and family, instructor and student alike will naturally turn to the Internet, but there are some high-quality print sources—in particular, the volume of photographs put together by Peter Urban, *Anton Čechov: Sein Leben in Bildern* ("His Life in Pictures"). The Russian *A. P. Chekhov: Dokumenty: Fotografii* (*А. П. Чехов: Документы: Фотографии*; "Anton Chekhov: Documents: Photographs") has an appendix tabulating and identifying the photographs in English.

Caution is always in order when it comes to the study of Chekhov's biography. Chekhov strove to keep himself out of his works, and he advised others to restrain or eliminate subjectivity in what they wrote. He famously professed to having the "malady called autobiographophobia" (*Anton Chekhov's Life* 366 [to Grigorii Rossolimo, 11 Oct. 1899]), and memoirists tell many anecdotes demonstrating his discomfort with his fame. We might do well to introduce for class discussion Janet Malcolm's warning:

> Chekhov's privacy is safe from the biographer's attempt upon it—as, indeed, are all privacies, even those of the most apparently open and even exhibitionistic natures. The letters and journals we leave behind and the impressions we have made on our contemporaries are the mere husk of

> the kernel of our essential life. When we die, the kernel is buried with us. This is the horror and the pity of death and the reason for the inescapable triviality of biography. (35–36)

Undergraduate courses involving Chekhov are unlikely to gather enough of the husk to appreciate even the external shape of the seed.

Nevertheless, this does not mean that Chekhov's life is irrelevant to his work; on the contrary, establishing that relevance is one of the most open and interesting areas of study today, and over the past few decades scholars have been excavating—not without controversy and dispute—what might be called a lyrical or expressivist dimension to his work.[3] While this project requires nuance beyond what can be expected in the undergraduate classroom, it makes no sense to militantly exclude biography from the classroom.

Most of our students expect that what they read will help them make sense of their own lives, and they are invariably interested in the person of the author. Although users of this volume are unlikely to take a systematic approach to Chekhov's biography in their classes, why not use those aspects of the biography that tend to capture the imagination of students and other readers and offer a pathway toward a broader understanding of Chekhov's social and historical context? Instructors will no doubt be pained at times by the reductive and narrowly informed interpretations of Chekhov's works that result from attempting to incorporate such facts; but this may be where the thinking process needs to start. Indeed, generating interest in and some knowledge of this larger picture—or better, these larger pictures—has value in and of itself. In any case, virtually anybody teaching Chekhov will want to offer some sort of narrative about the author's life and career and the place and time of his living and writing.

There have been four dominant ways of periodizing Chekhov's career, with Chekhov scholars often combining them in their approaches. The first, which tends to be most graspable for undergraduate students who are reading a significant body of work, involves indentifying shifting thematic dominants, which are often understood as reflecting key turning points in Chekhov's personal and professional life. A good example of this methodology may be found in Thomas Winner, *Chekhov and His Prose*, which tells an evolutionary story, each stage of it identified by a grouping of literary works with common themes and, to a certain extent, formal features. The second way of periodizing involves following the development of Chekhov's narrative technique, often with rhetoric that frames this process as progressive. The benchmark study of this sort is Aleksander Chudakov's enormously influential *Chekhov's Poetics*, which traces dominant tendencies and patterns of change in Chekhov's handling of narrative point of view and voice (among other features); the study's theoretical idiom may be a bit challenging for most undergraduates. The other two sound rather empirical but can lead to very interesting results. One involves considering where and how much Chekhov published; this is very nicely tabulated in an appendix to Hingley's biography. The last periodizes Chekhov's career on the basis of where he lived. Rosamund Bartlett's recent *Chekhov: Scenes from a Life* accesses Chekhov and his works through visiting Chekhov's places, as does Malcolm's less comprehensive but insightful *Reading Chekhov*.

What are the moments in Chekhov's biography that might help illuminate his texts in an undergraduate classroom? One can hardly mention his birth year of 1860 or explain his social background—quite different from that of the great figures of Russian literature who preceded him—without discussing the 1861 emancipation of serfs in Russia. This and the other so-called great reforms that took place in this period led to the further breakdown of traditional class boundaries and expectations and to the expansion of the professional classes (including the medical) that feature so centrally in Chekhov's oeuvre. Instructors must be selective—especially if they are unfamiliar with Russian history—but one should certainly introduce students to the institution of the zemstvo (a rural district council, the organ of local government in the countryside), which Chekhov would serve as a physician. And of course serfdom was the heritage of his family: his grandfather Yegor bought their independence when Chekhov's father was in his teens (1841). How this story resonates with students will vary, depending on where one teaches and the student population one serves, but in public institutions especially there are likely to be first-generation college students who will find it inspiring. In the wake of the recent housing bubble and wave of home foreclosures in the United States, the story of the bankruptcy of Chekhov's shopkeeper father in 1876, the loss of the Chekhov home, the family's struggles to begin anew in Moscow, and Chekhov's years alone in Taganrog while finishing gymnasium will also resonate with students. One might make available a map and perhaps some photographs: the geographic setting of Chekhov's childhood, including sea, steppe, Scythian burial mounds, and a multilingual, cosmopolitan population (to which Chekhov returned for artistic inspiration at key points in his writing career) can be difficult for both students and instructors to imagine without such visual aids.

What drew Chekhov into a medical career—the faith in science and social progress that prompted such a choice in the second half of the nineteenth century in Russia, the ideal of service despite poor remuneration—takes some explication for our students, whose notion of a doctor's life tends to be quite different. I also emphasize Chekhov's sheer capacity for work, demonstrated by his hardscrabble rise in the literary sphere while studying and then commencing the practice of medicine. His first known publications date from 1880. He began in the small press, a venue I liken, anachronistically, to a hybrid between *Reader's Digest* and *Mad Magazine*. The reading public these publications targeted was the newly literate lower and lower-middle urban classes: workers, clerks, sales assistants, and so on. Chekhov was proud of the trail he blazed for other aspiring writers of low provenance with his rise from a trivial and forgettable scribbler, appearing in lowbrow serials under pseudonyms, to an author whose works were sought by the most prestigious journals and book publishers and performed in leading theaters. He reflected on the social and psychological dimensions of this path, the difficult process by which one "squeezes the slave's blood out of himself" ("выдавливает из себя по каплям раба") to attain self-respect and independence as a man and an author, in a famous letter to Aleksei Suvorin (*Pis'ma* 3: 133 [7 Jan. 1889]).

Chekhov's dual professional identity as physician and author—his chasing of two hares, or living alternately with wife and mistress, as he put it many times (e.g., *Pis'ma* 2: 326 [to Suvorin, 11 Sept. 1888)—has been a favorite topic of the doctor-authors who continually publish on and with Chekhov. The medical stories have been grouped together for readers with this orientation in *Chekhov's Doctors*. The culmination of Chekhov's career as a doctor-author is certainly *Sakhalin Island*, his lengthy sociological and environmental study of the prison colony off the east coast of Siberia, to which Chekhov made the hard journey in 1890. For undergraduates, this work is probably not readable in its entirety, except perhaps in an advanced course focused on Siberia, exile and imprisonment, or the history of medicine. But the book, which does have some remarkable literary aspects, was preceded by a series of very engaging travel sketches that Chekhov largely wrote en route to Sakhalin, commonly published together with *Sakhalin Island* under the title "Across Siberia." These might be paired with a select chapter or two (in particular, the first and/or the last) of *Sakhalin Island*. Introducing excerpts from *Sakhalin Island* and the travel sketches facilitates discussion of distinctions between documentary literature and fiction. The essay in this volume by Conevery Valencius offers further recommendations on teaching *Sakhalin Island*.

The Sakhalin book and travel sketches are almost the only instances where Chekhov published under his own name a work in which his self—and at times an opinionated self—appears in his text. The author's textual presence is connected, of course, to the question of his use of pseudonyms. In the early years, he explained this strategy as motivated by a wish to reserve his family name for the research publications he anticipated in his "real" career in medicine. There were quite practical reasons for using pseudonyms as well, however: it was common practice in the "small press"; any author with ambition to be recognized as serious and publish in weightier venues risked embarrassment by freshman publications; and in the early period, Chekhov was subject to pressures from his publishers to reserve himself, as defined by a particular pseudonym, for their respective venues.

By early 1886, however, Chekhov had become quite visible. His first trip to St. Petersburg, in late 1885, involved meeting the capital's literary elites, who—to his great surprise—were aware of his writing. When he began appearing in Suvorin's *New Times* in 1886, with the story "The Requiem," he did so under his real name.[4] The story's theme of a famous but disowned and now deceased daughter, who had pursued a life in art that her father viewed as shameful, is not irrelevant to the question of publishing under one's true family name. Not long after "The Requiem" appeared, Chekhov received a letter from an eminent figure of Dostoevsky's generation, Dmitry Grigorovich, praising his talent and urging him to take it seriously: Chekhov ought to deal with weighty subject matter and avoid appealing to low tastes, tackle the novel form, and sign his works with his true name (*Pis'ma* 1: 427–28 [25 Mar. 1886]).

These moments typically comprise a key turning point in Chekhov's literary career. In *Anton Chekhov's Life and Thought*, for instance, they are treated in a chapter titled "Serious Literature." Correspondingly, much of Chekhov's work that was published prior to this period has been dismissed over the years as trivial and unworthy of careful translation or scholarly attention. By contrast, the 1888 publication of the lengthy story (or in Russian, повесть [povest']) "The Steppe" in the highbrow *Northern Herald* (*Северный вестник*; *Severnyi vestnik*) in 1888 is universally recognized as yet another important step forward for Chekhov, though the story has been relatively rarely translated and, for the most part, poorly translated. Even the fine translation of this rich, poetic, and unconventional work by Richard Pevear and Larissa Volokhonsky proves challenging to teach in an undergraduate course. Still, any course conducted with an eye to Chekhov's biography should include "The Requiem" and "Steppe."

The early 1892 purchase of Melikhovo, an estate about fifty miles south of Moscow, changed Chekhov's life and left echoes in his writings. In the summer of 1892, Chekhov signed on with the Serpukhov District, where the estate was located, as an unpaid zemstvo doctor and dedicated himself to battling the cholera epidemic threatening the area; he did the same the following summer and, while living there, regularly received local peasants for free medical care. His fiction inspired by life in the country culminates with the 1897 "Peasants," a story distinguished by its unromantic portrait of the rural underclass, very much at variance with the idealized peasants of Tolstoy and Dostoevsky.

Two turning points of a different sort in Chekhov's life were the death of his brother Nikolai, in 1889, and the resounding declaration of his own grave, tubercular condition with a massive hemorrhage in 1897, after which Chekhov became something of an invalid. Nikolai had been an immensely talented artist with whom Chekhov had collaborated in some early works (cartoons); but he was also highly irregular and unreliable, addicted to alcohol and opiates, and he also had tuberculosis. As Chekhov's career took off and Chekhov had opportunities to help his siblings, he tried to further Nikolai's career, but his efforts led to frustration. In the end it fell to him to collect his deathly ill brother from a flophouse when summoned and care for him in his final months, though Chekhov happened to be absent for a brief vacation when Nikolai actually died. Chekhov himself had suffered periodic bouts of blood spitting since 1884, the year he graduated from the Medical Faculty of Moscow University, but he avoided examination or treatment until the 1897 crisis (see Finke, "Heal Thyself"). He spent the winter of 1897–98 in Nice and the next winter in the Crimea. Soon he had bought property and was building a new home on the outskirts of Yalta; Melikhovo would be sold. "A Boring Story" (1889) is generally paired with the death of Nikolai; the odd and underappreciated "Story of an Unknown Man" (1895; "Рассказ неизвестного человека"; "Rasskaz neizvestnogo cheloveka"), while preceding Chekhov's 1897 health crisis, may be profitably linked with Chekhov's health crisis two years later. Among later works, "The Bishop" (1902; "Архиерей"; "Arkhierei"), one of Chekhov's last published stories, juxtaposes the sacred story of Passion Week with a high church man's illness and death and treats death as a kind of liberation from an alienating public role; and Chekhov's last play, *Cherry Orchard*, finished just half a year before his death, is suffused with the sense of an ending (it has been called his "last testament").[5] "The Lady with the Little Dog" (1899; "Дама с собачкой"; "Dama s sobachkoi") reflects something of his life in Yalta, which he likened to exile and which cannot have been beneficial to his health despite the therapeutic motivation for moving there: the "white dacha" that he built turned out to be difficult to heat properly, and neither his mother, who lived there with him, nor the family's cook saw to an appropriate diet for him. ("The Lady with the Little Dog" has been traditionally associated, too, with Chekhov's growing intimacy with Knipper, though his first notes toward the story precede that romance.)

Chekhov in Translation

Chekhov has long been considered one of the easier Russian classics to translate into English. D. S. Mirsky went so far as to claim that Chekhov "had no feeling for words," which "makes [him] (except for topical allusions, technical terms, and occasional catchwords) so easy to translate. Of all Russian writers, he has the least to fear from the treachery of translators" (262). Some validation for those who agree with this position may be found in the fact that Chekhov's stories are often read in low-intermediate courses of Russian; nevertheless, Mirsky's would have to be characterized as a minority position. Instructors interested in a wide-ranging and nuanced view of the matter from the perspective of both practicing translators and scholars should read the sections on translating Chekhov's prose and drama in *Chekhov the Immigrant* (29–100), where Richard Pevear in particular disputes Mirsky's judgment (33–34).

Indeed, there are subtleties in Chekhov's wielding of the language that, if missed or dismissed by a translator, can significantly impoverish the understanding of readers. Mirsky himself speaks of Chekhov's "lyrical art" (374) and a musical principle in the "architectural unity" of his prose (378–79), which is related, surely, to the importance Pevear and Volokhonsky attribute to consciously rendering the "rhythm" of Chekhov's prose (*Chekhov the Immigrant* 38). Chekhov scholarship of the past twenty-five years or so has dramatically increased our understanding of how much of the action in a Chekhov text takes place at the lexical level and in the handling of grammatical categories for which English has no direct analogues (such as verbal aspect).[6] Restraint in vocabulary, coupled with a high rate of exact or inexact lexical repetitions—both within a given work and across Chekhov's oeuvre, as convincingly argued by Savely Senderovich ("Towards Chekhov's Deeper Reaches") and Laurence Senelick ("Seeing Chekhov Whole")—create symbolic undercurrents and can reveal deeper planes of meaning in Chekhov's texts. So too can ambiguity and the use of ellipsis; what Chekhov leaves out, the spaces in between, constitutes a distinctively Chekhovian interpretive task. In Jakobsonian terms, we might speak of a poetic function to his prose, which translation tends to short-circuit. A translator who "corrects" Chekhov's "excessive" repetitions inhibits access to this dimension of his work.[7] And then there is the question of cultural competence. The contributions of Carol Apollonio and of Brian Baer and Maia Solovieva in this volume offer ways of teaching what might be at stake in translation for students without access to the original.

The most complete sources of Chekhov's texts in English suffer from these and other faults. The translations of Constance Garnett, who produced thirteen volumes of Chekhov's stories between 1916 and 1922, remain widely available in cheap editions or are free online because they are out of copyright. Many readers value them to this day, despite their Victorian idiom, which radically alters Chekhov's sentence structure and does not attend to his lexical subtleties.[8] There may be pragmatic reasons for using Garnett, but when doing so, one should be aware of what one is missing, of what has been added, and of the fact that Garnett published the stories without any regard to the order in which they were written and appeared.

Between 1965 and 1975, Oxford University Press published nine volumes of Chekhov's collected works, translated and annotated by Hingley (*Oxford Chekhov*), in an effort approximating the scholarly editions published by Soviet and post-Soviet academia. Perhaps the most scholarly and knowledgeable translator of Chekhov, Hingley was in some respects one of the least faithful. Senelick rebukes his "decision whenever possible not to follow Chekhov's sentence structures or word order, and to rely on English clichés and catchphrases when confronted with particularly flavorsome Russian idioms. He made no effort to preserve the careful repetition of words, let alone the rhythms, in Chekhov's later writing" ("Seeing" 71). Nevertheless, this annotated collection can be a good supplementary resource (though it neglects many early works by Chekhov).

Among collections of Chekhov's prose still in print, I find most reliable the two volumes of the translating team Pevear and Volokhonsky (Chekhov, *Complete Short Novels* and *Selected Stories of Anton Chekhov*), and those of Ann Dunnigan, also in two volumes (*Selected Stories* and "*Ward Six*"). Both are faithful to Chekhov's lexical choices, and Pevear and Volokhonsky are particularly attentive to his sentence structure, which does, however, lead some critics to remark on the occasional strangeness of their English. The Pevear and Volokhonsky volumes have helpful footnotes—perhaps not as many as one might like, but quite a concession from a trade publisher nonetheless; Dunnigan's do not. Dunnigan has more of the early stories—there are only a few in Pevear and

Volokhonsky. The best two sources for the early stories are the volume of translations by Patrick Miles and Pitcher (*Early Stories*) and the volume by Peter Constantine (*Undiscovered Chekhov*). Constantine offers Chekhov's very earliest publications, which can be of interest in monograph courses on Chekhov or perhaps in the discussion of verbal humor generally speaking. Both take some liberties with Chekhov's language, which, however, tends not to be so complex as that of his mature work.

Another source has become available recently: a new Norton Critical Edition of Chekhov's prose, edited by Cathy Popkin (*Anton Chekhov's Selected Stories*). Popkin consulted extensively with colleagues in choosing the stories for her volume, a lineup that covers the full range of Chekhov's publishing career. She paid a great deal of attention to translation, choosing the best available ones regardless of cost, commissioning new ones where no satisfactory variant was available, and extensively revising the Garnett translations she did use. In addition to offering a biographical essay, excerpts from letters, and a valuable selection of critical interpretations, the volume makes translation itself a theme for discussion, flagging particularly difficult passages or remarkably successful renderings and at times juxtaposing multiple translations of a single passage. Instructors may find this edition the single most useful book to order for courses treating Chekhov's fiction in English translation.

Selecting translations of Chekhov's plays is more difficult. With constant, market-driven demand for new and distinctive translations and adaptations for performance, there are a lot of them in print. Moreover, Chekhov's plays are often adapted by "English-language playwrights with little or no knowledge of Russian and Russian culture," who rework previous translations into idioms comfortable for the contemporary Anglo-American stage (Carnicke 89). Instructors must therefore have their goals firmly in mind in selecting a translation. Are Chekhov's dramatic works being read with an eye toward performance, or is the focus entirely on the text? Is studying the Chekhov play meant to provide access to turn-of-the-century Russian cultural and historical knowledge, or will an Americanized (or a Mametized or Stoppardized) version of Chekhov be just fine? While one of the distinguishing features of Chekhov's plays in the original is how remarkably well they work either for performance or for reading, a translator-interpreter tends to be oriented toward one or the other mode. And the hyphenation "Anglo-American" signals another distinction to consider, as did Paul Schmidt, with his determined effort to render Chekhov's plays in an American idiom (see Kirsch).

Heim's translations of the major plays were done for the stage and in collaboration with directors and actors; he found that he needed to hear his work uttered on the stage in early rehearsals to determine their speakability and finalize his text (84, 87). Perhaps because he was both a respected scholar and a professional translator with wide involvement in theatrical productions, his versions are faithful enough to Chekhov's text to serve courses where the approach involves close textual interpretation as well, and they also include helpful, if limited, annotations. The same may be said of the translations published by Sharon Carnicke, a leading expert on Stanislavsky and the Moscow Art Theater (Chekhov, *Four Plays*). Dunnigan's lexically reliable renderings of Chekhov's text have no such scholarly apparatus and serve the reader better than the actor (*Major Plays*); thus, Anna Pileggi used Dunnigan in staging *Seagull* at Washington University in the fall of 1994 but has since become a devotee of David Mamet's adaptations (see Pileggi's essay in this volume). Mamet's language may well define what American actors and audiences expect on stage, and he seems to be favored by those without Russian; while he cannot claim lexical fidelity to Chekhov's text, the more interesting question is how orientation toward page or stage conditions successful translation. Thus Senelick, the top American scholar on Chekhov's theater, who is also expert in Russian, determined that in order to publish translations of Chekhov's plays for the stage he would have to significantly redo the translations he had made for his Norton edition of Chekhov (*Complete Plays*), which is a volume designed for textual interpretation in the college classroom (Heim 83).

The recommendations of this volume's editors thus vary depending on a course's mission. In my own courses, slanted toward the prose and focused on textual interpretation, I generally order Heim's *The Essential Plays*; but I can also recommend Dunnigan's *The Major Plays* and Carnicke's *Four Plays and Three Jokes*, which has an introduction with particularly helpful remarks on the special features of Chekhov's language. Were I teaching a course more oriented toward Chekhov's drama, I would likely use one of the two weightiest, most comprehensive single volumes that can be ordered, which are both Senelick's: his Norton Critical Edition, which contains the mature, full-length plays and their variants, a couple of the one-act plays, as well as a strong selection of letters, criticism, and remarks of directors on Chekhov; or else his *Complete Plays*, also from Norton, which includes all the one-act plays (vaudevilles), the lengthy early play that Chekhov sought to destroy (untitled, but usually called *Platonov*), some comic dialogues and experiments at collaboration with other playwrights, and also variants of plays—it is truly complete.

For staging, or performance-oriented exercises or courses that employ dramatic reading, we recommend either the Heim volume or the Carnicke volume; the latter is best for those who want to read some of the one-act plays (which she calls, following Chekhov, the "jokes"). Fans of Mamet will probably want his treatments of *Vanya*, *Three Sisters*, and *Cherry Orchard*, which is to say that they will want Mamet. Nevertheless, it is difficult for a professor of Russian literature to encourage instructors to use translations produced without knowledge of the original language. Chekhov's famed laconicity and "deeper reaches" can be approached only through acute sensitivity to the lexical level of his text.With both the plays and the stories, cost and availability are always considerations. But the instructor who resorts to century-old American or British translations, because they are cheap or even free via the Internet, will severely diminish both the students' appreciation of Chekhov and what can be accomplished in the classroom.

Editions of Chekhov's Works

Most users of this volume will not have Russian, but those who do should be aware of the excellent scholarly resources that are available. First is the thirty-volume scholarly edition of Chekhov's writings, *Polnoe sobranie sochinenii i pisem* (*Полное собрание сочинений и писем*; "Complete Collection of Works and Letters"). This edition contains everything published that can reliably be attributed to Chekhov, with publication history, commentary, and much useful glossing on each work; all the letters that have survived, with annotation (though not without some censorship); essays that frame the periods covered by respective volumes; and a catalog of the changes Chekhov made when he republished works. Any instructor who can read Russian or get assistance with the language would do well to begin by reading the commentary on a given work in this edition, which can be accessed on the Web as well—use the site of the official Russian scholarly Chekhov organization, the Chekhov Commission (Чеховская Комиссия; Chekhovskaia Komissiia): www.chekhoved.ru/index.php/chekhov-all/pss.

Those without Russian might rely on Hingley's nine-volume *Oxford Chekhov* for a hint of the scholarly apparatus offered by *Polnoe sobranie*. But there are better choices to be made for translations to work with in class, as discussed above.

The Instructor's Library

Michael C. Finke, with Dmitry Tartakovsky

The wide variety of courses in which Chekhov might be read makes recommending the best and most useful secondary literature in English extremely challenging. The Norton Critical Editions of both Chekhov's prose (*Anton Chekhov's Selected Stories*) and drama (*Complete Plays*) will be extremely useful for instructors whether or not these editions are ordered for a course. The instructor will also want to be aware of English-language volumes with comprehensive Chekhov bibliographies: Kenneth Lantz's *Anton Chekhov: A Reference Guide to Literature*, Charles Meister's *Chekhov Bibliography*, and Senderovich and

Munir Sendich's *Anton Chekhov Rediscovered*. The most recent comprehensive source is Lauren Leighton's *A Bibliography of Anton Chekhov in English*.

A number of companion volumes, resources rather like this one but without the pedagogical orientation, are available: *The Cambridge Companion to Chekhov* has many useful essays, including contributions by top Russian scholars, but it is somewhat mistitled, being dedicated almost exclusively to Chekhov's drama and performance history. It includes appendixes with listings of select stage productions, screen adaptations, select bibliographies of primary and secondary sources in Russian and English, and a partial list collocating original Russian titles with the various ways they have been translated into English. Toby Clyman's older *Chekhov Companion* is more balanced if less weighty. There are many valuable monograph studies of Chekhov available in English. Peter Bitsilli's venerable and influential study, *Chekhov's Art*, is available in translation, and two other solid, accessible, and interesting overviews are Rayfield (*Understanding Chekhov*) and Winner (*Chekhov and His Prose*). There is one volume of the current czar of Chekhov studies in Russia available in English, Vladimir Kataev's *If Only We Could Know! An Interpretation of Chekhov*.

For courses on Chekhov's drama or theater, there are fine small volumes that introduce his major dramatic works in Routledge and Macmillan series that feature useful biographical introductions and bibliographies. Rose Whyman's *Anton Chekhov* offers a solid, contextualizing biographical sketch, and its bibliography is up-to-date and complete. Much of Senelick's short *Anton Chekhov* has been incorporated into his Norton volumes.

It is hard to pick and choose from the abundance of monographs on specific aspects of Chekhov's poetics of prose and drama and from the many excellent edited volumes of essays, which are often based on conferences devoted to particular themes. Two classic studies of the poetics of Chekhov's prose, with special emphasis on his handling of narrative point of view, are Chudakov's *Chekhov's Poetics* and Nils Ake Nilsson's *Studies in Čechov's Narrative Technique*. Two volumes with excellent selections of articles, some of them Russian and Soviet classics that have been translated, are Robert L. Jackson's *Chekhov: A Collection of Critical Essays* and René Wellek and Nonna D. Wellek's *Chekhov: New Perspectives*. Another outstanding collection, focused on the drama, is Jean-Pierre Barricelli's *Chekhov's Great Plays*. Harold Bloom edited a Modern Critical Views volume of Chekhov criticism (*Anton Chekhov*).

Without question, the first stop for anyone with an interest in Chekhov's performance history is Senelick's *The Chekhov Theatre*, which provides detailed commentary on some of the most exciting stagings of Chekhov, worldwide, in the twentieth century. J. L. Styan's *Chekhov in Performance* is also often used. A useful survey-style study of the plays for an undergraduate classroom is Richard Gilman's *Chekhov's Plays*: his interpretations can help spark discussion, though instructors in the know will find some irritating factual lapses and a disturbing obliviousness to the interpretive issues that arise from working with a text in translation. Other interpretive works are Beverly Hahn's *Chekhov*, Richard Peace's *Chekhov*, Pitcher's *The Chekhov Play*, and Maurice Valency's *The Breaking String*. Excerpts from memoirs by Stanislavsky and Nemirovich-Danchenko of the Moscow Art Theater are widely available—for example, in Turkov's *Anton Chekhov and His Times*; the memoirs can also be easily found in their entirety in English.

Courses on creative writing or reading Chekhov with a view toward his influence on American letters will want to turn to *Chekhov and Our Age*, a volume edited by James McConkey that contains essays by Harold Brodkey, John Cheever, Walker Percy, and Eudora Welty, among others who gathered for a symposium at Cornell University in the 1970s. A volume that assembles Chekhov's comments on writing has the title, surely conceived by a marketing specialist, *How to Write like Chekhov* (Brunello and Lenček). Courses with a focus on medical humanities may find useful my *Seeing Chekhov*; they should also be aware of the informative social-historical study of the medical profession in Chekhov's era by Nancy Frieden, *Russian Physicians in an Era of Reform and Revolution, 1856–1905*. Julie de Sherbinin's *Chekhov and Russian Religious Culture* will serve instructors interested in religious themes, but it is also exemplary in its nuanced approach to Chekhov's unorthodox handling of biblical subtexts. Courses emphasizing translation will want to consult Rachel May's *The Translator in the Text*, which has relatively few pages devoted to Chekhov but an approach that can really pay off in discussing his work. Finally, instructors will find pieces on translation, on Chekhov and Anglo-American letters, on Chekhov and the medical humanities, and on Chekhov in performance in *Chekhov the Immigrant*, edited by de Sherbinin and me.

There are other fine edited volumes of articles on Chekhov—too many call out from my bookshelf to list here. The instructor who wishes to dig deeper will find further references in the works mentioned above and in the works cited in the essays in this volume. Instructors searching the *MLA International Bibliography* online or resorting to *Google* to find articles on specific works should of course consider carefully the venue that has published a given article. Some of the peer-reviewed journals in the field of Slavic studies, which may be considered reliable, are *The Russian Language Journal*, *The Russian Review*, *Slavic and East European Journal* (*SEEJ*), *The Slavonic and East European Review*, *Slavic Review*.

Last, users of this volume may wish to begin the hunt for secondary materials with a relatively new Web site, created in the spring of 2013 and maintained by the Slavic Reference Service at the University of Illinois, Urbana. Their Chekhov *libguide* is accessible at http://uiuc.libguides.com/chekhov. Though oriented toward the graduate student or professional scholar who has Russian, the site itself is in English and does have links to many primary and secondary materials in English. The tab "Chekhov on the Web" will guide users to the Web sites of the various Chekhov home museums; of the publication of the North American Chekhov Society, where one can find reviews of the latest publications, performances, and film adaptations, as well as interpretive articles; of the Russian Chekhov Commission, which is the chief, official scholarly organizer of conferences and other events as well as publications on Chekhov in Russia; of out-of-copyright translations of Chekhov's works into English, which can be downloaded. The Chekhov *libguide* also has the pages "Chekhov's Life and Times," "Search Strategies," and "Archival Sources." It is also a rich source of links to audio and visual materials—the tab "Chekhov's Works" includes a link to the *Internet Archive*, where some fifty audio files of Chekhov stories read in English can be freely downloaded.

For those wishing to work with film and video adaptations of the plays or stories, the *Cambridge Companion to Chekhov* has both an overview article on the topic by Philip French and a select list in an appendix (260–62). The most comprehensive list of screen adaptations, as well as a number of review articles, both about particular films (a cluster treats adaptations of *Uncle Vanya*) and relevant scholarship from the 1990s, is to be found in a special issue of the *North American Chekhov Society Bulletin* 8.3 (1999), devoted entirely to Chekhov and film (*Special Focus Issue*)—but new Chekhov-related films continue to appear with great frequency: in May 2013 the IMDB webpage on Anton Chekhov listed fifty-three new items since 1999. For those who read Russian, a more recent listing of Chekhov on film may be found in the "Chekhov and Cinema" entry in *A. P. Chekhov: Entsiklopediia* (Smirnova 615–20); this listing may be the best source for Russian and Soviet productions (dating back to 1909), but in the category of non-Russian titles it is less comprehensive, and it offers those titles only in their Russian translations, so that tracking down the original may be difficult at times. (A chronic problem for those seeking film adaptations of Chekhov, as A. P. Smirnova points out, is that roughly one-third of film titles pertaining to Chekhov do not correspond to those of the relevant works by Chekhov [610].) The very best place to begin one's research, however, may be the "Chekhov on Stage & Screen" tab on the Chekhov *libguide* of the University of Illinois Library, periodically updated.

How to select video materials to work with? There are many versions of all the major plays to choose from. Perhaps the richest possibilities relate to *Uncle Vanya*, which was adapted in the United States, the United Kingdom, and Australia in the 1990s. Of these, Louis Malle's *Vanya on Forty-Second Street* is treated by two essays in this volume (MacKay and Safariants; Garner). Malle's adaptation might be compared with Anthony Hopkins's *August* or Michael Blakemore's *Country Life*. One might profitably screen select scenes from these works as well as any number of filmed stagings, like the 1963 British film starring Laurence Olivier and Michael Redgrave (*Uncle Vanya* [dir. Burge]). Among the prose works, one rich possibility pertains to what is likely the most frequently anthologized of Chekhov's stories, "The Lady with the Little Dog": there is the 1960 "Thaw" masterpiece of Iosif Kheifits, *The Lady with the Little Dog* (*Dama*; see the essay of MacKay and Safariants here) and the 1987 *Dark Eyes*, by Nikita Mikhailkov, which was shot in Italy and starred Marcello Mastroianni.

There are multiple film versions also of "Ward No. 6," "The Duel," "Black Monk," and "The Kiss," among many others. Two recent adaptations are the 2009 *Ward No. 6*, directed by Karen Shakhnazarov (Russia), which sets the action in Russia of the 2000s, and the sultry *Anton Chekhov's The Duel* (2010), directed by Dover Kosashvili, was filmed in Croatia and features British actors. Shakhnazarov's *Ward No. 6* is available on *YouTube* with English subtitles. Mosfilm has put its catalog of films, including its Chekhov adaptations, on *YouTube*.

The very earliest silent films in prerevolutionary Russia inaugurated a central tradition in Russian cinematography of adapting literary works. The earliest known Chekhov film was the 1909 *Khirurgiia* (*Хирургия*; "Surgery"), by P. Chardynin. By 1920 Russian cinema boasted more than fifty films based on Chekhov's works (Smirnova 608), and at least one of these is readily accessible in the collection Early Russian Cinema from Milestone, the 1911 *Romance with a Double Bass*. (The 1974 nude romp of Monty Python's John Cleese and his [then] wife Connie Booth in their film treatment of "Romance with a Double Bass" may be out-of-bounds for classroom screening.)

NOTES

[1] For further suggestions on foregrounding translation in the classroom, see Carol Apollonio's essay in this volume.

[2] The *Dictionary of Literary Biography* is often accessible for students online through a library Web site. A shorter dictionary entry is that of Hugh McLean in Victor Terras's *Handbook of Russian Literature*.

[3] For an early, influential example of such approaches in English, see Senderovich, "Anton Chekhov." This essay is an abbreviated version of his subsequent *Chekhov—s glazu na glaz* (*Чехов—с глазу на глаз*; "Chekhov—Eye to Eye").

[4] But he occasionally used his name earlier. See the discussion of his "At Sea" (1883; "В море"; "V more") in Finke, *Seeing Chekhov* 38–50.

[5] See Senderovich, "*Cherry Orchard*." For a discussion of teaching Raymond Carver's story about Chekhov's death, "Errand," see the essay by de Sherbinin in this volume. Katherine O'Connor offers an interesting treatment of Chekhov's impending death as figured in his letters.

[6] On aspect, see Apollonio.

[7] On Chekhov's inbetweenness, see Lapushin, *Dew*; de Sherbinin, "Poetics." On the propensity of translators to remove ambiguity, see Apollonio.

[8] For allegations that Garnett (or her ghost helpers in translation) used the French translations of Denis Roche as a crib, resulting in French spellings for Russian names and the feeling of an underlying French syntactic structure, see "Forum" 35.

Part Two

APPROACHES

Introduction: Teaching Chekhov, Chekhov Teaching: "A Boring Story" and Critical Thinking

Michael Holquist

. . . parables are older than reasoning.

—Johann Georg Hamann

1.

Chekhov loved teachers. He felt they were the great hope for a better Russia and had a historical role to play. Maxim Gorky recounts how Chekhov again and again returned to the theme of education in the Russian countryside. Chekhov did not just talk about teachers. It is widely known that after he became a famous author and was able to buy a small estate, he served as a doctor to the peasants on his land. What is sometimes overlooked is that he also established schools. In czarist Russia, teachers were, in Chekhov's words, "famished, downtrodden . . . in perpetual fear of losing their livelihood." And yet, "the teacher ought to be the first man in the village" (Gorky 272). As Gorky recounts, "Again and again I would hear from him: 'Listen—a teacher has just arrived . . . he's ill, he has a wife—you couldn't do anything for him, could you? I've fixed him up for the moment. . . .' Or: 'Listen, Gorky! A teacher wants to meet you. He is bedridden, sick. Won't you go see him?'" (273).

Chekhov's training as a physician has often been cited as source of the humane vision that pervades his literary practice. Surely this is true. But Chekhov also wanted to teach medicine. Teaching is another profession that plays a role in shaping his stories and plays. Pedagogy of a specific kind served to frame what we have come to recognize as a distinctively Chekhovian ethic and technique. It is not merely something that Chekhov put into his works but also something that we as readers and teachers can take out of them.

Like Shakespeare's plays, Chekhov's stories lend themselves to an unusually broad array of approaches. The essays in this volume demonstrate that variety, but they all address Chekhov's ability to defy the expectations of readers based on their previous reading. The fruitful ambiguity of Chekhov's plots is a gift to teachers who wish to improve their pupils' reading skills. Class discussion of Chekhov provides a forum in which to explore the complexity not only of formal narrative but also of life experience. In this essay, I emphasize some aspects of Chekhov's art that are helpful in teaching Chekhov, particularly in the present moment.

Chekhov was aware that he lived in a rapidly changing culture whose new challenges gave an urgency to teaching young people. Now, in the early years of the twenty-first century, we are in a period of even greater change. Chekhov's art takes on new meaning as we enter a digital age in which the need for acuteness and discrimination in evaluating a rapidly changing world—critical thinking—becomes more urgent with every passing day. Vast stores of data are now produced exponentially. They are so large that new orders of magnitude have had to be employed to describe them, such as the terabyte (10^{12}) or zettabyte (10^{21}). The tsunami of information has created a revolution in hermeneutics.

The new emphasis on recognition of general patterns (as opposed to attention to detail) sometimes puts a premium on information as opposed to wisdom. This tendency challenges traditional humanist core values, preeminently humanism's focus on pain and pleasure as experienced by individual persons. From Socrates's "Know thyself," to modernist thinkers obsessed with the existential crises that each of us must face on our own, humanist thought has focused on the distinctive place in existence we occupy as unique individuals.

Wherever we find ourselves, at each moment of our existence we inhabit a locus both in space and time that is ours alone. How we connect these moments is a challenge we must all face. Generationally shifting attitudes and the individual abilities and deficiencies of our students continually prompt us to reflect on the different ways that contingent lives are transformed into coherent narratives. Reading Chekhov is a good way to teach students that the singularity of the physical space and time we occupy has perceptual and ethical implications for how to live and die.

Chekhov can help us better understand how to coexist in a world in which we are all alone together. It is in this context that his emphasis on the dignity and value of individual human beings as they are present in unique moments becomes increasingly important.

Even a cursory acquaintance with Chekhov's biography makes it clear that his life was guided by devotion to a set of high principles rooted in an unflinching recognition of human frailty. His sympathy for his flawed (and sometimes quite repellent) characters springs from himself and his circumstances, of course, but it also derives from a powerful strain in the Russian liberal intelligentsia, best represented by Alexander Herzen (and Isaiah Berlin), a tradition that never loses sight of the ineluctable individuality that is our key attribute as human beings and thus resists universalizing absolutes of any kind, religious, political—or algorithmic.

The singularity of human existence is a key to understanding (and teaching) some of the basic formal features of Chekhov's literary experiments. I use a single aspect of his art, narrative, in "A Boring Story" to highlight the central place of what Walter Benjamin called "Jetztzeiten." Such now moments are to be found in all Chekhov's work, both early and late, in the fiction and in the plays. These are the points at which we experience feelings and perceptions that are absolutely unique to us as individual human beings.

Readers over the years have recognized Chekhov's unnerving emphasis on presentness (*nunc stans*) in his stories. In such moments, past and future fuse as characters fully inhabit the distinctiveness of an existential present. (A sensitive treatment of this Chekhovian dominant can be found in Gary Saul Morson's *Narrative and Freedom* and in his essay in this volume.) Metaphysics has evolved the concept of *qualia* for the uniqueness of individual perception: the infinitely precise way I see red or taste a lemon versus the way you see red or taste a lemon. Various religious faiths assume the existence of a soul that is uniquely tied to individual bodies. At the most immediate level, most human beings—no matter how conventional their lives may appear when viewed from the outside—sense that they are, at some deep level, singular beings who have experiences, moments of awareness, that are utterly their own. Chekhov is a master at realizing these nonfungible moments.

Throughout "A Boring Story," the narrator strives to understand his impending death. His interpretations can be contradictory at different points in the narrative. For instance, he says of his youth as a poor seminarian:

> I dreamed of going to university. . . . [I'd] imagine myself a doctor. . . . And so, as you see, my dreams have come true. . . . For thirty years I've been a beloved professor, have had excellent colleagues, have enjoyed honorable renown. I've loved, married for passionate love, had children. In short, looking back, my whole life seems to me like a beautiful composition, executed with talent. (83–84)

But elsewhere, in different now moments, he views his life quite differently: he finds his wife boring and ugly ("flabby, ungainly" [58]), his daughter and son selfish (59, 60), his career, titles, and many honors hollow ("the sixty-two years I have lived should be considered a waste" [90]).

Each of these paired now moments is fully realized and conveys deep conviction, yet they absolutely contradict each other. They both (as do others) claim the authority and immediacy that accrues to a voice in the first person. The problem for the reader is how to stitch these different moments into a coherent image of the narrator. Each occurs in the present (even when remembered) of the speaker's consciousness: there is an unbreakable bond between I and now that makes each a moment noninterchangeable with any other. But how, out of these moments, are we to define a single, coherent persona? Such a composite definition is necessary, of course, both from inside the individual, as he constructs a self, and for those who perceive him from outside. But insofar as such a blend of unique moments into a patterned character is a generalization, it will necessarily turn the character's discrete experiences of the existential present into an abstraction. The obvious solution is to create relations among now moments such that they figure as components of an essence larger than any one of them in isolation—in other words, to make a single pattern out of manifold events.

Such a strategy approaches interpretation architectonically: much as the architect creates a single building out of discrete materials, Chekhov creates unified characters out of discrete now moments. The resulting construction requires readers to see how the characters' now moments connect to those of other characters and how one character relates to the now moments of another. Understanding how disparate things relate to one another is the discipline at the heart of architecture. It is the reason why the cliché that architecture is frozen music contains so much truth. The question raised by Chekhov's work is how to construct such a general design without impairing the uniqueness of singular moments.

2.

Chekhov despised the preachy political moralizing characteristic of Dmitry Pisarev and Nikolai Dobroliubov, leading critics of the generation that preceded him in the 1860s. Nevertheless, his stories contain lessons. His teaching is vastly more subtle and variegated than the crude didacticism of reformers such as Dobroliubov, who insisted that "literature's chief significance is that of propaganda" (309; my trans.). Chekhov abjured such simplistic ideology, but there is a pedagogical element in his stories: they teach us how to live with complexity. He denies the reductionist logic of those who, like Sartre's Roquentin, believe you must choose between living and telling. Chekhov was convinced that living *is* telling. He understood that narrative is a crucial experiential factor in the self-organization of all human lives. Alisdair MacIntyre has put it very well: "Stories are lived before they are told—except in the case of fiction" (212). Chekhov's stories are illustrations of how to tell better stories.

The art with which he ambiguously concludes a tale is frequently put forward as the prime example of his technical mastery. This observation has become so formulaic that student-aid Web sites emphasize this aspect of his artistry, as when *Sparknotes* tells us, "[Chekhov] developed a technique of ending stories with what have been termed 'zero endings'—or anti-climactic conclusions" ("Chekhov Stories"). The suggestion is that his endings surprise, by being, according to the rules of conventional narrative form, nonconclusive.

But another cliché, almost equally entrenched, says just the opposite: Chekhov is characterized as a master of precisely calculated plots that provide subtle hints along the way of events to come. This foreshadowing has its own *Wikipedia* entry: "Chekhov's Gun" relates Chekhov's repeated admonition in letters and conversation that if there is a gun on the wall in the first act, it will be fired in a later act.

Both clichés capture something that is indeed characteristic of Chekhov's style. As teachers, we should draw attention to his obvious foreshadowing and enigmatic endings. But in focusing on Chekhov's beginnings and endings, let us not ignore his middles. Much of the distinctiveness of his art is found in the subtle turns that are the building blocks of a Chekhov tale. By middles, I mean the various disconnects and silences that are so numerous in Chekhovian narrative. Music is frequently invoked as a metaphor for Chekhov's technique, because Chekhov so well illustrates the truth of the mot often ascribed to Mozart, that music is what happens between the notes. These architectonic moments are difficult to characterize, because they differ from conventional constituents of either story or plot (the formalist distinction between *fabula* and *siuzhet* in narrative). We might think of these middle plot elements as now moments of the kind suggested above. Several examples of these are found in "A Boring Story."

3.

Chekhov makes clear from the outset of "A Boring Story" that nonlinear moments shape his story: it is not a connected narrative but a series of excerpts "from an old man's notes." The six divisions marked in the story can be interpreted as six different notes, each focused on an event in the narrator's life. Although given in rough chronological order covering his last six months, they are notes precisely because they emphasize, like diary entries, the immediacy of the moment in which they are recorded. The text insists on the presence of gaps between the events it includes, requiring the reader to fill in the blanks between them—as well as the blanks between events within each note.

We are told at the beginning of the story that the author is losing his ability to organize even so casual a sequence as the genre of notes demands: "My memory has weakened, my thoughts lack consistency, and each time I set them down on paper it seems to me I've lost the intuition of their organic connection . . . when I get to the end, I often forget the beginning" (56). We sense the honesty in these words: the reliability of the narrator consists precisely in his unreliability. The reader is challenged: How can a coherent narrative be organized from such jumbled information? It is this kind of artful metacriticsim, incised in the notes themselves, that makes reading—and teaching—Chekhov such a joy.

Oppositions dominate the text and recur throughout the notes. The most significant opposition is the difference between the world's external view of the doctor whose notes we read and his perception of things from inside the qualia of his consciousness. From the story's first words, we become aware of this distinction at the basic level of grammar: "There is in Russia an honored professor named Nikolai Stepanovich So-and-so, a privy councilor and chevalier. . . . He is a member of all the Russian and three foreign universities. And so on and so forth. All this and many other things that might be said constitute what is known as my name" (55). He begins by proclaiming that the convention of his name does not define who he is. He is not his name. In fact, he will say at the end that his name has betrayed him (103). The shift from third to first person is repeated throughout the story, whenever a distinction is drawn between empty forms and authentic existence.

Nikolai Stepanovich—first name and patronymic: significantly, we get only his name, not his family's—the distinguished professor of medicine whose notes are the story, will again use pronouns to indicate the distance between his worldly persona known to others and the self of which he alone is aware in section 4. Liza, his beloved stepdaughter, invites him for a carriage ride: "Let's go, *Your* Excellency." And the dying doctor recounts what happens next by distorting the conventional possessive in his title: "*My* Excellency is taken outside . . ." (90).

While the opposition is the same in both instances—a contrast between empty titles and the living subject whom they name—the tenor of each is different. On the first page of the story, the tone is somber, world-weary. Later, in response to Liza's playful use of his honorific, the narrator's tone is lighter, an ironic solecism that parries the irony in Liza's invocation of his title. That is, the same trope can have different meanings in Chekhov. The emotional weather, constantly shifting, can change from one sentence to the next. The Chekhovian plot is like a string of moments, each moment independent, a unit in itself.

In other words, Chekhov experiments with the temporal character of meanings that are localized in individual moments. Examples of the distinction between external conventions and the living persons they clumsily seek to define recur in different ways at chronologically separated moments in the text as instances of self-awareness in the present.

"A Boring Story" is a narrative very different from classical definitions of plot. Aritotle's *Poetics* prizes a flowing connection between episodes that are organically connected to one another. For Aristotle, plot is the most important element of a well-made tragedy because it is what shapes the whole:

> Now a whole is that which has a beginning, middle, and end. A beginning is that which is not itself necessarily after anything else, and which has naturally something else after it. An end is that which is naturally after something else, either as its necessary or usual consequent, and with nothing else after it; and a middle is that which is by nature after one thing and has also another after it. (1462)

The now moments of immediacy that make up "A Boring Story" ill comport with the classical demand for natural sequence. Aristotle, who invented the syllogism as well as narrative theory, calls natural those beginnings, middles, and ends that are logical: they are algorithmic insofar as they have a lawlike relation to one another. The source of authority for determining what Aristotle calls natural narrative is the presumption of absolute time. Time is conceived as absolute because it is in and of itself and thus has its own nature, independent of human beings. It flows uniformly, without necessary reference to anything external to it. It is the kind of time that is measured by the refrigerated atomic clocks in the vaults of the Naval Observatory in Washington.

But Chekhov is concerned with another kind of time, a time that must be measured by another kind of clock. Such a clock can be found, first of all, in language—specifically, in the uniqueness of the first-person pronoun. As Émile Benveniste, the great French linguist, reminds us, "I" is how human beings locate themselves in time and space first, then in the more complex conceptual realm of values that govern our lives (226). Linguistic time is always self-referential to the speaker. It is oriented around the now of the subject who says, "I."

The narrator of "A Boring Story" tells us, as he shares a meal with his family, that "I have the feeling that once upon a time I lived at home with a real family, but now I'm a dinner guest of someone who is not my real wife and am looking at someone who is not the real Liza" (78). Using his life as a timepiece, he compares his self as it is in the present with what it was in the past. As a result of his present eminence as a privy councilor and distinguished professor, he sees that his family has changed to keep up with that acquired dignity. They insist on fancy tableware, a new servant, more formal dress, and so on, all of which goes with a different kind of discourse at the table. The narrator compares the kidneys and Madeira he is now consuming with the fish and kasha of earlier days, when instead of the polite chatter of his arriviste wife and daughter there was a lot of noise and surprise: "a fight between the cat and dog under the table, or the bandage falling from Katya's cheek into her plate of soup" (78).

The details remembered in such now moments (the kasha, the fallen bandage, etc.) contrast with the ritually patterned behavior of those around him. Chekhov goes out of his way to make clear that the conventions that dominate the narrator's family in the current moment are ordered by a false logic. Externally imposed social norms rule the dinner table, stifling spontaneity and the play of chance. In such scenes we perceive the narrator's acute awareness of habit that makes questioning repetitive pattern a preoccupation in his life. His day always begins with his wife's appearance in his study (they have long since ceased sleeping together): "She enters my room in a petticoat, her hair not yet done, but already washed, smelling of flower cologne. . . ." She enters always "with the air of having come by chance," aware, as he is, that there is something inauthentic, dishonest, about habitual behavior. So she must disguise her predictable entrance by making it appear to be spontaneous, even though "each time she says one and the same thing . . ." (57).

Habit rules not only the wife's relations with her family but also her whole perception of the world. We are told that the professor, for all his honors and titles, is living beyond his means (he is "ashamed of his poverty"). The emptiness—and danger—of sheer repetition rather than the use of critical judgment is demonstrated by the wife's handling of the family's finances: "Everyday experience might have convinced my wife that expenses are not diminished by our frequent talking about them, but my wife does not recognize experience . . ." (58).

The relation between habit and ethics is most pronounced in moments when Chekhov invokes the metaphor of education, as we can see in the narrator's anger directed at students who come to the narrator for topics: "I don't deal in topics! . . . I'm not running a shop! . . . Why don't you want to be independent? Why are you so against freedom?" (69). Education comes up again when he is visited by his young ward, Katya, who has come back after an unsuccessful career as an actress in provincial theater. Despite her failure, she retains "a passionate love" for the theater and tells the professor that what happens in the theater is higher than what happens in an auditorium, it is "higher than books, higher than anything in the world" (72).

The professor takes quite another view. He finds actors "bound from head to foot in theatrical traditions and preconditions. . . . I feel the same routine wafting from the stage that I already found boring forty years ago. . . ." He connects the rigid stasis of the theater to its failure to instruct. After a long paragraph condemning present performances (in which he says, "As before," four times in his list of unchanged habits), he adds, "The sentimental and gullible crowd may be convinced that the theater in its present form is a school. But no one acquainted with school in the true sense can be caught on that hook" (71).

What school might look like "in the true sense" is dramatized in the story in two ways. The first is relatively straightforward: Katya's condemnation of young actors who lack passion in the theater (73). The second is the narrator's equally harsh comments on his indifferent students (87–88). These comments can spark a lively discussion among one's own students. What about their passion? What about their habits?

Education, at a subtler, less thematic level, is present on every page of the story. Chekhov challenges the reader to recognize complex relations without at the same time becoming the dupe of patterns—or, as we might now say, to discriminate between information and semantics. Teaching Chekhov has always been done under the influence of critical models in fashion at the time. However, one feature of his work that is an unchanging source of instruction for students—no matter what theoretical frame in which he is taught—is the exercise of having to make complex connections between moments of intense immediacy. Careless readers like to slot a text into currently fashionable reading habits, but Chekhovian texts make it difficult for them to do so. Whatever the ism that dominates the reading and teaching of literature at the moment, the need for architectonic interpretation in Chekhov demands critical thinking.

Examples of Chekhov's emphasis on hermeneutics—as opposed to mere calculation—are to be found throughout "A Boring Story" as its narrator seeks to make sense of his life under the imperative of his impending death. We are told—but only in passing—that he has six months to live. He is aware that there is a conventional expectation that he should somehow render his end meaningful: he knows that "something strange is happening to me" and that "it would seem I should now be most occupied with questions about the darkness beyond the grave and the visions that will haunt my sepulchral sleep." Yet "for some reason my soul rejects those questions, although my mind is aware of all their importance" (65).

The narrator, a doctor who has seen much death in his six decades and knows more about the workings of the body than most laymen, here makes an important distinction between "soul" and "mind." *Soul* is the term we use for the core of our individuality, that thing for which only the I, not the we, is mortally responsible. *Mind* is that part of our being that engages the world outside our soul, that thinks impersonally as we strive to make connections with nature and other minds. The narrator at this early stage in his dying rejects inquiry about the meaning of his life ("my soul rejects those questions"). His mind clings to faith in the impersonality of science: "[I]n the face of death I am interested only in science. Breathing my last, I will still believe that science is the most important, the most beautiful and necessary thing in man's life . . . only by science will man conquer nature and himself." His soul is aware that such "faith may be naive and incorrect in its foundations," but in his mind he believes in science and "cannot overcome this faith."

Although the plot of the story is not linear in any conventional way, there is a chronological progression in the notes that chart different stages of the narrator's journey toward the grave. In the first note, we learn he has six months to live (65). In the fourth note, he tells us, "I still find nature beautiful, though a demon whispers to me that none of these pines and birds and white clouds in the sky will notice my absence when I die three or four months from now" (96).

At this more advanced stage of his illness, the important role that Katya plays as his other self emerges. It is she who asks the questions of soul that the narrator's mind suppressed earlier in the name of science. She reminds him of his distinctiveness, his unique place in existence: ". . . there's no actor who could play you. Even a bad actor could play me . . . for instance, but no one could play you." The dying doctor is moved to think about the benefits of valorizing uniqueness in interpretation, although in terms that are scientific: in medicine, one is advised " 'to individualize each particular case.' One needed only follow that advice to be convinced that the remedies recommended by textbooks . . . for the standard case prove completely unsuitable in particular cases. The same is true for moral illnesses." But he is unable at this point to apply to his own case this general recognition of the importance of the particular. It is Katya who must ask the great Chekhovian question, "What am I to do?" (96). And he is unable to answer her—or himself.

In the final note, the scene changes, as the narrator announces out of the blue, "I'm in Kharkov" (102). He is months closer to death, "sitting all alone in a strange town, on a strange bed. . . ." In other words, he is approaching the ultimate now moment, after which his I will perish and all time will be then instead of now. In the presence of this finality, he is moved to ask himself the questions he has been avoiding. "How, then, does the exclusiveness of my position manifest itself?" (103). He specifically conflates this way of putting things with the Delphic maxim "Know thyself." After ruefully noting, "the ancients never thought of showing how to use this advice," the dying doctor concludes that the self is what is desired: "Tell me what you want, and I'll tell you who you are" (104).

He dutifully lists the things he has desired, such as love from his family and students, but he feels they do not add up to any definitive identity: "[I]n all the thoughts, feelings, and conceptions I form about everything, something general is lacking that would unite it all into a single whole. Each feeling and thought lives separately in me . . . even the most skillful analyst would be unable to find what is known as a general idea . . ." (104–05).

Society has provided him with many ways in which he could endow the contingencies of his life with a single overarching meaning. But throughout his notes, he rejects these social algorithms as false and inadequate, because they presume an inclusivity to which the randomness of separate moments in his life will not yield. His name (which we are never given in full) is the recurring master trope for false patterning. His I is a nonlexical entity; it can never signify who he is in the way that the concept of tree identifies all the trees in the world.

This is why the narrator's I moments are simultaneously now moments and why, in the end, the narrator finds that the patterns his society makes available for encapsulating a life's meaning are inadequate. Captious journalists who report on little old ladies who believe they can see the face of Mother Teresa in their cinnamon bun provide a humorous example of believing in false patterns. But apophenia, the technical name for perceiving pattern where there is none, is, as "A Boring Story" makes clear, a metaphysical as well as an existential problem, for it goes to the heart of what we can—or cannot—believe in as real (see Shermer).

As the narrator sits in the squalid Kharkov hotel, he is visited one last time by Katya. She is in yet another of her existential crises. She cries out, "I can't live like this" and implores Nikolai Stepanych, as her teacher and father, to tell her what to do (106). She is seeking a pattern in her life that will reveal its order and meaning. He cannot help her, having just concluded that such universalizing patterns don't exist. He is happy that he made this grim discovery only at the end of his life. He pities Katya and is ashamed that he, the dying one, is happier than she, because, he says, "I've noticed the absence in me of what my philosopher colleagues call a general idea only shortly before death . . . but that the soul of this poor thing has known and will know no refuge for all her life, for all her life" (107).

There are many ways to interpret "A Boring Story," but one aspect of Chekhov's tale has the power to instruct in any age: its meditation on the importance of pattern in human lives is, if anything, more pertinent to current and future generations than it was to his own time. Nikolai Stepanych may be right or wrong in his final judgment that the meaning of a human life cannot be reduced to a single, monologic structure or idea. It could be argued that he goes too far in denying the power of patterns to render a life meaningful. Surely, he does go too far in perceiving pattern as available only to science, completely rejecting it as a source of meaning in individual lives. But even if he is wrong, his suspicion is a healthy antidote to the growing faith in numbers and prediction that digital technology, big data, and the algorithmic power to see the future stochastically have inspired.

"A Boring Story," from its title, through its architectonically structured narrative, through the ambiguous meanings that accrue to the narrator's end at its open conclusion, is a master lesson in the virtue of mature irony. There is much to learn—and teach—in the lively art of "A Boring Story."

APPROACHES TO CHEKHOV'S PROSE

Chekhov and the Anglophone Short Story

Julie W. de Sherbinin

> Ask any thoughtful reader—a student or teacher of literature, a critic or another writer, and you will find agreement: Chekhov is the greatest short story writer who ever lived.
>
> —Raymond Carver, *No Heroics Please*

Chekhov can more than hold his own. Then why design an undergraduate course to read luminaries of short story writing in English alongside him? Because a multiple-author course can serve both institutional and intellectual purposes. It proves an attractive means for students to fulfill a college-wide literature requirement with the promise of exposure to a number of writers; indeed, single-author courses have little appeal for first-year students. More important, to study Chekhov's poetics and then read authors who, broadly speaking, count themselves as his literary heirs gives students the opportunity to practice identifying and analyzing some of the principles of the protowriter and his legacy in anglophone letters: the thwarting of narrative expectations, the displacing and inverting of meanings, the elevated status of seemingly irrelevant details, the constructed nature of reality, and the indeterminate ending. Such a class attempts to address several questions—albeit at a first-year college level. What is Chekhovian about Chekhov? What does it mean for a successor of Chekhov to engage with Chekhovian principles? What has made Chekhov relevant to short story writing over time?

The selection of anglophone authors for such a course depends on instructor discretion, with the caveat that the ubiquitous epithet *Chekhovian* may mean little in terms of shared poetics. Certainly Katherine Mansfield and Raymond Carver belong in the course: each saw in Chekhov a model for her and his own art and life. Short stories by writers who have written essays on Chekhov—Virginia Woolf, Frank O'Connor, Eudora Welty, Vladimir Nabokov, and others—can be good topics for comparison and contrast. There are strong affinity writers, such as Sherwood Anderson, although he claims that he'd not yet read "the Russians" when he wrote *Winesburg, Ohio* (Stewart 30). Oddly enough, James Joyce's "The Dead" reads well with Chekhov's "The Teacher of Literature." I have taught stories by writers with an atmospheric link to Chekhov, such as Alice Munro ("our Chekhov," in Cynthia Ozick's famous words [Thacker 443]) and Bernard Malamud ("Chekhov of the East Side," "Chekhov of the urban Jewish milieu").[1] A nearly requisite comparative pairing is Chekhov's "Lady with a Little Dog" and Joyce Carol Oates's "The Lady with the Pet Dog."

The key to a successful course has to do with a relevant reading lineup that excites the instructor. Then the goal is to equip students with the ability to articulate some basic ideas about the Chekhov short story before they begin comparative or freestanding readings of anglophone authors.

Chekhov's Poetics 101

An undergraduate once wrote in an anonymous course evaluation of me, "The professor wouldn't show us the point of all the stories." While flattered to be confused with Chekhov, I observe in the dismay of this student the major challenge to teaching Chekhov to undergraduates unpracticed in literary inquiry. Accustomed to the neat endings with which popular culture ties up its narratives, students balk at indeterminacy, which is the thrilling hallmark of so much Chekhov. As Woolf writes:

> Where the tune is familiar and the end emphatic—lovers united, villains discomfited, intrigues exposed—as it is in most Victorian fiction, we can scarcely go wrong, but where the tune is unfamiliar and the end a note of interrogation or merely the information that they went on talking, as it is in Tchekhov, we need a very daring and alert sense of literature to make us hear the tune, and in particular those last notes which complete the harmony. (240–41)

The question of narrative expectations can be addressed from the outset in a humorous fashion through one of Chekhov's two inaugural print publications, the jocular "Elements Most Often Found in Novels, Short Stories, Etc." In this short ditty of a text, Chekhov enumerates hackneyed ploys of traditionally plotted fiction. Among his inventory (in Peter Constantine's translation) are "The hero—whisking the heroine off a bolting horse . . . ," "Fair-haired friends and red-haired foes," "Inadvertently overheard words that suddenly make everything clear," and "Gentle hints at portentous circumstances" (*Undiscovered*

Chekhov 175–76). Unpracticed readers will not necessarily get the joke; to some, these literary moments may seem fairly engaging. To make the point, it can be helpful to have a class brainstorm popular television, film, and light reading genres that thrive on predictable plot and foreseeable outcome, then link them to the irony in Chekhov's piece. The result should be the dawning sense that one of Chekhov's innovations is the utter eschewal of predictability, of "[s]even deadly sins at the beginning and a wedding at the end" (177). In time, a class should begin to see that there is absolutely no blueprint for a Chekhov story.

In order to assign comparative readings, it is essential that students first grasp the poetics of the protowriter, at least to some extent. One strategy here is to elicit student participation in creating a chart of Chekhov's poetics. This exercise can involve three intermingled activities: studying excerpts from Chekhov's letters that speak of writing,[2] reading selected essays on Chekhov, and reading a lot of his stories. Directed to keep a record of statements that bear on how we as a class read a Chekhov story, students are motivated to be attentive to elements of poetics. As a collective, the class is charged with compiling all student observations—by way of any electronic platform, such as a *Moodle* blog or *Google Docs*, or in print form—to create a map that will guide reading and help generate ideas for papers.

Essays on Chekhov penned by anglophone short story writers play an important role here. Selection from an extensive menu of such essays reinforces the course premise that the Russian writer's influence runs wide and deep and at the same time allows for selection of aspects of Chekhov's poetics that the instructor wishes to emphasize.[3] A personal favorite of mine is Welty's "Reality in Chekhov's Stories." Students often select citations from Welty that accord with scholarship of the last decades that understands Chekhov as a phenomenologist: "Chekhov's perception of our differing views of reality, with its capacity to understand them all, may have done more than anything else to bring about his revolutionizing of the short story" (62); "Chekhov leads us to discover that what we should have thought the most incongruous detail is in fact the most probable" (65); each unique story "took form from within," operating on a "principle of growth" (74). Any one of the points about poetics that the group generates can then be used as a springboard for a student paper investigating a specific story or comparing stories, from Chekhov's famous statement on the need to avoid labels and ideologies to Flannery O'Connor's insistence that, like Chekhov, "you have to let the things in the story do the talking" (83–84). Below is a brief discussion of two anglophone stories that can be fruitfully read through the lens of Chekhovian poetics.

Reading via Chekhov

Mansfield (1888–1923), New Zealand–born, and Carver (1938–88), an American, invite comparison with Chekhov on several grounds. Both fashioned themselves as his heirs: Mansfield wrote in marginalia, "I am the English Anton T." (Kurylo 15), and Chekhov has been called Carver's "double, mentor, and companion soul" (Stull 199). Both consciously modeled their writing on their sense of Chekhov—Mansfield to the extent of borrowing plots, while Carver expresses his debt in brief essays. Both were diagnosed with terminal illnesses (Mansfield died of tuberculosis, as did Chekhov; Carver, of cancer) and relied on Chekhov as their solace in illness. Carver's final story, "Errand" (1988), is an account of Chekhov's death in a mixed biography-and-fiction genre—a story aesthetically unlike anything Chekhov might have written but essential reading for a course of this nature (see K. O'Connor).

After lecturing on these biographical affinities, I have the class take on two sets of paired readings in order to explore very different understandings of Chekhov on the part of these two heirs, each a gifted writer in a different way. A good strategy for approaching these rudimentary comparative readings is to reformulate Flannery O'Connor's statement and ask, "What do the things in the story say?"

Mansfield's "Bliss" (1918) reads well alongside Chekhov's "The Fidget" (1892). Both stories relate the circumstances in which a young married woman comes to a new understanding of her marriage. In Mansfield, Bertha Young discovers that her husband is having an affair; in Chekhov, Olga Ivanovna has an affair, then faces the death of her husband at the story's conclusion. Each story tracks the woman's illusory construction of her life but to different ends.

The imagery in Mansfield can be rewarding for students to tackle because of its accessibility. "Bliss" brims with anatomical symbols and indications that, with a little help, students can piece together and relate to Bertha's repressed sexuality. The heroine imagines a body "shut up in a case like a rare, rare fiddle" (143) but ignores the thought, relegates her daughter to surrogate care, and prepares to preside at a dinner party. She arranges sensuous fruit in two breastlike piles; banters with her husband, Harry, a man with ample animal appetite; entertains witty, modern friends nicknamed Face and Mug; and becomes enthralled with Pearl Fulton, who possesses all the sensuality and passion absent in the sexually frigid Bertha. Motivated by this overwhelming voluptuousness, Bertha finally, and for the first time, feels sexual desire for her husband; but her euphoria abruptly ends when she sees him embracing Pearl. An undisguised reference to the blooming pear tree in the garden, which appears through the story, confronts Bertha at the end ("Oh, what is going to happen now?" [156]).

Students will identify the hinge of Mansfield's things, and the story's operating narrative principle, as irony. This irony and open endings that nonetheless imply morals may be Mansfield's major borrowings from Chekhov. Irony is a Chekhovian trademark, yet it rarely constitutes the major idea of a Chekhov story. In fact, just as her irony is relatively transparent, so is her admiration for her writing guru. In "Bliss," Mansfield has Bertha think about her party guests: ". . . what a decorative group they made, how they seemed to set one another off and how they reminded her of a play by Chekhov!" (151). Students won't get the allusion without an explanation, won't get the simplified notion of a Chekhov play the allusion represents. But perhaps they will come to see the circumscribed reach of Mansfield's writing when held up against Chekhov's. In "Bliss," irony overrides the text without giving breath to complication.

In Chekhov's more sophisticated "Fidget," Olga Ivanovna, like Bertha, fabricates a bourgeois domestic nest to display to society. However, in this story things serve not as symbols but as theatrical props to facilitate the heroine's second-rate performance of life. Like her home décor ("Chinese parasols, easels, colorful rags, daggers, little busts, photographs" [139]), Olga Ivanovna adorns her life with people whom she imbues with the status of thing (she imagines her husband variously as a Bengal tiger, a Bedouin, a deer, a bear, and a portrait of Zola). She seeks out celebrities yet fails to recognize her husband, a scientist, as anyone beyond mediocre, until he dies of an infection and she finds out that he was famous. This is straightforward irony if the story is read as one in which the heroine experiences a life-changing epiphany at the end—and students will want to read it this way. But Olga Ivanovna's persistent staging of life precludes such a reading. The wording of her vow at the story's end to "worship him and feel a holy dread" (160) promises a perpetuation of the people-as-things theme, for she turns him almost literally into an icon. The ending, in a sense, belies the story's Russian title, "Poprygun'ia" ("Попрыгунья"), the root of which, *-pryg-*, means to jump around. Chekhov's deeper meaning is that, although she jumps from one thing to the other, her fixation remains constant, immobile, an inanimate thing itself. The story points to unchangeability in a character who constructs herself as energetic, creative, with it, and on the move. Chekhov goes well beyond situational irony to show the common disjuncture in many of us between the imagined self and the operational self.

We turn to a different kind of pairing, two fish stories, by Chekhov and by Carver. Students can be encouraged to do online biography searches on both authors to understand their personal passion for sports fishing. Chekhov's "The Fish" (translated also as "The Burbot") is one of his early humorous stories from 1885. Its only comparative purpose here is to link the authors' interests and illustrate the well-known narrative of fishing as a display of masculine prowess that serves as a backdrop for Carver's story. Chekhov's "fish that got away" story seems to lampoon the Russian folktale motif in which one person after another comes to pull out a giant radish, but they succeed only by pulling together. In "The Fish," one male after another, each having higher status than the previous one, jumps into a pond, insistent that he has the know-how to catch the crafty burbot hiding by the bank in willow roots. At the triumphant moment—all five men now in the water—when the landowner himself finally gets a purchase on the fish and holds it up, the burbot thrashes out and escapes. The story, funny in many details, can be used to list the aspects of masculinity in fishing: competition, one-upmanship, sexual conquest suggested by nude men pursuing a long fish. Chekhov's narrative joke is funny, too: we expect something different from the "fish that got away" tale . . . and we get a "fish that got away" tale.

In Carver's "Nobody Said Anything," it is the fish that does the talking. The story engages a theme widely associated with Chekhov: the way that individuals crave communication with others, but words of every kind—hopeful words, angry words, poorly timed words, and lack of words—thwart the communicative act. If Carver's text abounds in crude divulgences untypical of Chekhov's indirect sexual allusions, the story matches Chekhov in the matter of, as Carver put it, "how consequence is delivered" (*No Heroics* 156).

The boy narrator in "Nobody Said Anything" struggles with his parents' dysfunctional relationship even as his own sexuality awakens. He pleads ill on a school morning, engages in sexual fantasies and masturbates, goes fishing, and returns home in the evening triumphantly bearing the day's prize catch, a big fish, only to be summarily dismissed by his father: "Take it the hell out of the kitchen and throw it in the goddamn garbage!" (*Where* 20). Threading through the story are phallus-shaped things that suggest the boy's desperate yearning to master the terms of "fishing," as he believes his father has: cigarettes; the hunting knife, boots, and fly rod with which he sets out; the name Birch Creek; the "boner" he gets when imagining sexual exploits; the crawdads, stick, and rooster pheasant at the creek; the wish for a gun and use of a club by the boy he meets at the creek; and, of course, the two-foot-long "queerly skinny" fish he catches that "gave a long slow tremble and was still" (8). His parents' rejection of the half-fish he brings home—the two boys decide to cut the fish in two since they caught it together—does not tell the full story, however, because, as in much of Chekhov, the real story is about personhood.

Like Chekhov's boy protagonists in "Vanka" and "Grisha," Carver's boy is in many ways naive: the adult world has begun to infringe on him, the way the smudge pots in the orchard leave a "black ring of stuff in your nose" (*Where* 7) or the way the tires have "smacked down" and "left oily skid marks" around the "flowers growing in the cracks in the pavement" that the boy stops to observe (10). The boy is so sensitive that he can narrate the experience of the cornered fish with certainty: "There's no place for him to go. . . . He's scared shitless. . . . He can't go anyplace. He knows that. He knows we're going to nail him. He knows it's tough shit" (13). The boy intuits the abusive power behind unbridled masculinity because he understands both the place of the victim and the place of the perpetrator.

The final lines of the story deliver consequence with a Chekhovian light touch. Students may read the ending as a study in hopelessness, yet with luck their ears will now be attuned to final notes that yield unexpected meanings. Although Chekhov's endings are often read pessimistically, his elegant solutions to individual problems, minimalist as they are, celebrate human ingenuity and perceptiveness: Iona's intimate sharing with his horse at the end of "Misery" (see Jackson, "Kontsovka"), Misail's work as a construction contractor in "My Life" (*Complete Short Novels* 533–38), Nina's career in third-rate provincial theaters at the end of *The Seagull*. In these cases and many others, a character in compromised circumstances discovers a way to create meaning for himself or herself that makes no sense according to conventional measures. I encourage students to see in this way the final lines in "Nobody Said Anything," when the narrator refuses to relinquish his triumph. Banished outside with the creel, the boy relates, "I lifted him out. I held him. I held that half of him" (*Where* 20). With no sentimentality, Carver points to the most precious resource that any of us has in defeat: the possibility of nurturing our diminished and battered personhood. The title of Carver's story, like the title of Chekhov's, is belied. In "Nobody Said Anything," the social world may respond to pain and distress with silence, but the boy, through his ability to describe his world articulately and vividly, has said everything that needs to be said.

No matter what materials an instructor chooses to put together for a comparative course on Chekhov and the anglophone short story, the result will be rewarding. Instructors will be stimulated by reading short story writers from new angles; students will acquire a confident grasp of one of the world's most frequently evoked authors, and they will also acquire a taste for many other writers. The broad objective of my course is to wean students from predictability and steer them toward the ability to read complexity. I want them to be curious about and grapple with the unexpected, to accept ambivalence and absorb multivalences, each valence laying a valid claim on a story—in short, to become critical readers of Chekhov and of every other short story writer they encounter. At the last class meeting, I ask students to spend five minutes writing about the author from the course who made the biggest impression on them. It is, perhaps, an unfairly stacked question. A vote or two will go to most of the writers we have read, but many students leave the class agreeing with Nabokov about Chekhov: "It is *his* works which I would take on a trip to another planet" (*Strong Opinions* 286).

NOTES

This brief piece is dedicated with profound gratitude to an extraordinary and incomparable mentor in reading Chekhov, Savely Senderovich.

[1] Sobriquets attached to writers deemed Chekhovian fluctuate over time. For the phrases cited for Malamud, see Gladstone; "Bernard Malamud."

[2] See Chekhov, *Anton Chekhov's Life and Thought*. Excerpted quotes can be found on many online sites.

[3] A partial list of essays is Frank O'Connor, "The Slave's Son"; Nabokov, "Chekhov"; essays by Cheever, Brodkey, and Welty that appear in James McConkey's *Chekhov and Our Age*; essays by Claire Messud, Francine Prose, and James Wood that appear in *Chekhov the Immigrant*, which also contains (in print and on DVD) an interview of Robert Coles about William Carlos Williams and Chekhov (Coles and Finke). The DVD makes for excellent showing with a set of Chekhov stories on medical themes: "Anyuta," "A Medical Case," "Ward No. 6," "The Black Monk," "Enemies," and others (for more on Chekhov as doctor, see Finke, *Seeing Chekhov*, esp. 51–98).

Reading Chekhov's Short Fiction: The Invisible Language of Culture

Brian James Baer and Maia Solovieva

While Western critics have long celebrated the universal humanism of Chekhov's fiction — Donald Rayfield famously referred to Chekhov as "the most approachable and least alien" of all the Russian classics (*Anton Chekhov* xv) — Russians perceive the writer and dramatist to be thoroughly Russian. There are fundamental differences between the reception of Chekhov's works in Russia and their reception in the West. A 2001 survey by Sergei Pshenitsyn, a Russian translation scholar, showed that Russian and American lay readers interpret Chekhov's *Uncle Vanya* in radically different — and culture-specific — ways: the Russian readers found the main characters to be "educated," "soulful," and "self-sacrificing"; the American readers typically found them "lazy," "self-pitying," and "weak" (361). Vladimir Nabokov, a central figure in the canon of world literature, insisted on the cultural specificity of Chekhov's works: "For the Russian philosophical or social minded critic [Chekhov] was the unique exponent of a unique Russian type of character" ("Chekhov" 253).

In search of a more productive way to read Chekhov's prose fiction in English translation, this essay proposes a pedagogical method that explores the cultural perspectives underlying his short stories, that "[locates] the text in a rich cultural and linguistic context" (Appiah 427). This approach seeks to enable new interpretive possibilities for American readers by suggesting an alternative prism, or prisms, through which to view the motivations, emotions, and judgments of Chekhov's characters while, at the same time, sensitizing readers to the cultural specificity of perception and experience in general.

Reading Culture

Although Gilberte Furstenberg's notion that "there are many parallels to be drawn between the reading of a culture and the reading of a text" (76) is certainly true, teaching culture through literature presents many challenges. On the one hand, cultural perspectives are often elusive, as Edward Hall argued in his seminal works *The Silent Language* and *The Hidden Dimension*. Hall asserts that culture is a form of communication governed by hidden rules, that it involves both speech and actions, and that it exists outside the range of people's conscious awareness. On the other hand, when we make cultural differences too visible, we risk reducing complex cultural phenomena to simplistic stereotypes. As Nicolas Shumway remarks, "the most difficult aspect of cultural studies is not learning facts, but learning new ways of seeing" (252). This challenge is especially acute in reading the works of Chekhov, where so much is expressed in silences and ellipses. As Julie de Sherbinin argues, Chekhov's works contain "layers of meaning not immediately accessible on the surface" ("Chekhov" 286).

The methodology we propose for rendering visible some of the hidden cultural concepts, values, and beliefs animating Chekhov's short fiction is intended for instructors of literature who may not be well-versed in Russian language, history, and culture and for instructors of Russian literature who may not be sure how to lead students to unpack the thick cultural context of Chekhov's short fiction. Our goal is to help instructors and students resist the temptation to ignore the culture-specific dimension in Chekhov's works—which often occurs when his stories are read as expressions of a universal humanism—or to trivialize culture-specific references as merely contributing to what Roland Barthes referred to as a "reality effect" ("Reality Effect"). But discussion of culture-specific references in a work should not be used to reinforce common stereotypes about Russian culture and society. We therefore begin with the caution, made by Rachel May in *The Translator in the Text*, that works in translation are not about the source culture; they are of the source culture, which reminds us that culture is not so much reflected in literary works as it is refracted through the author's creative point of view and specific sociohistorical reality.

Our approach is based on many years of teaching Chekhov, both in English translation and in the original Russian, both in a traditional classroom setting and in the more exclusive study-abroad setting of Chekhov's hometown of Taganrog. The methodology is adapted from the ACTFL standards for the teaching of culture in the foreign language classroom. It is intended to help students "gain knowledge and understanding of other cultures," as elaborated in ACTFL's two culture-related standards:

> Standard 2.1: Students demonstrate an understanding of the relationship between the practices and perspectives of the culture studied.
>
> Standard 2.2: Students demonstrate an understanding of the relationship between the products and perspectives of the culture studied.

ACTFL defines cultural practices as "patterns of behavior accepted by a society [that] deal with aspects of culture such as rites of passage, the use of forms of discourse, the social 'pecking order,' and the use of space. In short, they represent the knowledge of '*what to do when and where.*'" Products, on the other hand, are defined as

> tangible (e.g., a painting, a piece of literature, a pair of chopsticks) or intangible (e.g., an oral tale, a dance, a sacred ritual, a system of education). Whatever the form of the product, its presence within the culture is required or justified by the underlying beliefs and values (*perspectives*) of that culture, and the cultural practices involve the use of that product" (*Standards*).

Our approach makes a distinction between visible aspects of culture and more elusive, at times invisible or at least unstated, perspectives. Easily adapted to the study of literary works in translation, it allows for a spiraling upward from the concrete to the abstract through guided student research and reflection. By focusing on culture-specific products, practices, and perspectives, we believe, the discussion of world literature in the classroom can problematize a simplistic identification with the characters in a text and avoid the domestication of a work into a universal humanism that is often not universal but a reflection of the values and beliefs of the dominant culture.

We model this approach using one of Chekhov's best known short stories, "The Student." It presents an encounter on Good Friday between a young student at a theological seminary and two peasant women. It was originally published as "In the Evening" ("Вечером"; "Vecherom"), but the title was later changed to "The Student," focusing greater attention on the main character, Ivan Velikopolsky. Chekhov claimed it was his favorite story (Bunin, *O Chekhove* 57).

Exploring Products and Perspectives

Although only a few pages long, the story is dense with unarticulated cultural perspectives and contains many cultural products, designated by nouns and noun phrases that were clearly chosen by Chekhov to support the story's theme. Generally speaking, products function to define or describe space in literary works, whereas practices, which have a temporal dimension, function to define time. The unpacking of the cultural specificity of the products and practices that appear in "The Student" can initiate a discussion of the nature of space and time in the story and of the extent to which that representation is distinctly Russian.

Isolating culture-specific elements for discussion is easiest when the translator renders them through the strategy of borrowing, often italicizing the foreign words. When translators choose to preserve foreign words in their translations, it is typically because the source text object has no perceived equivalent in the target text. "Samovar," for example, is a borrowing found in translations of Chekhov's "Student." Other words may lose their cultural specificity in translation. For example, the stove mentioned in the story may conjure up the image of a modern gas or electric stove. But because Ivan's father is lying on the stove, Chekhov means a traditional Russian stove (печь; pech'), made of brick, which was used both for cooking and for heating the home. The Russian stove was designed to retain heat for long periods of time, and in winter people would sleep on top of it to keep warm. Pictures of traditional Russian stoves available online show that the stove was the physical center of the Russian home.

In addition to the samovar and the stove, other products or artifacts that might be explored are the forest, the snipe, the fire, the leaky thatched roofs, the man's coat worn by Vasilisa, and the cauldron and spoons being washed by

Lukerya. Names in literary texts can also be treated as culture-specific products—Ivan Velikopolsky, Peter the Great, Rurik, Vasilisa, and Lukerya—as can the names of occupations, such as *sacristan* and even *student*. Research on the word *sacristan* (дьячок; d'iachok) will introduce the hierarchical aspect of the Orthodox clerical world: that sacristan was the lowest rung on the clerical ladder indicates the social position of Ivan's father. Research on students in late-nineteenth-century Russia will make it clear that educational opportunities were still restricted but expanding. What does it mean to be a student in a society where such a small percentage of the population is educated?

After an initial reading, students are asked to make a list of the culture-specific objects mentioned in the story, which they easily do. They are then asked to research these objects or products and present their findings to the class, along with their personal reflections on how this cultural background knowledge affects their perception of the story. Finally, students are placed in small groups and asked to organize the products thematically. The students often come up with many thematic groupings, such as the oppositions inside versus outside, home versus world, and hot versus cold. Discussion of these oppositions typically reveals that they are emotionally charged—for example, inside is related to warmth, shelter, and stasis (the stove, the samovar, the home); outside, to coldness and change (the wind, the snipe's erratic flight, Vasilisa's weeping).

During subsequent discussion of how the juxtaposition of inside and outside in the story plays out thematically, the students often note the distinction in the story between the inner world of Ivan's thoughts and feelings and the inscrutable outer appearance of the characters, also expressed as a distinction between the material world, a world of things, and the world of thoughts, ideas, and feelings. The relations between the two as presented in the story, however, is not direct or easily interpreted. This difficulty is seen in Vasilisa's failure to recognize Ivan (outward appearances cannot be trusted) and in the Apostle Peter's denial of Jesus (words can hide the truth).

Some students also note an opposition between high and low in the story: Ivan's mother and Lukerya are sitting on the ground, whereas Ivan stands throughout. Moreover, unlike the women, Ivan moves—he comes from elsewhere and ascends from the riverbank to a hilltop at the end of the story. One student saw a connection between Ivan's ascent to the hilltop and his upward social mobility as a student. The women, not moving, are left behind. The association of social mobility with ambition and pride is suggested by Ivan's invocation of the great men who changed the course of Russian history: Rurik, Ivan the Terrible, and Peter the Great. Students may observe that only the first names of the women are given, while Ivan appears with both his first and last name.

Having students research the meaning of Russian names is usually a productive exercise in almost any class on Russian literature, particularly because the device of talking names—names that indicate qualities of characters—was extensively used by nineteenth-century authors, such as Gogol, Dostoevsky, and Chekhov. Chekhov employs the device less obviously than, say, Dostoevsky, but many of his characters' names hold symbolic, even allegorical meaning: Ivan Velikopolsky (Иван Великопольский), Vasilisa (Василиса), and Lukerya (Лукерья) have cultural associations and even intertextual references. The geographic associations of *Velikopolsky*, formed from the words *velikii* (великий; "great"), and *pole* (поле; "field"), also serve to situate the character in the opposition of home versus the wide world.

Directed research, reflection, and discussion of these cultural products in "The Student" typically lead to an understanding of the encounter in the story as a clash between traditional and modern ways of life, which was especially acute in Chekhov's lifetime as Russia underwent an unprecedented period of industrialization and internal migration. Because college-age students naturally identify with the story's hero, some cultural background on traditional Russian spiritual culture and, specifically, Russian views on humility, acceptance of suffering, and fate may prompt them to reevaluate their initial assessment of both Ivan and the old women, whom American students often describe on their first reading as frightening and strange. Moreover, the high-low opposition ties nicely into notions of pride and humility, which are emotionally charged concepts in Russian culture. Humility is perhaps the supreme Russian virtue, often opposed to the perceived materialism and arrogance of the West. The central tension in the story between spiritual wisdom and intellectual wisdom, between soul and mind, is often lost on American students, who may not see humility and acceptance of suffering as virtues at all.

At this point, the instructor can introduce additional readings to deepen the students' understanding of the Russian cultural context in which Chekhov's story unfolds. Especially useful are the sections on soul (душа; dusha), painful longing (тоска; toska), acceptance of suffering (смирение; smirenie), and fate (судьба; sud'ba) in *Semantics, Culture, and Cognition: Universal Human Concepts in Culture-Specific Configurations*, by Anna Wierzbicka, a linguistic anthropologist. Also helpful are the sections devoted to Russian names, eating habits, and hospitality in Genevra Gerhart's *The Russian's World: Life and Language*. Finally, Robert C. Williams's article "The Russian Soul: A Study in European Thought and Non-European Nationalism" offers an overview of the value of soulfulness in Russian culture, comparing it with soulfulness in African American culture. These readings may help the students develop paper topics dealing with the tension between traditional and modern culture in Chekhov's short fiction.

From Practices to Perspectives

A number of meaningful culture-specific practices in "The Student" can open up a productive discussion of time and movement through it. Most of the practices are religious and involve preparations for Easter. The Lenten practices mentioned serve in large part to organize the plot. Ivan's encounter with the two women takes place on Good Friday, the day that marks the crucifixion and death of Christ. In two days it will be Easter. Students can be asked to research Russian Easter and Lenten observances. They will learn that Easter was by far the most important holiday in czarist Russia and that Orthodox practices required the proper observation of rituals, such as cleaning, fasting, and the reading of the twelve Gospels. Ivan's father's profession of sacristan also underscores the idea of ritual observance, of "right worship," a direct translation of the Russian word for Orthodoxy, *pravoslavie* (православие).

Another culture-specific practice occurs when Ivan first approaches the two women by the campfire. Vasilisa does not recognize him at first. When she finally does, she says, "You'll be a rich man" (264), alluding to a Russian folk superstition that says wealth will come to a person when he or she is not recognized. Students can research superstitions in Russia and discuss the persistence of superstition in the face of evidence-based science—Chekhov, a doctor, would be on the side of science—and the relation of superstition to official religion, not to mention the relation between Ivan's long-term commitment to education and the superstitious prediction that he will, through no effort of his own, become wealthy.

After the students have researched these culture-specific practices and presented their findings to the class, they can discuss how ritual relates to time. Students typically raise the notion of repetition, or what could be referred to as a cyclical model of time. They can then discuss how Ivan's wish not to return home and his invocation of great men in history suggest a different model of time, of time as progress or succession.

The cultural perspectives opened up by these practices suggest a tension between the cyclical time of traditional, agrarian societies, which does not value the individual, and chronological time, represented by the history of great men and the student's desire for a future different from that of his parents. Instructors might explore the cultural perspectives informing these practices as a reflection of Chekhov's historical moment, when agrarian Russia was being transformed by industrialization, or as a clash of literary chronotopes, as elaborated by Mikhail Bakhtin in "Forms of Time and of the Chronotope in the Novel." The introduction of additional readings, such as Michael Holquist's discussion of chronological versus kairotic time in *Dostoevsky and the Novel* (102–23), may help students unpack more fully the cultural concepts underlying Chekhov's work, as would the sections on superstition and religion in Gerhart's *The Russian's World*.

The importance of exploring the cultural context of translated fiction was underscored by David Damrosch in *How to Read World Literature*:

> Reaching back over nearly five millennia and extending today to almost every inhabited region of the globe, world literature offers its reader an unparalleled variety of literary pleasure and cultural experiences. Yes this very variety also poses exceptional challenges, as we cannot expect to

> approach all these works with the fund of cultural knowledge that readers share with writers within a single tradition. (1)

The temptation to ignore cultural context is especially great with a writer like Chekhov, who leaves so much unsaid and whose fiction has for so long been presented as universal. But developing an understanding of the cultural perspectives through which Russian readers make sense of Chekhov's fiction is all the more important, because, as Kwame Anthony Appiah notes, "in the easy atmosphere of relativism—in the world of 'that's just your opinion' that pervades the high schools that produce our students—one thing that can get entirely lost is the rich differences of human life in culture" (427).

Teaching Chekhov in Translations

Carol Apollonio

More Is Better

Chekhov wrote in Russian, and yet he finds passionate readers all around the world and in every language. Since most of his readers will encounter his works only in translation, it makes sense in the classroom to develop an awareness of the role translation plays in interpretation. What would seem to be a loss—that readers do not have access to the original text—may actually turn out to be an advantage, for there are many more translations than there are originals. Despite the widespread assumption that there is only one best translation of a work, the fact is, most published translations are just fine. If instructors assign several different versions of a work, a broader range of interpretations will be possible than from reading one translation, or even from just reading the original.[1] Not only does the tactic of studying different versions foster close reading skills and a respect for the structure of the text, but it can also lead to exciting discoveries and stimulating classroom conversations. This essay analyzes various translations of three key passages from Chekhov's short stories. Where the translations differ, one can deduce that (barring outright error, which in fact is rare in reputable published translations) Chekhov's Russian allows different interpretations. By developing sensitivity to these differences, the reader, and the classroom community, can gain insights into the depth and rich potentialities of the original text.

Human Nature

Chekhov offers a distinctive vision of the way people are situated in the natural environment. It is not always clear where a person ends and nature begins. "The Grasshopper" serves as a particularly sophisticated example.[2] In this 1892 story, a frivolous young wife, Olga, chases after celebrity through an affair with a famous painter, without realizing that her husband, Dymov, is far more eminent than her acquaintances in the art world. At the center point of the story, the heroine is spending the summer out in the country with her lover, who, bored with her and sated, stares moodily out at the Volga River and its banks. A meticulous reading of different translations reveals many fruitful lines of comparison for classroom discussion. I focus on just one: the ambiguity in pronoun referent. Who is "bare," Olga or the river? In the Russian language, all nouns are gendered: masculine, feminine, or neuter. The noun for river, like the heroine, is feminine, as are the adjective ("naked or bare") modifying it and the pronoun referring to it. Translators' choices as to how to convey this ambiguity are underlined:

Garnett:
And it seemed as though nature had removed now from the Volga the sumptuous green covers from the banks, the brilliant reflections of the sunbeams, the transparent blue distance, and all its smart gala array, and had packed it away in boxes till the coming spring, and the crows were flying above the Volga and crying tauntingly, "Bare, bare [no pronoun]!"
("Grasshopper" [*"Wife" and Other Stories*] 105)

Chamot:
It seemed as if the sumptuous green carpets that were spread on the banks, the reflections of diamond rays, the transparent blue distance and the whole of the elegance of stately nature had been stripped off the Volga and packed away in a trunk till the next spring, and the ravens flew along the Volga mocking her: "Bare! Bare!"
("Grasshopper" [*"Grasshopper" and Other Stories*] 32)

Litvinov:
It seemed as if the lush green carpets on the banks, the diamond-like reflections of the sun's rays, the transparent, blue distance, and all the elegant show of nature had been taken from the Volga and laid away in a chest till next spring, and the crows flew over the river, teasing it: "Bare! Bare!" ("Grasshopper" 78)

Magarshack:
It seemed that nature had taken from the Volga the luxuriant green carpets on her banks, her diamondlike reflections of the sun's rays, her transparent blue distances, and all her gala splendour and smartness, and put it away in chests till next spring, and that the crows flew over the river teasing her: "Naked! Naked!"
("Grasshopper" [*"Lady with Lapdog"*] 115)

Hingley:
Sumptuous, green-carpeted banks, brilliantly reflected sunbeams, translucent blue distance . . . nature seemed to have taken everything showy and flamboyant from the Volga and packed it away until the coming spring, while crows flew above the river taunting its nakedness with their raucous caws. ("Butterfly" 10)

Pevear and Volokhonsky:
And it seemed as if nature now stripped the Volga of the luxurious green carpets on its banks, the diamond glints of the sun, the transparent blue distance, and all that was smart and showy, and packed it away in trunks till next spring, and the crows flew about the Volga, teasing her: "Bare! Bare!" ("Fidget" 147)

All the translations are accurate reflections of the original. Some translators chose to convey the river's feminine gender, thus encouraging the reader, looking through the eyes of the disillusioned lover, to associate the denuded river with the heroine, who herself has lost her appeal—her gaudy exterior. Indeed, the lover has stripped her himself, through his summer activity of painting the river landscape, transferring it onto canvas. She *is* the river. The association is deepened by sound play in the Russian text involving the *o*, the hard or soft (palatalized) *l*, and the *g*, as well as the feminine-gendered *-a* endings: the heroine's name is Olga; the river is the Volga.[3]

Such connections nearly always spread out into the broader text, expanding the circles of significance from the individual person into nature, and even into the moral universe. Based on this distinctive feature of his works, it is often said that Chekhov is a poet of mood. The term implies a certain haziness of tone, although Russian readers are struck by the precision of his language. To some extent, this apparent haziness may be rooted in an important feature of Russian, the impersonal expression. Many conditions and emotions are expressed without an explicit subject; the implication is that the state may originate outside the individual. For example, where English says, "I'm bored," Russian will say, "It is boring." Where English says, "I'm thirsty," Russian, bizarrely, will say, "It wants itself to drink for me." Where English says, "I have to," Russian will say, "It is necessary to." This basic difference affects the interpretation of some of Chekhov's most famous stories. An example is the translation of the title of the 1888 story variously translated as "Sleepy," "I Want to Sleep," "Sleepy-Eye," "Sleepyhead," and "Let Me Sleep." The sleepy person is not mentioned in the Russian title, and the story is not told in the first person, so the addition of a pronoun is the translators' decision.

Chekhov uses impersonal expressions liberally in his works to cast doubt on the boundaries that divide people from one another. The first paragraph of chapter 2 of his "The Lady with the Dog" serves as an example:

> It was a thirsty day. . . . One did not know what to do with oneself.
> ([trans. Garnett] 7)
>
> All day long he was plagued with thirst. . . . It was impossibly hot.
> ([trans. Koteliansky and Cannan] 210)
>
> It was a parching day. . . . The heat was overpowering.
> ([trans. Litvinov in *Anton Chekhov's Short Stories*] 223–24)
>
> One was thirsty all day. . . . One did not know what to do with oneself.
> ([trans. Yarmolinsky] 415–16)
>
> It was a thirsty day. . . . There was no escaping from the heat.
> ([trans. Coulson] 274)

> All day long Gurov was plagued with thirst. . . . There was no refuge from the heat. ([trans. Payne] 287)

> All day long one felt thirsty. . . . There was nowhere to go. ([trans. Magarshack] 267)

> One felt thirsty all day. . . . They could not think of a place to go. ([trans. Fen] 226)

> It was a thirsty day. . . . There was no escaping the heat. ([trans. Hingley] 9)

> They felt thirsty all day. . . . There was no escape. ([trans. Pevear and Volokhonsky in *Stories*] 364)

> It was a holiday. . . . All day one felt thirsty. . . . But there was no escaping the heat. ([trans. Wilks] 226)

> They were thirsty all day. . . . They did not know what to do with themselves. ([trans. Bartlett] 169–70)

In grappling with the characters' (or the day's) thirst, the translators have offered a wide variety of solutions, from using the nonspecific pronoun "one" to switching the grammar to describe a "thirsty day" to attributing the thirst to a specific person or persons in the story: "they," "Gurov," "he." As for the problem of not knowing what to do or where to go, the Russian says, literally, "There was nowhere to put oneself" ("Некуда было деваться"; "Nekuda bylo devat'sia" [*Sochineniia* 10: 131]). The idea here is that the characters, still just beginning to get to know each other, are out in the open air, and the forces of nature, circumstance, and the mysterious processes of their inner souls are all conspiring to send them into each other's arms—somewhere, but not out in public. The whole story traces the couple's search for a place where they can nurture their love, out of sight of other people and away from society's inevitable condemnation. The absence of a subject conveys the shared nature of this quest and the characters' lack of control over the circumstances of their love. The translation solutions for this use of the impersonal construction, taken collectively, communicate a range of nuances inherent in the Russian phrasing that are impossible to grasp in a single translation. The issue of interpersonal boundaries is vital to an interpretation of "The Lady with the Dog," whose plot shows the miracle of love that comes when such boundaries are crossed. Chekhov's characters, even as they maintain their human uniqueness, merge into a landscape that is both socially constructed and natural and filled with moral significance.[4]

A Symphony of Translations

Consider the following riddle:

> I am the beginning of the end,
> And the end of time and space.
> I am essential to creation,
> And I surround every place.

The answer is the letter *e*. The only way to answer the riddle is to turn attention away from the denotation—what the words mean—and focus on their form. It's a matter of perspective. Chekhov manipulates all the features of the Russian language, but his attention to sound is especially elusive to the non-Russian reader. Heeding the sound and rhythm of words in his works is something like listening to them as musical compositions. Narrative, like music, unfolds its meaning through time. By muting the referential meaning of the words (who is doing what, where, and when), we can come to appreciate the rhythm of the words, sentences, and paragraphs and the story's entire flow of sounds. Translators often do an excellent job of conveying the rhythm, the text's crescendos and decrescendos, on the level of syntax. But when it comes to a text's phonetic level, comparing a number of translations can pay off.

"Sleepy" tells the story of Var'ka, a young girl who as a nanny is forced to care for a colicky baby who cries constantly and will not sleep. After she stays up day and night, her exhaustion and desperate need for sleep cause her to smother the baby—whereupon she sinks into blessed sleep at last. The syllables of the classic Russian lullaby, *baiushki baiu* ("баюшки баю" [*Sochineniia* 7: 8]), that Var'ka sings to the baby serve as a refrain (both in the song and in Chekhov's story overall) that marks her gradual descent into irrationality until she realizes with maniacal joy at the story's climax that the baby is her enemy. The *bu-bu* sounds of the lullaby serve as a transition between the present-day plot (Var'ka as an oppressed nanny) and the backstory (how she was forced to become a nanny after her father died suddenly). The father in her memory moans *bu-bu-bu* ("Бу-бу-бу" [8]), echoing the syllables of the song. Different translators offer different solutions to this challenge, only some of them reflecting the musical echoes between the two plots:

> "Bayu-bayushki-bayu,
> A little song I sing . . ."
>
> . . . .
>
> The pain is so strong that he is not able to speak even one word and only draws air into himself and beats with his teeth like a drum:
>
> "Boo-boo-boo-boo . . ." ("I Want")

> "*Bayu, bayushki, bayu*
> Nurse will sing a song to you."
>
> . . . .
>
> The pain is so intense that he cannot utter a single word, and only inhales air and emits through his lips a drumming sound. "Bu, bu, bu, bu, bu—"
> ("Sleepy-head" [trans. Long] 181)
>
> "Hush-a-bye, my baby wee,
> While I sing a song for thee."
>
> . . . .
>
> The pain is so violent that he cannot utter a single word, and can only draw in his breath and clack his teeth like the rattling of a drum: "Boo—boo—boo—boo . . ." ("Sleepy" [trans. Garnett])
>
> *Hush-a-bye, hush-a-bye,*
> *I'll sing you a song . . .*
>
> . . . .
>
> The pain was so fierce that he was unable to speak a single word. He just sucked in the air and expelled it from his mouth with a sound like the rolling of drums.
> "*Bu, bu, bu, bu . . .*" ("Sleepyhead" [trans. Payne] 131, 132)
>
> "*Bayu-bayushki-bayu*,
> I'll sing a song for you . . ."
>
> . . . .
>
> The pain is so great that he cannot utter a single word, only draw in sharp breaths and beat a tattoo with his teeth: "Bm-bm-bm-bm-bm . . ."
> ("Let Me Sleep" [trans. Miles and Pitcher] 192)
>
> "Hush-a-bye, baby,
> I'll sing you a song . . ."
>
> . . . .
>
> The pain is so intense that he cannot utter a single word and only sucks in air, his teeth chattering like a drum roll: "Rat-a-tat-tat-tat."
> ("Sleepy" [trans. Pevear and Volokhonsky in *Stories*] 50)

This manipulation of language at the phonetic level is representative of Chekhov's distinctive genius.[5] One difficulty for translators is that teeth in the real world make dental sounds (*ddd-ttt*) rather than bilabial ones (*bbb-ppp*). One translator (R. E. C. Long) changes "teeth" (*зубами*; *zubami*) to "lips" (*губами*; *gubami*). Another translator, the clever and evasive Robert Payne, replaces the part (teeth) with the whole (mouth). Pevear and Volokhonsky abandon the *bbb* sound for what is lexically the safer version in English, "rat-a-tat-tat-tat," essentially exchanging tympani for the snare. The point here is that the sound play is not gratuitous but serves as a link between the story's two plots: it is the father's death, after all, that left Var'ka to fend for herself among hostile strangers. The *bu-bu-bu* sounds her father makes not only shift the reader's perspective from present to past but also keep this backstory ever present, subconsciously as it resounds in the sounds of the lullaby, in the moral drama that is unfolding in the present.

In the process of conducting close readings of Chekhov's stories, students and instructors can be alert to broader rhythms and sound play on the sentence and paragraph levels. At important moments in his stories Chekhov sometimes constructs long lyrical paragraphs culminating in a short but powerful phrase, often repeated, that carries a sonic and moral punch. The Olga-Volga passage from "The Grasshopper" quoted above is an example; the repetition of the word "Naked!" at the culmination of the paragraph marks the heroine's moral fall—not bearing authorial judgment, as would be inevitable in a work by a writer like Tolstoy, but communicating this moral tension as part of the overall sound texture of the story. Once students and instructors are aware of this feature of Chekhov's style, they can seek out similar passages at climactic moments in his other stories.

Reminding students that the text they are reading was originally written in a foreign language is in itself pedagogically worthwhile—worthwhile even, or especially, when the teacher or the students are unaware of the specifics of that language. Using multiple translations of the same story offers a rich range of educational and conversational opportunities. In addition to discussing textual differences in class, students can be assigned to write papers comparing several translations of a story. In the process, they learn about Chekhov's language and style and, what is more, may even discover errors in a translation; this sometimes happens, and discovering errors can be an exciting experience. Comparing translations in this way helps develop a rigorous approach to close reading, an attention to detail that can lead to stimulating class discussions, and, ultimately, a deep appreciation for Chekhov's art.

NOTES

[1] It is easy to obtain online versions of most of Chekhov's stories and plays. Some are clumsy, unattributed, error-sprinkled, or incomplete, but even such defective texts can spark excellent discussions. An indispensable source is Cathy Popkin's Norton Critical Edition of Chekhov's short stories, which foregrounds problems of translation (*Anton Chekhov's Selected Stories*).

[2] Translators have given this story various titles, including "The Butterfly" and "The Fidget." Generally speaking, instructors should know a story's date of publication and narrow their search accordingly. Of course, a sure-fire way of identifying a story is by

comparing translations of the first sentence. Online translation programs may also be of help in tracking down different versions.

3 The phonetic reinforcement of the theme continues in the Russian text; the word for "bare" or "naked" is *golaia* (*голая*).

4 I analyze this example from "The Lady with the Dog" in my essay "Gained in Translation."

5 Chekhov is a great master of onomatopoeia; my personal favorite is the *r-r-r-nga-nga-nga* ("ррр . . . нга-нга-нга-нга . . . ррр . . .") growl of the dog under the table in the story "The Teacher of Literature" ("Учитель словесности"; "Uchitel' slovesnosti" [*Sochineniia* 8: 313]). These nonsense syllables have no denotative meaning whatsoever and therefore can be universally appreciated.

A Tolstoyan Narratological Lesson: Teaching What Chekhov Learned

Michael C. Finke

Among the works by Tolstoy that Chekhov engaged, both in his art and in his life as a consumptive and a physician, was the story "Death of Ivan Ilych" (1886; "Смерть Ивана Ильича"; "Smert' Ivana Il'icha"). This masterpiece features in surveys of nineteenth-century Russian, European, and world literature, as well as in philosophy and medical humanities courses focused on the body, illness, death, and dying. I have found it particularly useful to pair this story by Tolstoy with several of Chekhov's commonly taught stories, and this essay outlines how this works in reading "The Kiss" (1887), "A Boring Story" (1889), "Gusev" (1890), and "Ward No. 6" (1892).

In Russia of the late 1880s, Tolstoy's influence was felt by every serious author of prose fiction. Chekhov was particularly sensitive, however, to how Tolstoy represented illness, doctoring, and physicians. Although far from uncritical toward his own writings, Chekhov recoiled at Tolstoy's grossly unbalanced treatment of physicians: when rereading *War and Peace* in the early 1890s, he thought that Tolstoy "must have been thoroughly saturated with hatred for medicine" (*Pis'ma* 4: 291 [to Aleksei Suvorin, 25 Oct. 1891]); amid praise for Tolstoy's "Kreutzer Sonata," Chekhov indicted "the audacity with which Tolstoy treats topics about which he knows nothing . . ."; he should have read "two or three books written by medical specialists" (4: 18 [to Aleksei Pleshcheev, 15 Feb. 1890]).

And yet, had Chekhov realized his ambition, strong in the mid-1890s, to become a professor of medicine at Moscow University, he might well have had his students read "Ivan Ilych." Why so? What would they have learned? The story's themes of alienation and death never fail to arouse and engage students. My strategy exploits this to conduct students to a place they might not willingly go otherwise. Proceeding from thematics to stylistics, we focus on the story's narratological features, and then observe their echoes in Chekhov's own art. We move from the "what" to the "how" of the two authors, and we register its meaningfulness.

But first, a couple of relevant words about the "why" of "Ivan Ilych." Death was one of the master themes of Tolstoy's art and life both. Mikhail Bakhtin and scholars working with Bakhtin's theoretical framework have offered some powerful generalizations.[1] Among these is that death and revelation are always paired in Tolstoy, and death is always for oneself in Tolstoy, having meaning only for the individual who is dying—not for those who gather to mourn or bury. With a few notable exceptions,[2] Tolstoy's artistic treatments of death were experiments in seeing it from the inside, or in dramatizing the difference between that perspective and the exterior one. In 1897, when Chekhov lay hospitalized after the nearly fatal hemorrhage by which his advanced TB declared itself,

Tolstoy rushed to his bedside and very nearly talked Chekhov to a literal death. He came to talk about death, and it was the smell of death, and the prospect of hearing someone of Chekhov's sensitivity and intellect reflect on death as he lay dying, that attracted Tolstoy.

This is not unrelated to the "how" of "Ivan Ilych." However gripping the topic of death, the key to the story's effectiveness, from which Chekhov learned a great deal, may be found in its formal aspect. Tolstoy's story works on a rather simple, binary logic, whereby everything that takes place in Ivan Ilych's life is either good or bad, and what's positive and what's negative undergo reversal by the story's end. The story sets up a constellation of motifs placing in opposition the social code, propriety, and decorum, on the one hand, and awkwardness, stumbling, scandal, bad smells, and screams, on the other. Ivan's life has been all about mastering and implementing the code of a comfortable and successful bourgeois life, about being comme il faut. By the end of the story, however, the values associated with propriety and with scandal have been reversed. Words and phrases with positive associations for Ivan and their opposites are easily elicited from students and tabulated on a blackboard.

The most important of these reversals, arguably, involves the binary of other and self and is tightly connected to the handling of narrative point of view. It's he who's dead, not me, and a good thing too—so reflect the colleagues who read the announcement in the newspaper at the story's beginning. But the story's design breaks down this psychological difference through its handling of narrative point of view. Students will discover this on their own when prompted by some open-ended questions about how the story is told.

"Ivan Ilych" opens with an omniscient, third-person narration of his colleagues learning of Ivan's death in a newspaper obituary. There could be no greater narrative distance on Ivan when he is introduced. And all the colleagues who see the announcement immediately think: how can I (or a relative) take Ivan's place—his place in the workplace, that is. The narrative's brutally calculated manipulation of narrative point of view gives the reader exactly what Ivan's colleagues dream of obtaining: Ivan's place. We take his place not at work, but as an intensely suffering, dying human being. We start with maximum distance on Ivan. We see Ivan's wake largely through the eyes of the detached and unsympathetic Pyotr Ivanovich. We then get Ivan's biography, told with unmistakable irony. We know that the narrator means the opposite when he says, mimicking Ivan's view, that all was going just right for Ivan Ilych: "So that on the whole [his] life continued to flow as he considered it should do—pleasantly and properly" ("Death" 112); "Everything was as it should be" (118); "So they lived, and all went well, without change, and life flowed pleasantly" (119). And in catching the irony of that double-voiced discourse we have been invited to share the narrator's supercilious view of Ivan. We are observing him; we are safely distant from him; we are superior to him—just like the doctors who examine Ivan, just like Ivan had been as a judge in his own courtroom. And the narrative still promises voyeuristic pleasure in the spectacle of impending death.

But then, quite subtly, our point of view merges with that of Ivan: although the story continues to be told in the third person, narration becomes—without any overt marking of this shift—almost entirely personal, free indirect discourse attached to the point of view of Ivan. This tricks readers into a kind of identification with Ivan. Some of the students invariably notice that the narrative manner has changed somewhere between the story's beginning and its end. They can be asked to locate in the text the place where this change occurs: the scene in which Ivan undergoes medical examination, submitting to the putatively scientific, objectivizing gaze of a professional. From here to the end of the story, readers are compelled to feel what the patient feels. The narrator's distance from and irony toward Ivan disappear, and Ivan as other has become Ivan as us.[3]

So, what of Chekhov? There is only one remark about "Ivan Ilych" in Chekhov's letters, but, though offhand and appearing a few years after Tolstoy's story was published, it is telling. In a letter to Aleksei Suvorin of 5 or 6 October 1888, Chekhov says that Viktor Burenin, who has been ailing, should quit reading "Ivan Ilych" and, by extension, quit worrying about death from rheumatism (*Pis'ma* 3: 15). Tolstoy's story is pathogenic, Chekhov suggests; how the narrative works over its readers was a lesson that he learned well.

Several of Chekhov's most remarkable stories from the next few years experiment with the handling of narrative point of view;[4] in some, he practices the same sleight of hand that he likely observed in "Ivan Ilych." Certain of these stories involve doctoring, death, and dying; others do not. The following sections sketch how reading and discussing "Ivan Ilych" can enrich the reading of other stories by Chekhov.

"Ward No. 6" begins with a very chatty, overt narrator who offers readers great distance from all the characters and settings he describes, and expresses his own likes and dislikes—of Gromov, for instance: "I like his broad, high-cheekboned face, always pale and unhappy, reflecting as in a mirror his soul tormented by struggle and prolonged fear. . . . I like the man himself . . ." (173). This "I" narrator addresses a "you," the readers, in a perpetually present tense, and he invites these readers to take a risky expedition into the ward, where "we" will see "them," the madmen: "If you are not afraid of being stung by nettles, let us go down the narrow path that leads to the annex and see what is going on inside" (171). After introducing the "caretaker Nikita," who is "convinced that *they* [Chekhov's emphasis] must be beaten" (171–72), we enter a room with people on beds screwed to the floor: "These are the madmen" (172). The rhetoric of the opening figures the readers as sightseers who, even if they are not afraid to get close, remain alien to this world. But while presenting the case history of Gromov, the narration shifts into a free-indirect-discourse representation of the madman's thoughts, so that the narrator's perspective and voice merge with Gromov's:

> He was not guilty of anything that he knew of and could pledge that he would never kill, or burn, or steal; yet it was not difficult to commit a crime

> accidentally, inadvertently, and was slander or, finally, a judicial error impossible? . . . Those who take an official, business-like attitude towards other people's suffering, like judges, policemen, doctors, from force of habit, as time goes by, become callous to such a degree that they would be unable to treat their clients otherwise than formally even if they wanted to; in this respect they are no different from the peasant who slaughters sheep and calves in his backyard without noticing the blood. (176)

The same merging occurs with Ragin. First his physical appearance is described, then his biography is given, also from an outside perspective, but soon the narration shifts to free indirect discourse: "Then, too, why prevent people from dying, if death is the normal and natural end of every man? So what if some dealer or clerk lives for an extra five or ten years? If the purpose of medical science is seen as the alleviation of suffering by medication, then, willy-nilly, the question arises: why alleviate it?" (183). Beginning with chapter 9 (191), the narration attaches to Ragin's point of view and remains there until the end, when two short paragraphs tell how the doctor's corpse is disposed of after his death (220–21).

The powerful effect of "Ward No. 6" on readers results, arguably, from Chekhov's clever handling of point of view, which begins by maximizing the distance of the readers ("we") from the madmen ("they") but then merges the perspective of the narrator and the readers with that of the madmen. When the doctor enters the asylum and begins speaking to Gromov, during which the doctor refers to himself and Gromov as "we," the reader is ushered into Ragin's perspective unmarkedly, by sleight of hand. This sharing of his internal experience facilitates the readers' psychic identification with the doctor and makes the story's shocking finale of his beating and death experienced from within all the more effective.[5]

In "Gusev," one of Chekhov's boldest experiments in the handling of narrative point of view, free indirect discourse from the point of view of the character Gusev seems to remain in operation after his death, which is itself unmarked in the narration: when Gusev is fetched for burial at sea, we have no clue at first that he has died: "He sleeps for two days, and on the third day two sailors come from topside and carry him out of the sick bay" (121). When his corpse is tossed overboard, the narration, hitherto issuing from his point of view, does not leave him, giving the story's ending an uncanny feeling and leading some readers to believe that he has been buried at sea while still alive. The character's proper name and pronouns referring to him remain the grammatical subject in active constructions following the unremarked death. It is not Gusev's corpse but Gusev doing these things, and the point of view proceeds undersea, where only Gusev goes: "He goes quickly toward the bottom. Will he get there? . . . But now he meets on his way a school of little fish, which are known as pilot fish" (120).

The ensuing return of the narrative to the surface of the sea, which plays a great role in the uncanny effect of the story's ending, arguably continues this pattern of free indirect discourse attached to the point of view of Gusev.

Although there are no overt indications that Gusev's body resurfaces together with the narrative point of view, the laws of physics suggest it: once his shroud has been ripped open by a shark and the weights that were dragging his corpse downward have fallen out of it, the buoyant corpse is likely to be moving upward. Readers, conditioned by the stylistic pattern established from the story's start, and confused by the way Gusev is brought up on deck for burial at sea without any mention of his death, cannot help but continue to associate the narrative point of view with Gusev's consciousness, and the use of the present tense supports that association. Asking the class what exactly happens at the end of this story always provokes lively discussion. Some readers assert that the shark eats Gusev. Is it there in the text? How do they know? How can I argue that my hypothesis regarding Gusev's resurfacing is more valid than this alternative?

Finally, the class can be asked to relate the story's narrative stragegy to its ending: the description of the cloud shapes and the final image of an anthropormorphized nature that casts off human language, a nature that is unapprehended (paradoxically) by human consciousness.

The Chekhov story most often associated with "Ivan Ilych," "A Boring Story," seems to diverge from its model precisely in terms of the handling of point of view and emplotment. Thematically close to "Ivan Ilych," this first-person narration, in which a mortally ill professor of medicine becomes increasingly alienated from those closest to him and his own self as seen by others (his name), does not adopt but rather inverts or negates key narrative features of Tolstoy's example. The professional, objectivizing gaze that Ivan Ilych had practiced as a judge, and which he recoiled against when he came to occupy the position of patient, is turned by the brilliant physician-researcher-lecturer upon himself and his intimates. The result is quite destructive. Rather than begin with distance between viewer and object, this first-person narrative depicts a process of alienation from one's self, family, and friends, as analytic powers are turned inward.

Finally I turn to a story that, while chronologically close to "Ivan Ilych," is thematically unlike it and has not been associated with it: "The Kiss." Once again, the class is asked to describe how narrative point of view is handled. "Kiss" begins with an impersonal narration that gives a wide-angled perspective on an artillery brigade's arrival in a little town en route to a summer encampment. The story's first line might be an unsigned newspaper dispatch: "On the twentieth of May, at eight o'clock in the evening, all six batteries of the N___ Reserve Artillery Brigade halted for the night on their way to camp in the village of Mestechki" (95). At times point of view and voice do approach those of the officers who, it seems, will be the focus of the story. Eventually, however, the narrative's focus narrows and narration itself becomes solely and overtly attached to the perspective of its late-appearing main character. This occurs over the course of the long paragraph at the end of the cited passage that first introduces Ryabovich, beginning with the words: "The most ill at ease of them all was Second Captain Ryabovich, a short, stooped officer with spectacles and whiskers like a lynx" (98). The exterior view of Ryabovich given here would seem to signal that we have not yet come to inhabit his point of view, though a close analysis not possible here reveals important nuances (see Finke, "Of Interpretation" 134, 140–41). Regardless of where this process starts, by the end of the paragraph, the narration has clearly become personal and attached to his point of view. Students readily indentify this section of the narrative as involving a shift, and then are asked what textual features tipped them off. Here I often introduce the operation suggested by Roland Barthes ("Introduction" 262): if one replaces the name Ryabovich with the first-person singular pronoun and adjusts the verbs accordingly, the narrative still makes sense.

Why, I ask students, does Chekhov introduce the main character only after three pages into a far from lengthy story?[6] And why the tricky handling of point of view and voice, whereby the reader's consciousness, having been well aligned with an outside perspective on Ryabovich, is manipulated into that of Ryabovich himself? These formal features of the narrative are tightly tied to its thematic development of Ryabovich's character. Ryabovich becomes the central character in the very passage that defines him as unlike the other officers and peripheral:

> While some of his comrades assumed serious expressions and others forced smiles, his face, his lynxlike whiskers, and his spectacles all seemed to say: "I am the most shy, the most modest, and most colorless officer in the whole brigade!" On first entering the room, and later . . . all merged into a single, overwhelming impression which inspired in him a feeling of alarm and a desire to hide his head. (98)

Notice that Ryabovich's speech first occurs as quoted speech—and not even directly quoted, because the words are imputed to him from an outside perspective on the basis of how he looks ("all seemed to say"). As the paragraphs proceed to describe Ryabovich's disorientation, the objective narrator's discourse retreats to the parenthetical: "(physiologists call such a condition, in which the subject sees but does not understand, 'psychic blindness')" (98–99). By the end of this paragraph, which began with a description of Ryabovich's extraneousness, Ryabovich has become, ironically, the narrative's center of attention, and from here to the end of the story free indirect discourse attached to his point of view predominates.

This stylistic shift brilliantly parallels the development of the story's psychological theme. Ryabovich's self-image—his feeling that he does not belong in this milieu, that all the pleasures of this house (family, women, easy social interaction) are not for him—alters as his imagination works over the mistaken kiss. Suddenly he no longer sees himself as peripheral; now at ease, he even imagines himself as a center of attention, with all the others arrayed around him:

> He completely forgot that he was round-shouldered and colorless, that he had lynxlike whiskers and a "nondescript appearance" (as he had once been described by some ladies whose conversation he had accidentally overheard). . . . [A]fter his conversation with her Ryabovich began to

> smile even more tenderly, and to think that he was surrounded by splendid people. . . . (102)

Students can be asked to find other evidence of this shift in how Ryabovich imagines his position in space and among people. For instance, in building his fantasy out of the woman's kiss, he substitutes himself for its intended addressee, thus becoming a hero worthy of narrative focus; and on the walk back to his night's lodgings from the general's house, when Ryabovich looks at a fire on the other bank of the river, it seems that even the fire is looking at him. Chekhov's handling of narrative point of view in the story is calculated to enhance this thematic aspect.

It may be impossible to prove that Chekhov's mastery of this narrative technique is at least in part due to his reading of Tolstoy,[7] but there is nonetheless great pedagogical value in reading these works of the two authors together. In Chekhov's case there is a further argument to be made: contemplating the ethics of narration went hand in hand for Chekhov with contemplating the ethics of medical practice.

In the mid-1890s it appeared possible that his book on Sakhalin might earn Chekhov a doctorate and teaching position at Moscow University. He hoped to teach the introduction to internal medicine to first-year medical students. In discussing this prospect with his medical school colleague Grigorii Rossolimo, who was now on the faculty, he imagined imparting a new way of seeing the patient, a teaching project that anticipated today's field of medical humanities:

> I, for instance, suffer from intestinal catarrh and well understand what such a patient feels, what sort of mental tortures he experiences, but this is rarely comprehensible to a doctor. If I were a teacher, then I would try to draw my audience as deeply as possible into the realm of the subjective feelings of the patient, and I think that this could really be of use to the students. (Rossolimo 436)

Chekhov's plan involved implementing the lesson Tolstoy had delivered with "Death of Ivan Ilych." And for Chekhov, the lesson was both medical and literary: it would have been how he handled narrative point of view in telling a patient's story in his lectures as a professor of medicine that conditioned how his "audience" (of budding doctors) saw that patient. Discussions of Chekhov's two professional identities invariably make claims about what being a doctor gave to his art. But it was a two-way street.

NOTES

Translations from the Russian are mine, unless otherwise indicated.

1 For a sharp summary of this theme work (esp. about Tolstoy as contrasted with Dostoevsky), see C. Emerson 160–64.

[2] The most striking exception, perhaps, is the death of Petya Rostov in *War and Peace*, precisely because of its meaninglessness.

[3] Preliminary drafts of the story had a different narrative strategy: Ivan's sufferings have been entered into a diary, which is read and related by his friend Pyotr Ivanovich. Considering why Tolstoy revised this approach, if a class can afford to address it, fits in well with the interpretation I'm suggesting.

[4] Some experiments with point of view precede "Ivan Ilych"—for example, the 1884 serialized detective novel *The Shooting Party* or *Drama during the Hunt* (*Drama na okhote*; *Драма на охоте* [*Sochineniia* 3: 241–416]), where the detective-narrator is revealed at the end as the killer in the crime he is investigating.

[5] On readers' response, see the editors' commentary in *Sochineniia* 8: 463.

[6] The oddness of this narrative tactic for Chekhov is noted by Lapushin ("Potselui" 154).

[7] The shift in narrative point of view in "Kiss" differs from the earlier experiment referred to in note 4, and is emblematic of a pervasive change in Chekhov's inning at this time. According to A. P. Chudakov, whose monograph *Chekhov's Poetics* remains the benchmark study of this aspect of Chekhov's stylistics, 1888 is marked by a new prevalence of "narrative [. . .] saturated with the heroes' voices" (44) and point of view, in what he calls "the objective manner," in which "the narrator's subjectivity is eliminated and the hero's point of view and his words predominate" (33).

Chekhov in the Undergraduate Creative Writing Classroom

John Griswold

Unused Resources

I've always assumed many writers in the academy feel a debt to Chekhov and want to pass on their appreciation to undergraduate students. After all, as Claire Messud says, "To trace the influence of Chekhov on contemporary fiction is like searching for the original cutting from which a vast plant has grown" (170).

But when I started looking for this formal influence, I didn't find it. *Writing Fiction: A Guide to Narrative Craft* (Burroway, Stuckey-French, and Stuckey-French), which is marketed by its publisher, on the Web site *My Pearson Store*, as "[t]he most widely used and respected text in its field," has no Chekhov stories in it; neither do other popular texts, such as *The Sincerest Form: Writing Fiction by Imitation* (Delbanco) or *Shaping the Story* (Baechtel).

The Writer's Chronicle, a magazine published by the main professional organization for writers in the academy, lists in its indices only three craft essays devoted exclusively to Chekhov since 1980. (Though a hundred essays mention his name at least once.) Thirty years of the archives of *Poets and Writers Magazine*, published by "the nation's largest nonprofit literary organization serving poets, fiction writers, and creative nonfiction writers," as described on its Web site, includes six essays tagged "Chekhov," which are on contemporary writers deemed American Chekhovs (e.g., Andre Dubus) or on writers who are also medical doctors (e.g., Ethan Canin).

In responses to a survey of faculty members at the top twenty-five American creative writing MFA programs, only twelve teachers said they'd ever used his stories in an undergrad class.[1]

One anonymous respondent said that he did not use Chekhov stories but did use the essay "Learning from Chekhov," by Francine Prose. Many students told him that the essay made them want to read Chekhov. In general the respondent tried to limit his course packs to work "from the last few decades" and to work that was originally in English.

Infamously, only three percent of literature published in the United States is in translation (Rohter). As for "the last few decades," I've often heard colleagues speak of noncontemporary literature in ways that echo Gertrude Stein on Hemingway: It "smells of the museums."

More than anything, though, the benevolent curse "a writer's writer" is applied to Chekhov, referring perhaps to the quietude, the elliptical endings, and his "he and she" domesticity. It is hard to teach what Vladimir Nabokov called "a tint between the color of an old fence and that of a low cloud" or "a world of waves instead of particles of matter" ("Chekhov" 253, 262). The stories are, in Seinfeldian terms, often stories about nothing. Like irony, this quality is much praised but little understood by undergraduate writers, whose own writing often starts with rants, set pieces of grotesque violence, weird dreams, and drug trips.

"A story is just a bunch of stuff that happens," one student told me.

So what in Chekhov might be transmitted to undergrads in an age of canonical suspicions? How might Chekhov be useful when they say they want to write like Thomas Pynchon instead of a more Chekhovian writer, such as Jhumpa Lahiri? What models can Chekhov provide to students heavily influenced by simplistic narratives from digital media?

The answer, I believe, is that he can help students learn to see, find their own stories, and begin to understand the complexity of art.

Seeing

Denise Levertov says, "[I]t was Chekhov's vision of life that I received and cherished, and which, however imperceptibly, affected my own vision and consequently the course of my life" (146). For me, too, Chekhov's way of seeing has remained valid through marriage, children, the death of my parents, and the struggles of career. But what will students see when I ask them to slip on the pince-nez?

As Simon Karlinsky has pointed out, ". . . Chekhov is not the hazy writer some . . . take him to be, but a very precise and observant one" (Chekhov, *Anton Chekhov's Life* 142). Philip Hensher says, "Overwhelmingly, that sense of life [in the stories] arises from the astonishing, unelaborated concreteness of Chekhov's evocations of the world." He goes on to list dozens of words for things in just a couple of stories—unpressed caviar, mud, acetic acid, a thicket of wild pears—which "create . . . a world of unprecedented solidity." The lesson he draws is that "it would be truer to say that Chekhov's manner reflects a conviction that there is nothing for the writer to talk about but the physical world and people's lives in it" (128). This statement covers a lot of creative writing's old saw "Show don't tell" and provides guidance for beginning writers, who almost without exception are anxious not only about filling portfolios by the end of the semester but also about what to write on their first pages.[2]

"No ideas but in things," as William Carlos Williams says (6), or, more understandably for students who've written solipsistic meditations instead of short stories: No life for your characters but in the context of their world, so please take note of concrete, sensory details—made significant by being the ones that characters experience or surround themselves with or that are emblematic of their problems.

But the impulse toward "people's lives" includes something beyond the physical world, what Vladimir Kataev calls Chekhov's tendency to epistemology (24). That is, with Chekhov, the dramatic interest often lies in what characters think they know about their worlds, how they're mistaken, and how they take their worlds inside to manipulate them emotionally.

That passage in "Lady With the Dog" in which Gurov returns home after another affair—Nabokov says it's an example of "what in Chekhov's quiet stories may be called the climax" ("Anton Chekhov" 259)—is one of my favorites in all literature:

> He returned to Moscow on a fine frosty day, and when he put on his fur-lined overcoat and thick gloves, and sauntered down Petrovka Street, and when, on Saturday evening, he heard the church bells ringing, his recent journey and the places he had visited lost their charm for him. . . . [O]nce more [he] glowed with the flattering consciousness that well-known lawyers and actors came to his house, that he played cards in the Medical Club opposite a professor. He could once again eat a whole serving of Moscow Fish Stew in a pan.
>
> ([trans. Litvinov, in *Anton Chekhov's Short Stories*] 226)

I don't even like chowder, but that fish stew served in a pan makes me crazy with hunger. Just three paragraphs later, Gurov's feelings about the very same place and people are reversed by his emotions. Touched off by an acquaintance's comment that the fish dinner was "a *leetle* off," his rage is so sudden, it's comic:

> What savage manners, what people! What wasted evenings, what tedious, empty days! Frantic card-playing, gluttony, drunkenness, perpetual talk always about the same thing. The greater part of one's time and energy went on business that was no use to anyone, and on discussing the same

> thing over and over again, and there was nothing to show for it all but a stunted wingless existence and a round of trivialities, and there was nowhere to escape to, you might as well be in a madhouse or a convict settlement. (229)

These paragraphs cover the same data of Gurov's physical and social world but point to the impressionistic nature of subjective experience, as surely as do serial paintings of haystacks or water lilies.

This is the basis—the storyhood, or storyness, one might say—for Chekhov's fiction, and Chekhov developed it early on. One of his first published stories, "Oysters" (1884), is built almost entirely around misunderstandings by the narrator. The word "oysters" on a placard over the door of a restaurant signifies in quick succession for the child: "the name of the restaurant-keeper" (3); "something midway between a fish and a crab . . . a very nice hot fish soup with savory pepper and laurel leaves"; "a creature in a shell with claws, glittering eyes, and a slimy skin . . . grown-ups would take it and . . . eat it alive with its eyes, its teeth, its legs! While it squeaked and tried to bite their lips . . ." (4). These impressions, along with description of the action—father and son standing starving outside a restaurant—make up the bulk of what's on the page.

The corrective for the boy's impressions comes from the world itself, as it so often does in Chekhov—and in life. When at last two chortling swells in top hats give the starving boy oysters, he tries to eat them shell and all, and they are entirely different from what he'd imagined, almost insignificant: "I sat at a table and ate something slimy, salt with a flavor of dampness and moldiness" (5).

Chekhov's stories, then, are partly about how well or poorly his characters see, a sort of narrative metaseeing that may account for his famous demand for total objectivity (see his letter to his brother, dated 10 May 1886, containing six precepts for successful short stories [Turkov 240–41]). What "Oysters" is about, what writing teachers sometimes call "the so what," is not far away at this point in a classroom discussion: Other characters' (and readers') understanding of oysters, and of money, triangulates with the narrator's changing impressions to make a poignant story about class, empathy, and the near madness of a father desperate to provide.

Moving the focalization out of one's own view and empathetically into a character's is a valuable lesson for apprentice writers, whose prose often unwittingly communicates their own immaturity, inexperience, or ignorance.

Stein wrote, "Gertrude Stein never corrects any detail of anybody's writing, she sticks to general principles, the way of seeing what a writer chooses to see, and the relation between that vision and the way it gets down." But I cannot say to a student, as Stein could say to a young Hemingway, "[A]fter all, you are ninety percent Rotarian." In the sly pedagogy of the creative writing classroom we talk instead about Chekhov's "The Darling," which miraculously builds sympathy for a character who, in lesser writers' hands, would be the object of scorn. Chekhov sees, and helps us see, that the character will never reconcile her outer world with her inner one, because "there is no there there," as Stein would have it.

This empathy is an important lesson for undergrads, even when virtually none of them, statistically, will go on to be writers. When Prose was asked recently what one book the newly reelected president of the United States should read, she replied, ". . . *The Complete Stories of Anton Chekhov*. Chekhov helps you imagine what it's like to be someone else . . ." ("Francine Prose").

Finding Stories

If a friend would like a story called "The Ashtray," Chekhov famously teased, fingering an ashtray on the table, he could have it for him the next morning (Constantine xiii). This claim is often reported as boasting, but it's not boasting if a writer has the method and craft to write some eight hundred stories in a relatively short life.

But what *is* a story? students demand anxiously.

"Damned if I know, for sure," admits John Barth (126).

Undergrads, who often view their own daily experiences as too prosaic to write about, get frustrated with this uncertainty. That's why many write melodrama or invent grinding engines of plot to make sure readers are moved. (When peer readers are not moved by the melodrama either, it creates more frustration.)

Chekhov's stories provide narrative models unreliant on trick endings, prurient details, pornographic violence, or sentimental suicides. They aren't about running barefoot on broken glass while machine-gunning terrorists, and they're not about copulating with fruit pies. Their dramatic basis is the conflict between inner and outer lives. This working method—addressing the mind/body problem itself—allows for a profusion of stories. Even Chekhov's notebook is filled with what we now call microfictions: "Every day after dinner the husband threatens his wife that he will become a monk, and the wife cries" (*Note-book* 92). Or:

> The spiritual life of these women is as gray and dull as their faces and dresses; they speak of science, literature, tendencies, and the like, only because they are the wives and sisters of scholars and literary men; were they the wives and sisters of inspectors or of dentists, they would speak with the same zeal of fires or teeth.
>
> (132; this note probably led to "The Darling")

It's often said in creative writing classrooms that change is the measure of whether story has been achieved; in Chekhovian terms, change is usually emotional-psychological. And so students and I read to find how his people are fooling themselves, or trying to understand, or coming back to something time and again to be more certain yet seeing something different every time they look.

The storyness of "The Kiss" is that Ryabovitch is savagely disappointed at being unable to reconcile imagination and reality, so he refuses to go out again and fulfills his own worst fear of being alone.

The storyness of "In Exile" is that, for the Tatar, forgoing the struggle between outer and inner means becoming less than human. Trapped by sentencing in a Stygian setting with a false preacher of satanic glee, who insists on accepting fate, the Tatar says, "You are bad . . . you are a beast, bad! [A] dead carcass . . . you are not alive, you are stone, clay!" (97).

The lesson for students is that our characters hope to live in the gap between outer world and inner feelings, without becoming golems—or Pollyannas. This is as valid a method for finding stories in dorm rooms as it was in Imperial Russia.

Complexity

Some student usually works up the courage to ask, "Why's literature always about *bad* stuff?" The easy answer is that drama requires conflict, which many will read as unpleasantness. Think of all the unpleasantness in Chekhov: failure, death, madness, loneliness, boredom, disappointment, poverty, and so on. Yet there's also deep comedy in him, which is important for writing students to realize, for their own sense of roundedness.

As Renato Poggioli says in his study of failed communication in Chekhov:

> Chekhov . . . never changes his laughter into a sneer, or his smile into a grimace. He constantly avoids the temptation of the grotesque, as if he knew that its nemesis is to degrade the comedy of life into a farce. While tragedy is self-sufficient . . . comedy is always a mixed genre, and needs a certain amount of tragic sense to achieve the catharsis of its own pathos and form. (315–16)

Or as Messud says, "[Chekhov's] is not a broad comedy of situation, nor is it farce. His is the subtle comedy of the everyday, the small tragicomic ironies that are often internal, invisible" (173). There are metastatements in Chekhov's stories that announce this method. Gurov, in "Lady with the Dog," "began to judge others by himself, no longer believing what he saw, and always assuming that the real, the only interesting life of every individual goes on as under cover of night, secretly" ([trans. Litvinov, in *Anton Chekhov's Short Stories*] 233).

It's been said that comedy comes from partial understanding: if you knew too much about someone's troubles, you'd no longer laugh. Yet the deepest comedy, from Cervantes and Shakespeare to Steve Martin and Bill Murray, embraces complex awareness. Chekhov's way of seeing is a cosmic point of view—the travails of humankind watched by a god with total empathy but no agency. His characters are not monochromatic but shaded, a useful model for students who have a hard time imagining beyond clichés.

It's important that students become aware of all they're presenting, even when their characters are not aware, to prevent unintended comedy. A young protagonist can be tragic all he wants, wondering why everyone is so mean to him, but the story itself, as a consciousness, must see the bigger context and somehow cue readers, explicitly or with irony, of the self-defeating actions that led to the occasion for self-pity. This capacity for complexity is what Ralph Waldo Emerson advocates when he says, "The wise man shows his wisdom in separation, in gradation, and his scale of creatures and of merits is as wide as nature. The foolish have no range in their scale, but suppose every man is as every other man. What is not good they call the worst, and what is not hateful, they call the best."

Discussing gradations in Chekhov can help writers who've drafted nice, wish-fulfillment stories with stock characters, or stories that in the first sentence announce bad people and ride them unrelentingly to their deserved end. Neither type of writing does justice to the potential of its situation, and none of us want our readers to say, as Chekhov said of Ibsen, "Listen, [he] just doesn't know life. In life it simply isn't like that" (Stanislavsky, "A. P. Chekhov" [Turkov] 113).

Specific Assignments

The course packet for my introductory fiction workshop is divided into three sections: craft essays, what I call "other sorts of stories" (poems, nonfiction, journal entries by famous writers, and so on), and an array of short stories, including at least two by Chekhov. I usually pick among "Lady with the Dog," "The Darling," "Oysters," "Gusev," "In Exile," and "The Kiss."

At the start of the semester I often begin with a game: What do you see in the stories, and what makes you say that? Students must use evidence from the text to back up their assertions, so, "The story was gloomy," is discovered to have been caused in the reader's mind by descriptions such as "In front of [Anna's house in "Lady"] was a long gray fence with inverted nails hammered into the tops of the palings" ([trans. Litvinov, in *Anton Chekhov's Short Stories*] 230). This exercise moves us past emotional responses, which can vary and be more or less relevant (less relevant might be, "I've never been to Moscow, so I just can't get into it"). As I explain, Tolstoy believed art is an "infection" (*What Is Art?*), and I want them to seek how the infection is transmitted.

Once a week students read an assignment from the packet and type a two-to-three-page response paper to my focused question. (In addition to this paper, they write comments on peer stories for the next meeting.) Though I usually assign two texts at once (a craft essay with a short story, for example), I've found that one longer Chekhov story is plenty for vigorous discussion. All response papers are collected and marked on a check system, for twenty percent of the final grade.

By playing my game, students can begin to apply answers to their own work. Sample questions might include, Is it love, in "Lady with the Dog"? I warn them that the simpler the question seems, the harder it will be to answer, because they'll need to dig for craft explanations for their emotional responses. Raucous discussion is proof that Chekhov lives. Some point to Gurov's long history of callousness, even cruelty, as when he crunches watermelon while Anna weeps. "Dmitri . . . [refers] to women as 'the lower race.' Does a man who holds women in such regard even have the capacity to love an 'inferior' being? After all, a man may love his dog, but he is not, as they say, in love with it."[3]

Others quote from Chekhov, "He and Anna Sergeyevna loved one another as people who are very close and intimate, as husband and wife, as dear friends love one another" ([trans. Litvinov, in *Anton Chekhov's Short Stories*] 234), as pure authorial evidence and add, "I believe that every great love starts out as lust and blossoms into something greater[,] because what would a great love story be if the two people who are fated to be together had no [desire] to make passionate love? It wouldn't be anything I would want to read. I believe that this is a story of modern love, a love story for us jaded souls."

Some students point to qualifying phrases such as, "they felt that" and "it seemed to them," as potential irony, because of their impressionism: "[T]here is a spectrum between obsessive lust and eternal love that can be hard to examine from the outside. It's like that gross saying about friendship and peeing your pants. Everyone can see it, but only you can feel the warmth."

Other questions I ask are:

How, in "Oysters," do we get a complex understanding of adult behavior *despite* the child's limited view?

How does the story "Gusev" survive the death of its point-of-view character—something often castigated as a narrative no-no? (Here I refer to the account of the first British printing of *Moby-Dick*, which accidentally left out the epilogue that explains Ishmael survived to tell the tale. It's said that this omission created confusion—would we still be confused now?)

In what way does "In Exile" create a story from a battle over the loss of necessary illusion? What conclusions do you reach about the outcome of the battle?

Trace, step by step, how Ryabovich in "The Kiss" creates a fantasy from a very concrete world, how it necessarily collapses, and how this leads the protagonist to spite himself.

Success

How will I prove empirically that Chekhov is a valid pedagogical choice for a creative writing course? I can't, of course, but I offer this anecdote. I had a Russian student, once, whose parents were scientists on exchange. Natasha (not her real name) was expected to be a scientist as well, but she wanted fiercely also to be a writer. She was smart, well-read for a freshman in the United States, and could critique peers' work as well as any senior in my advanced workshop. But her stories were fantasies written for herself. One was about a spunky gal starting work at a New York fashion house. There was no *there* in her fashion house, no Manhattan, and no job search. Weirdly, her protagonist giggles and blushes over her new boss's sexual harassment, and she falls in love her first day. Unfortunately, the boss uses her, then discards her for a transvestite (I think). The ending sounded something like this:

> "*MOI!? Je ne travaille pas ici? Ohhh, je travaille. Je travaille TRES BIEN*," she whipped her face up at hers with streams of expensive mascara uselessly running down her face; her elegance melted right off her face in a matter of minutes; pathetic little puddles surrounded her. "I see what happened!" she burst out loudly. "He got you too didn't he? He made you fall in love with him only to fuck your heart later to pieces with another man's ass!"

At the end of the semester, after much discussion about seeing truly, finding stories, and building complexity, and after Natasha voluntarily revised maybe twice as much as I asked, she wrote a final draft of the story that started like this:

> The sun was just rising and light shone through the white birch trees of Akademgorodok, a small academic suburb of Novosibirsk, in Siberia. The door of Room 312 of a youth hostel creaked open slowly and a girl walked out, shuffling her slippers on the old carpet under her feet; she brought a roll of toilet paper, a towel, and a bar of soap with her. "Good morning, Maria Ivanovna," she cheerfully murmured to the heavy-set woman in a skirt that broke her body into two halves, like two packaged sausages. . . .

In my end comments I wrote, "*Yes*, Natasha. Finally the story I've been hoping you'd write. It's rough yet beautifully done; imagine what you can make of it in revision. . . . I am the best teacher in the world. Thank you for this draft, which confirms it. I'm going to buy myself a cake."

In truth, Chekhov deserved much of the credit.

NOTES

[1] I conducted the decidedly informal survey using *SurveyMonkey* and social media; there were only twenty-four respondents total, despite a raffle for two cash prizes. The top twenty-five American creative writing MFA programs were listed by annual rankings in *Poets and Writers Magazine*, December 2012.

[2] This is one of the strangest phenomena of teaching creative writing. Students have, nearly without fail, read at least one short story and know what the mix (usually) of de-

scription, action, and dialogue looks like on the page. Yet asked to create their own, they freeze and go blank. I can remember this happening to me as well.

[3] These quotations come from response papers in Engl 442A at McNeese State University, in the fall of 2012. The students quoted in this essay are, in order, Alex Lopez, Luke Crowe, and Luci Thomas.

Adapting Chekhov: A Primer for Dramaturgs

Valleri J. Robinson

Theatrical adaptation is conversational and interactive. It is an interpretive practice that enables dramaturgs to engage deeply with a source text and in a dialogue with its author. In this essay, I outline how I integrate adaptation into my dramaturgy course as a means of building students' analytic, interpretive, and practical dramaturgy skills, while encouraging them to converse with Anton Chekhov.

For several years, I have used the slim volume *Orchards: Seven Stories by Anton Chekhov and Seven Plays They Have Inspired*, as a springboard for teaching Chekhov and adaptation for dramaturgs (Chekhov, Fornes, et al.).[1] This volume resulted from an event organized by the Acting Company, the national touring company for the John F. Kennedy Center. In 1985, the company commissioned seven prominent American playwrights to write plays inspired by Chekhov short stories. As noted in the book's foreword, the company's dramaturg, Anne Cattaneo, selected the stories and assigned them to the playwrights represented in the volume (n. pag.): Maria Irene Fornes, Spalding Gray, John Guare, David Mamet, Wendy Wasserstein, Michael Wellen, and Samm-Art Williams. The playwrights, among the most notable in American theater at the time, approached Chekhov with distinctive interpretations that highlighted their own diverse personal playwriting styles. The Acting Company prepared a production of the plays and toured it around the United States in 1986. The volume created out of this work provides an extremely useful foundation for teaching dramaturgy through Chekhov.

The collection offers an opportunity to introduce theater students to Chekhov's world and writing before they move into readings of his mature plays, which often overwhelm and frustrate undergraduates. In addition to presenting short works by Chekhov, the collection demonstrates the curatorial activities of dramaturgs and literary managers. It provides an array of distinctive American voices and theatrical styles for analysis, raises questions about translation, and lays out a variety of approaches to theatrical adaptation. It prepares students to discuss the question, "Why do so many American playwrights adapt Chekhov?" The plays in the collection also serve as models for an assignment, late in the semester, in which students write adaptations of Chekhov's "A Joke" or "The Man in a Case."

One concern with the volume is its use of poor and anonymous translations of the short stories. This problem can be a productive one in the dramaturgy class, however, because my students, who do not read Russian, compare the translations with other translations (such as those by Richard Pevear and Larissa Volokhonsky) in order to understand the ways in which translation can greatly affect interpretation. I refer to the stories as they appear in the *Orchards* volume, making transliteration adjustments as needed.

The course I teach, Dramaturg's Workshop, commonly combines upper-division undergraduate students and graduate students and is the sole offering in dramaturgy in our theater department at the University of Illinois. It introduces students to the variety of activities dramaturgs perform and begins to develop their dramaturgical skills. The course emphasizes practice, and exercises in adaptation are ideal for combining critical analysis and practical work.

The profession of dramaturgy developed in the United States in the 1960s in concert with the regional theater movement.[2] Since then, the profession has expanded, and dramaturgs often work in film and dance as well as theater. Production dramaturgs are specialists in dramatic literature and performance history and theory who engage with practitioners to develop new works and revive existing ones. In-house dramaturgs at institutional theaters also work with artistic directors to compose the production season and commission playwrights. They provide critical analysis of dramatic texts and performances as those texts and performances take shape in time and space, and they offer support for understanding the context or contexts of a text and its earliest performances. These theater professionals must have a broad knowledge of dramatic literature, dramatic structures, theatrical styles, and performance theories as well as superb verbal and written communication skills and an understanding of the rehearsal process in order to collaborate productively with playwrights, directors, designers, actors, and audiences.[3] So that students might begin to understand dramaturgical practice and develop and enhance the critical skills needed to perform dramaturgical tasks, I have created an instructional approach that combines deep textual analysis with broad research and practical application centered on Chekhov.

Chekhov and Dramaturgy

Dramaturgical skills can be developed using any playwright as a touchstone, but Chekhov offers unique challenges and possibilities. Early in their academic careers, students are resistant to Chekhov. They find his full-length plays impenetrable at first because of the unfamiliar names, distant locales, and uncommon dramatic structure. They overlook the subtlety of change and action and find the plays static or dull and the characters unsympathetic. Eliminating this resistance is step 1. In a large introductory-level course, I introduce students to Chekhov through his one-act plays, usually "The Bear" or "The Proposal." These plays reveal aspects of Chekhov's worldview and sense of humor and introduce Chekhovian characters who lack self-awareness, become obsessed with an idea, or suffer physically (but comically). Because the dramaturgy course is for a small group in a discussion-workshop format, we take more time to explore Chekhov than we can in the large course. Nevertheless, preconceptions must be addressed here as well. Chekhov's stories offer some of the richness and complexity of his writing in ways that his short plays do not, and theater students usually do not have presuppositions about the stories. Working freely with his short stories, they encounter a Chekhov who hasn't already been revered or been dismissed as staid.

Chekhov continues to be one of the most often produced playwrights (in America, just after Shakespeare), so dramaturgy students should be able to engage with his plays on a practical level—that is, they need to consider how the plays have been and might be staged. Because the Moscow Art Theater's (MAT) approach to producing Chekhov, under the direction of Konstantin Stanislavsky and Vladimir Nemirovich-Danchenko, has greatly influenced how American theater artists imagine Chekhov in performance, students need to consider other possible approaches. Laurence Senelick's *The Chekhov Theatre: A Century of the Plays in Performance* provides an effective overview of some Chekhovian productions that break with the MAT model. The chapters "Breaking with Tradition" and "Out of the Rubble" and the adaptation readings and assignments help eliminate preconceptions that limit interpretive potential, and they encourage students to explore and take risks in their approaches to Chekhov.

Chekhov has been adapted by such stellar playwrights as Tennessee Williams, Mamet, Brian Friel, Tom Stoppard, and, more recently, Suzan-Lori Parks, Adam Rapp, Sarah Ruhl, Annie Baker, and Tracy Letts. Understanding his dramaturgy enables students to see his influence on contemporary playwrights, too, and provides students with a vocabulary for the discussion of contemporary dramatic literature.

For one approach to dramatic analysis, the students read Elinor Fuchs's influential "Visit to a Small Planet: Some Questions to Ask a Play." With Chekhov, we can study the groupings of characters and their typical interactions, search for the emergence of patterns and tonal shifts, and explore distinctive linguistic features (indirect language, self-consciously literary language, nonsense phrases, clustering, monologues and speeches, interruptions and interjections, echoic effects, quotation, foreign language use) and movement designations (arriving, eating and drinking, playing games, tripping, hiding, breaking things, playing instruments, sleeping, fighting sleep, departing). We explore how spaces shift between interior and exterior, private and public, literal and symbolic. We note how the offstage action influences the stage action. We identify the many objects (guns, gifts, galoshes, birds, newspapers, letters, maps, books, flowers, clocks, bookshelves) and examine their literal, practical, symbolic, and affective functions. How do these objects serve in social exchanges and as plot devices? We imagine Chekhov's textured landscapes and vivid and rhythmic soundscapes. We watch time pass, noting change. Only then do we begin to discuss themes. By the end of the semester, we read the exclamation of Baker, a contemporary playwright, to Adam Szymkowicz, an interviewer, about her influences. She echoed Williams with, "Chekhov! Chekhov! Chekhov!" The students should be able to identify elements of Chekhov's dramaturgy in Baker's.

Introducing Chekhov and the Adaptations

After students have spent time developing play analysis skills and have been introduced to adaptation through selections from Julie Sanders's *Adaptation and Appropriation*, we move on to the *Orchards* text. Adapters have their own distinctive aims, but, like translators, they inevitably extend the life of the source text by engaging it in a new context. They provide new avenues for understanding, critiquing, and re-visioning the original. We discuss various approaches to adaptation from Sanders, such as transference (moving from one genre into another), analogue (updating a work for a contemporary audience or moving it into a contemporary period), and commentary (using adaptation to critique viewpoints of the original or to critique aspects of contemporary society). The students also explore the problems and impossibilities of fidelity raised by our readings.

Next, we read several of the selections from *Orchards* to closely analyze how the playwrights have interpreted, tightened, or expanded Chekhov's stories. This analysis usually includes "A Joke," "The Man in a Case," and "Drowning," along with the plays inspired by them—respectively, Guare's *The Talking Dog*, Fornes's *Drowning*, and Wasserstein's *The Man in a Case*. The selections pose unique problems and solutions for theatrical adaptation. Guare attempts to transfer and update Chekhov's story, locating it in a contemporary environment. Fornes dispenses with Chekhov's story, setting, and characters entirely, replacing them with characters who resemble "shapeless potatoes" to explore Chekhov's themes of humiliation, isolation, and suffering (Chekhov, Fornes, et al. 55). Wasserstein, more than the others, focuses on transferring Chekhov's short story from the page to the stage. She uses his events, characters, and environment but eliminates the framing story and narration and centers the play on the relationship between Belikov and Varenka. Of course, she has to invent dialogue and create elements not existing in the story to illuminate and develop the characters and setting. We look for what the playwrights find and enhance through adaptation, not just for what they change or eliminate.

Our discussions appreciate the stories as literature but also analyze them as potential theatrical vehicles. We search for clues about the use of space and objects, analyze the depiction and development of character, chart the events and basic story structure, note the physical and linguistic interactions that reveal relationships, and make lists of color palettes and soundscapes. We carefully record the changes that occur. We analyze the narrator's position and point of view as they help establish the tone and style of the piece and how they may translate to the stage.

When we work with "A Joke," students read both story and play before the class meeting, and then we read the texts aloud together, stopping along the way as ideas emerge, often going back and forth to compare phrases and expressions. The story appears to be a very simple one, of a young man playing with the affections of a young woman. He teases her by saying, "I love you," as they descend a steep slope on a sled. But the tiny story's complexities begin to reveal themselves. It is "a bright winter's day" (perfectly at noon), and the characters appear at the summit of a steep hill. The students note the Romantic descriptors: the "steep incline . . . reflected the sun's rays like a mirror." The brightness, referred to four times in the opening paragraph, contrasts with the frightening slope, depicted as a "terrible, yawning chasm" (Chekhov, Fornes, et al. 120). As the man and woman descend the hill, the wind becomes violent: it howls and threatens furiously. The narrator invokes "the devil himself," and the descent is imagined as one into "the infernal regions" (121). The landscape remains full of dangers and terror (and, metaphorically, sexual temptation) until the scene shifts to the neighbor's gardens separated by a fence with iron spikes. The hillside has grown dark and dull (123). The landscape essentially dissolves in the final paragraphs as the narrator wraps up the story after the two have parted. One imagines a dull, characterless domestic environment, though it is not described. Students observe how the passage of time affects both the relationship and the setting. Memory emerges as a central motif. A close analysis of this play prepares them to understand the irreversibility of time and the play of memory in Chekhov's mature drama.

As we analyze character, new problems and possibilities emerge. The narrator's first descriptions position the young woman as diminutive, timid, naive, youthful, simple, and beautiful. Using the reading strategies from David Ball's popular *Backwards and Forwards: A Technical Manual for Reading Plays*, I pose the question, "What exactly does she do in the story?" We chart the following: she fears, she hesitates, she rides, she questions, she hesitates, she takes his arm, she searches, she hesitates, she suggests riding again, she rides, she searches, she suggests riding again, she searches, she struggles, she rides again and again, she craves the pleasure, she rides alone, she longs for pleasure, she stretches forth her arms. Then, after the shift, she settles and she remembers. Descriptions of the silvery down on her upper lip, her delicate blush, her longing, and her radiant beauty disappear into a dull domesticity. Thus the innocent young girl becomes daring and adventuresome before settling into a nondescript middle age. Students challenge the end: why so dull and lifeless? Is this a depiction of her true existence or only what the narrator sees for her as he considers himself the heroic figure of her life. Students question his representation of her throughout: he assumes her feelings and responses on the basis of facial signals and body movements: "Every inch of her, even her muff and her hood, every line of her little frame expressed the utmost uncertainty" (Chekhov, Fornes, et al. 122). His Romantic descriptions reveal his inability to view and represent the past objectively.

We turn to an analysis of the narrator. What do we know about him? He sleds. He is preparing to move to St. Petersburg. What does he do in the story? He begs the young woman to coast, he rides with her, he says, "I love you," he smokes, he watches her, he agrees to ride again, he whispers, "I love you," he repeats this, he watches her, he watches her, he says, "I love you, Nadia." He also remembers and tells the story. Has he assigned his own feelings to her? Can the passion and longing he describes in her be applied to him? Did he have a sexual awakening too, or was he just tempting and joking with her? Why does he place himself so centrally in her life story? The ambiguity of Chekhov's writing emerges vividly as the students suggest possibilities and look for how a single description can evoke many different meanings. They see how Chekhov deals with indirect speech and body language in the story and discuss how he uses these methods in his plays. They are reminded of Nina and Trigorin of *Seagull*, who may share a similar courtship and descent (with much higher stakes). The close analysis of character enables students to consider how Chekhov's dramatic characters often lack self-awareness, view the world through literary tropes and ideals, act against their impulses, and mask their true feelings.

We next consider Guare's *The Talking Dog*. By now the students have developed a keen interest in and sensitivity to Chekhov's writing and are prone to evaluate the adaptation chiefly on the basis of its fidelity to the original story. Instead, we analyze Guare's play on its own merits, then look for links between it and the story. Guare sets his play in the Catskills, and his two characters, designated only as M, the man, and F, the woman, are going hang gliding. She is "in her twenties," he "in his late twenties" (128). We meet them at the top of a mountain; she hesitates, but he encourages her to take risks and show courage. They hang glide, the wind roars, and he says, "I. Love. You" (132, 133, 134). As in Chekhov, the woman asks to go again and again, becoming more courageous and passionate. After the second flight, the man tries to resist with such lines as "There's a long line," "It's by the hour," and "I have to get back to work" (133–34). In a more decisive break with Chekhov, the characters discuss spirituality, and the woman has misread his "I love you" as Nature speaking to her. The man, jokingly, tells her a story about a friend who taught a dog to say, "Hello, I love you" (137). He repeats the phrase, using a dog voice, several times. He's joking, but she doesn't laugh or understand that he's telling her that he loves her. So, he tells her that he is being transferred, then moves backstage, whispering, "I love you." She hears but doesn't acknowledge him, stretching forth her arms "to infinity." He then directly addresses the audience, stating that he saw in the paper that she married "some nerd" (138). He resolves that he's glad he didn't end up with her because she "couldn't take a, take a, take a, take a joke" (139).

Unlike the relationship between Fornes and Chekhov, that between Guare and Chekhov is apparent. His male character jokes in order to guard or mask his feelings. The woman grows more courageous and passionate but ends up in what he presumes to be a dull marriage. However, Guare makes certain elements in the Chekhov story more explicit. For example, he draws out the sexual parallel of the source text when the characters joke about how long the man can "stay up," referring to hang gliding with obviously sexual double entendre (130). He also shifts the power dynamics of the relationship by aging the female charater: she is more knowing in her sexual joking with her companion. That their relationship is less dangerous is in part a reflection of a shift in social attitudes. Guare places more emphasis on the man's inability to express his feelings. Students sometimes note that these two resemble Lopakhin and Varya from *The Cherry Orchard*, a couple that just never hit the same wavelength and miss opportunities to express their feelings. Adaptations often have more than one source text, and this sort of intertextuality can augment an adaptation's power.

Now the students must write their own adaptations of Chekhov. They may choose "Joke" or "Man in a Case" for the project, because everyone in the class knows them well. Each student writes a play and also serves as dramaturg for a play written by another student in the class. Familiarity with the stories allows students to respond more precisely to the decisions made by each adapter. They can offer theatrical solutions when adapters say which aspects of the story they wish to explore. This exercise gives the students the practical skills of working collaboratively with authors even as they learn how a playwright might feel during the writing process. The adaptations are always diverse in approach and style. Some stick closely to the original in terms of character, plot, dialogue, and environment; others create new characters and situations that highlight the themes or moods of the source text; others put the characters in a new setting such as the inner city or, in one case, the wild West. Their adaptations are usually highly personal and reveal which aspects of Chekhov's story captured their interest. Their conversations with Chekhov show how they interpret his work. For "Joke," students have written plays that interrogate the narrator's ability to know the truth or investigate his resistance to a relationship. One student transferred the couple, both men in her version, to a high-stakes motorcycle ride in which one attempts, but resists, coming out. Another wrote an adaptation of "Joke" that centered on the loss of a carefree, exciting youth. Student adaptations of "Man in a Case" have also been wide-ranging. One writer rendered the "case" as heteronormative sexuality; another placed the story in a harsh, urban setting and explored a complicated interracial relationship. One student wrote his entire adaptation using only Chekhov's framing device of the storytellers, highlighting the companionship of the male campers and the act of storytelling. Some wrote short realist dramas; others experimented with a highly stylized approach, including one entirely movement-based critique of "Joke's" gender implications. Many, having discovered that one word can shift a relationship or mood or even augment a joke, consulted multiple translations for more possibilities. Students often consulted Chekhov's plays, looking at how Chekhov presented a theatrical solution in depicting a relationship or signifying environment or tone.

In the final days of the semester, students present their completed plays in class. (Many of the scripts have subsequently been fully produced in a campus venue, the Armory Free Theatre.) The class discussions that follow presentations are lively, and the student dramaturgs offer insightful and sophisticated responses to their peers' diverse adaptations. By this time in the semester, nearly all the students in the class effectively demonstrate a facility with the course's concepts and the ability to converse productively and freely with Chekhov.

NOTES

[1] No editor or translator of Chekhov is credited in the book. The translations are Constance Garnett's.

[2] For background on dramaturgy, see Cattaneo.

[3] For an extended list of a dramaturg's responsibilities, see Katz.

A Performance-Based Approach to Play Analysis Using Anton Chekhov's *The Three Sisters*

Annamaria Pileggi

Unlike a novel or short story, a play is incomplete in its written form. It is fully realized only when it is embodied onstage. In this sense a play can be considered a blueprint for performance. That our understanding of a play evolves as it moves from the page to the stage must be considered when dramatic literature is read and analyzed. One way to approach a play is through the lens of acting. Actors begin by analyzing the written word, but that analysis continues in rehearsal, where language becomes action—a means of affecting another character or characters in order to accomplish something. As the actors interact onstage, they become embodied storytellers, using their language and movement to carry one another through the journey of the play, either toward or away from their objectives.

Analyzing a play from the actor's perspective gives students the opportunity to explore the play as something that transforms when it is performed, allows them to imagine how they might realize a particular character's journey and to explore the process of bringing a play to completion. Knowing how a play evolves from its written form to a fully produced event helps us understand how an actor transforms the written word into action; it also shows us how we, as human beings, interact with one another in pursuit of what we need. In short, it offers perspective on the human condition.

The study of acting is all about perspective. Actors cannot even begin their process until they know the character they'll be playing. Once that identity is established, they read the text on their own, then do table work, in which, as the play is read aloud, they test their understanding of the play in interaction with one another. The next phase of analysis involves script-in-hand rehearsals, during which the actors get on their feet and begin to interact not only verbally but also physically. Once the text is memorized, the actors explore the play off-book. In this phase, embodiment becomes complete. The final step of analysis is performance, when the play is shared with an audience: only then does the play, clarified further by the audience's response, become a living exchange.

I have suggested a linear process here, but in reality the implementation of these phases is not that linear. The reading and then rereading of a play, for example, continues for an actor well into the rehearsal process, sometimes even up to the performance. There are valuable discoveries to be made by revisiting the text, and the relation that actors develop with the written word continually informs their performance.

I teach all levels of acting in the BA drama program at Washington University in St. Louis. In first- and second-level acting courses, I focus on the actor's craft;

in the third-level course, after students have a foundation in craft, I emphasize analysis of the text. In that analysis, students work on four scenes, each scene an example of increasingly contemporary, nonrealistic theater. The first playwright we explore is Anton Chekhov, and I regularly use *The Three Sisters*.[1]

For many students, this class marks their first exposure to Chekhov. They find his plays difficult. The use of patronymics confuses them as they try to chart characters' identities. They are impatient with the seeming inaction of the plays—in *Three Sisters*, for example, they almost always complain that they wish the sisters would go to Moscow already! The historical context is also unfamiliar. Russia's social structure at the end of the nineteenth century is foreign to them, as is the sense of geographic isolation. Finally, the humor in these plays completely eludes the students.

Although historical context is important, it is not my main focus: I want my students to experience the ways in which Chekhov's writing transcends time and place, to understand these plays from their own lives and perspectives. I like to immerse them in the fiction of the play from the perspective of a specific character. It isn't until they act out the scenes in class that they begin to truly understand the plays and the humanity of the characters who inhabit them.

I developed an in-depth method of analysis and scene study based on the acting theories of Earle Gister.[2] In this method, five distinct readings of the text explore and chronicle particular elements. In addition, I have students record in detail their rehearsal process—both independent rehearsals and the coaching sessions I lead in class. Character analysis is treated as a fluid thing: discoveries made in the text lead to implementation in rehearsal. In this way, the actor is constantly applying page work to stage work. Readings of the text are tested in rehearsal.

The account of character analysis should reflect the journey that the student actors take to achieve a final, fully integrated understanding of their role in the play. I want to see every stage of the process. It is valuable for student actors to realize how their understanding of the play deepens and, in some cases, completely changes as they move through this creative process. Below is the basic format of the written analysis.

Reading 1: An Actor's Emotional Response

Students record in detail their emotional response to the play and the scene in which they have been cast. This is an essential first step for an actor. When they study the text from an emotional perspective, they begin to relate more personally to their character. I have found that having them describe their responses gives them valuable insight into the text.

A student in my 2009 Acting III class played Irina from *Three Sisters* in a scene with Tuzenbach at the beginning of act 4. She wrote this as part of her emotional response:

> When I first read the play, I found Irina annoying, at least until the end of the play. It seemed like all she did was complain either about working (or not working) or about her love life, or lack thereof. She seemed young and slightly naive, while always wanting to be treated like an adult.
>
> After class, I went back and reread act 4 and more specifically, the scene [my scene partner] and I will be working on. I was completely crushed when I realized the moment Tuzenbach leaves is [the] last moment Irina will ever see him because he dies and they never get married. It gave me goose bumps. Yes, she claims she is not in love with him, but she cares about him so deeply and wants him to feel cared for and loved and wanted. He, on the other hand, feels like he needs to compete with Solyony for her. It is just heartbreaking.

This student has found a strong emotional connection to her character.

Reading 2: Who Am I?

Reading the play from the perspective of the character that the actor is playing requires the actor to explore how this character views the world of the play and the character's place in that world. All these elements must be considered:

Place—the general world of the play as well as specific locales.
Time—the general time period as well as the specific chronology of events in the play. How much time passes throughout the course of the play?
Status—the character's social status, economic status, gender, status in a relationship.
Likes and dislikes of the character.
Relationship of the character with other characters.

By literally writing out the moment-to-moment journey that the student actors take, they learn to imagine from their own perspective what the character experiences, thus personalizing their character.

In the "Who Am I?" section of this analysis, one student describes the world of the play and the circumstances of the beginning of Irina's journey:

> We were planning to celebrate my birthday in true Russian fashion. All the men from town were invited to join us for a lovely breakfast prepared by Anfisa and Olga. By all, I mean those that my sisters and I remain close to, such as the men of my father's brigade, members of the district board, and colleagues of my brother. I remember that, when I was little, the whole house would be full of guests on our birthdays, and now we all fit around the dining room table. Ever since my father died, fewer and fewer guests come by on a regular basis. Naturally, Olga has to bring

> up our father's death because it occurred just a year ago today, on my birthday.

Writing this first-person account is a necessary step for student actors to make their character's journey more vivid and personal. The student can then test in rehearsal the sense of loneliness she describes that permeates the Prozorov household—an ironic loneliness, considering that their home is a constant gathering place. Their world is depicted as a kind of prison: educated, interesting people forced to live in the middle of nowhere. This insight can enlighten Irina's scene at the top of act 4.

Reading 3: What Do Others Say about Me?

To help the students focus on what all the other characters in the play say about their character, I ask them to make a chart. The first column contains verbatim what a particular character says; the second, when in the course of the play the statement is made; the third, the name of the character who makes the statement; and the fourth, what the students have discovered about their character. This exercise is lengthy and can be tedious at times, but it gives students specific insights into their character: how the character relates to other characters, what the character's status is in the world of the play.

Here is a brief example of a student's third reading, from act 2 (the chart is typically several pages long):

Quote of Statement Made to Irina	***Page***	***Character Speaking***	***Discovery of Student***
Such a young, Unhappy Little Thing	39	Tuzenbach	His way of saying, "Let me take care of you."
You're losing weight? And yes, yes you are, your face has lost its softness. You look like a young boy.	39	Masha	My job at the telegraph is taking a physical and emotional toll on me that I don't necessarily realize.
No, that's the hairstyle.	39	Tuzenbach	He stands up for me because he loves me.
I cannot live without you.	41	Chebutykin	In reference to card playing. This really shows how close we are to each other.
Do suffer me to take a seat. Yes. Oh, well. Sprawled all over it. Your cards, your tea.	48	Masha	Masha, though she and I always seem to look out for each other, can get fed up with me sometimes.

But you can understand me. I feel that. You are so far above the average of . . . intelligence, of . . . you are pure. I think that you are elevated. You perceive the truth. And you, alone, can understand me. And my love. I profoundly, I endlessly . . . adore . . . I cannot live without you. My angel. My bliss. My darling. You magnificent, you wonderful, such eyes, which no mortal . . .	57	Solyony	Solyony confesses his love to me, and it is the last thing that I want to hear. He thinks I am intelligent, pure, and beautiful. He claims I "understand" him, when really I cannot stand the sight of him.

Having students write their observations as the character and in the first person helps them personalize what happens in the play. It is clear from this student's comments that she is developing empathy for Irina and her situation.

Reading 4: What Do I Want?

The student actors identify what drives their character through the entire play: the character's super objective. This identification is essential, as it gives them purpose and motivates all verbal and physical life onstage. The objective transforms language into action. Through language, the character acts on the other characters to make them provide what the character needs. Finding what can be obtained from the others in the play will ensure that, in rehearsal, students focus on those with whom they interact: the other characters are the ones who make possible the character's journey.

Students must determine the objective of every scene in which their character appears. Each of these objectives should somehow relate to the super objective. A student has traced a clear path from her super objective to the objectives of each of the scenes that compose Irina's journey.

> My super objective:
> I want someone to give me the chance to be happy.
>
> My scene objective:
> I want Tuzenbach to give me forgiveness for not loving him.
>
> Relation to my super objective:
> If he can accept that I don't love him, then he will stay and we will get married and leave the town. Even though we are not going to Moscow,

getting out of town is the one thing I want to do. Even though he is not the man of my dreams, he still makes me happy and awakens in me a new spirit to work.

Act 1

Objective: I want my sisters to give me reassurance we will actually move to Moscow.

Relation: We have been talking of leaving this town and going to Moscow. That is where my true happiness lies. In going there, I will be able to find my husband, Andrei will become a scholar and we will all live as we did before we came to this town.

Objective: I want Tuzenbach to give me information about Vershinin.

Relation: This new man could be a potential husband.

Objective: I want my superiors to give me respect as an adult.

Relation: I do not like to be treated like a little girl anymore. My happiness will come from working as an adult and experiencing life as an adult—preferably in Moscow. I talk about how much I want to work and the way work will be the only way I will be happy.

Objective: I want my guests to give me attention.

Relation: I am used to being the youngest who is always given gifts and praised, and on my birthday I don't think it should be any different. Though I say I don't like presents and such things, I really do. Attention makes me happy.

The student charts a clear progression of action firmly rooted in objective. This exercise gives her the structure she needs to support her moment-to-moment journey through the play. Although she is performing only one of Irina's scenes in class, this analysis contextualizes that performance.

Reading 5: How Do I Get What I Want?

The student actors identify their character's first action in every scene in which the character appears. Because their objective is rooted in the other characters, action must also be rooted in them. Therefore the students are squarely focused on the other characters onstage.

Identifying the first action means entering the scene with a strong attack. All subsequent actions should be determined by the moment-to-moment journey of playing the scene with the other students. This involvement is fundamental to the evolution of the play from written document to live event. It is the interaction among actors that determines the journey. If students have personalized their character, they will experience the character's journey.

Act 3
Objective: I want Tuzenbach, Vershinin, and Kulygin to give me trust.
Action: I will make Vershinin feel welcome and at ease.

Objective: I want Solyony to give me space.
Action: I will make him feel unwelcome.

Objective: I want my sisters to give me peace of mind.
Action: I will make Masha empathetic.

Objective: I want Olga to give me advice.
Action: I will make her feel valuable.

The Rehearsal Journal

In the rehearsal journal, the document that accompanies the text analysis, the student actors detail how they applied all the discoveries they made in their various readings of the text. I encourage them to write rehearsal entries as they analyze the text.

It is impossible to convey in this essay the full effect of this phase in the analysis process. Rehearsal can be a difficult and frustrating experience. Often there is a chasm between students' intellectual and emotional understanding of a play. In one rehearsal journal, a student wrote very early in her analysis, after only two readings of the text:

> If my objective is to make him feel wanted, it makes what I am saying all the more heartbreaking, as unrequited love should be. I am simply trying to be open and honest with him and help him see things from my point of view. Yes I am not in love with him, but I don't want him to fight Solyony over me; I want to stay with him and I want us to have a happy life together. He is giving me everything I ever wanted, a husband, and a new life away from this town. Why can't I love him? I want to, I really do, but I just can't for some reason.

The next entry was written after the student's first on-book coaching session in class, in which I guided her to a stronger objective:

> This workshop peeled off a new layer of the scene for me. Going into it, I was aware of the given circumstances surrounding the scene and how I felt about Tuzenbach, but it never occurred to me that I want him to accept that I cannot love him, but more than that to give me a way to love him. Before, I always thought of the scene on a surface level. Yes I am not in love with him, but I care about him and he will be able to make me

> happy and has reinvigorated a new passion in me for work. Not to mention that because of him I am finally getting out of this town. In looking at it through the lens of wanting acceptance and even forgiveness for the way I feel, it makes me feel much more guilty for the fact that I don't love him.

The following entry was written after the final showing of the scene in performance in front of an audience:

> Over the course of these three weeks, [my scene partner] and I have really grown to trust and connect with each other on stage. I feel like there was a lot more silence in our scene today than there usually is, but I never felt like I checked out at any given point. I also think the presence of an audience helps. It is one thing to rehearse and rehearse by ourselves, but another to test that rehearsal work in a performance. I felt a sense of freedom to share our story with the audience as well as this connection to [my scene partner] that made it feel like we were the only two people in the room sometimes. Overall, I think working on Chekhov has been very beneficial to the things I know I need to focus on: trust in myself and others, going with my impulses, not thinking through a scene while on stage, and not "playing" my source on stage but using it to invest in the given circumstances. With these scenes you cannot try to make sense of them because of the emotional logic. You also really have to do your homework, both alone and in rehearsal, to reach the emotional place where these people lie.

In just these three entries it is evident how far the student has come in her journey toward embodiment, from intellectual understanding to emotional connection.

The Score

The final document in the character analysis is the score of the scene in which the student actors perform. It is a record of all their character's lines in the scene, with corresponding actions. This document is not finalized until the students consistently play the same actions in repeated performances of the scene. The rehearsal process must inform their choices. If they set their choices too soon, they may stop listening to their partner onstage. Documenting their score near the end of the rehearsal process, they can then test it in final rehearsals before performing the scene in front of an audience. Here is an excerpt from a student's score:

Scene Objective: I want Tuzenbach to give me forgiveness.

Lines	***My Objective***
(Moment before my entrance) The town will be empty now.	I want to make Tuzenbach feel concerned.
Where are you going?	I want to make Tuzenbach feel worried about me.
Is that true? No, it's not.	I want to make Tuzenbach feel caught in the act.
Nikolai, what was it happened yesterday? In front of the theater.	I want to make Tuzenbach feel cared for.

Students spend about three weeks working on Chekhov. They turn in their analyses after they have performed their scenes for an invited audience. On average, the analysis ends up filling twenty to thirty typed pages.

At the conclusion of this project, students have certainly gained a deeper understanding of Chekhov's writing. They appreciate the characters' struggles and find humor in their foibles. This progress results not just from intellectual engagement but also from an immersive experience. The work has both a critical, analytic component and, perhaps more important, an emotional engagement. It is through the process of embodiment that the students are able to empathize with the characters and thus recognize themselves in them. So, instead of seeing Chekhov's writing merely as a snapshot of the past, they encounter it in their own present, thus imbuing his plays with pertinence, viability, and immediacy.

Very few of my students go on to pursue acting professionally. That said, this training gives them valuable tools they can apply to whatever they choose to do. They definitely develop intellectual skills in critical thinking and analysis, but it is in the emotional area that perhaps their greatest learning occurs: they learn about themselves and grow in their capacity to relate to others.

NOTES

[1] I use David Mamet's adaptation of *The Three Sisters*, which is based on a literal translation by Vlada Chernomordik. I find Mamet's style very actor-friendly in its sparseness and immediacy. Mamet understands language as action and the play as a blueprint for performance. To illuminate his style as a playwright and adapter, I have students read another translation and compare it to his. They invariably find his writing more accessible and relatable.

[2] I was introduced to Gister's methodology when I studied with Gister at the Actor's Center in New York as part of its inaugural Teacher Development Workshop (summer 1997). My approach to actor-centered text analysis is based on my work in this workshop. On Gister's methodology in detail, see Alberti.

Introducing Chekhov's *The Cherry Orchard* with Method-Style Acting and *Facebook*-Style Reacting

Lisa Siefker Bailey

Several years ago, I found a fierce competitor sneaking into my classrooms and stealing scenes from my teaching stage, especially around midterm, when student focus decreases. My performance-based pedagogy was no match for such a powerful entertainer: the cell phone. Students appeared far more interested in their friends' latest updates than they were in my class activities. Text messages, or whatever they were, interrupted my class and made me feel that my students were disrespectful, uncivil, disruptive—even rude. I could see that they were not listening to me, and their gaze and hand movements distracted other students, too. Colleagues commiserated about the contribution of social networking to classroom incivility. As reported in *Pedagogy*, "Literacy practices that fall outside the realm of traditional academic writing, like *Facebook*, can easily be seen as a threat to print literacy by teachers, especially when [those practices] sneak into the classroom uninvited as students check their *Facebook* profiles instead of participating in class discussions and activities" (Fife 555). But I have embraced social media in my classroom and found a way to use *Facebook*, along with other social networking platforms, to teach *The Cherry Orchard*. The approach is very productive in composition, drama, and theater classes: it encourages imaginative analysis of characters' motivations and actions and promotes deep reading, in particular developing student understanding of subtext.

When Peter Elbow discusses ways to develop good writing in *Writing without Teachers*, he notes that writers can rarely "disentangle the good insight from the excrescence until *after*" they have "allowed the digression to develop" (34). I have found that the digression of a social networking exercise allows students to develop good insights with freedom of exploration and experimentation. My first integration of social media involved reworking a low-stakes, oral, summary-and-response assignment on a short story in my composition classes. I asked students to create a *MySpace* or *Facebook*-style profile page for a character that they selected from the story under discussion. They were to extrapolate from what they knew about the character to show that character's favorite music, films, artworks, activities, and other elements typically posted on social networking sites. I was astounded at the effort students put into their profile pages. They received only completion points (not a scaled grade), but the approval of their peers motivated them to produce impressive projects. Not all students respond equally, however.[1] In order to accommodate a variety of comfort levels, I showed students a sample of what a social networking profile might look like and allowed them to handwrite profiles in their journals if they weren't comfortable with technology. As I developed this assignment over several semesters, students asked if they could use *Photoshop*, *Excel*, *Publisher*, and more; my answer was a resounding, "Yes!" The only caveat was that they break no third-party rules. Students could also use sites such as *Fakebook* and *Fake Tweet Builder*, which offer online tools that imitate *Facebook* and *Twitter* for educational use.

Students who had been skipping class or were receiving failing marks often showed up for their presentations and turned in the most involved and well-constructed projects. In a reflection on her *Twitter* profile for the mobile app, one student wrote about the author, "[H]is stories are so deep and meaningful that if you do not completely immerse yourself in reading his stories, you will not completely understand them. . . . Overall I really enjoyed this project. It was a fun way to be able to establish a relationship with the characters in all of our stories and I took pleasure in tapping into the complexity." Her formal reflection does not capture the enthusiasm with which most students addressed these assignments, but it does suggest success in engaging students in deep and multiple readings, in helping them "wallow in complexity" (Ramage, Bean, and Johnson 27). It is a way of following the suggestion of John D. Bransford, Ann L. Brown, and Rodney R. Cocking that students taught to develop improved metacognitive skills are more likely to meet instructional goals and improve achievement. My students' appreciation of character depth certainly increased. It is a short step to analysis of characterization from the student insight that, in students' words, *Facebook* is "really fake," with profiles carefully constructed according to what people want others to think of them, "emphasizing socially desirable characteristics that may not be easily recognizable in offline encounters and hiding or deemphasizing socially undesirable aspects of the self" (Hyllegard et al. 603). My students' profiles helped students recognize the differences among how characters perceive themselves, how others perceive characters, and how characters want to be perceived.

After success in using a social networking assignment in introductory writing classes, I created one for my introduction to drama classes. In this assignment, I used *The Cherry Orchard*, both to address the lack of focus at midterm, and—more substantively—because I anticipated that it would help students develop an understanding of Chekhov's subtext. I had recognized that the kind of thinking about character involved in constructing a social media profile on his or her behalf might serve to parallel the careful approach that develops and deepens understanding of character that Konstantin Stanislavsky taught in his system of acting. To borrow Stanislavsky's words, I wanted my drama students to perceive how actors "bring to life what is hidden under the words," put their "own thoughts into the author's lines," establish their own relationships with other characters, and supplement materials from the director and the author out of their "own imagination" (*Actor* 49). Repeating my strategy from the composition classes, I made the social networking project an assignment that in an unpressured way prepared students for class discussion, essays, and exams. Once again, students loved the exercise and found that it really helped them grasp the motivations and complexities of characters.

The theme of social mobility (both upward and downward) and the ways Chekhov's characters cling to the past or jump blindly into the future are accessible to our students and can be appreciated in a *Facebook*-style assignment. The rapid changes around the cherry orchard leave its owners waiting for something that will not come and seemingly unaware of something else that surely will. I want my students to identify with the feeling of being suspended in time, of finding oneself caught in a moment that does not appear to exist in the world anymore but that still remains all-important in the mind. I want students to feel the space of the play, the literal space on the stage as well as space in terms of the energy of each scene. I help them see that Chekhov freezes the dramatic art of the play in isolated moments, which I argue are like photographs in an album—moments that stand out vividly for individuals despite greater changes to the larger world. Just as the album contains only small pieces of the whole of one's memory, scenes in *Cherry Orchard* show only small parts of the whole of Chekhov's meaning. His most dramatic moments are isolated physically when they occur offstage and isolated emotionally when they occur onstage. Daniel Gillés writes:

> Even more than Chekhov's other plays, *The Cherry Orchard* has "no fixed structure" and tells no story. Jean-Louis Barrault, who has staged it with admirable devotion, summed it up in a few lines: "Act I: the Cherry Orchard is in danger of being sold. Act II: the Cherry Orchard is going to be sold. [Act] III: the Cherry Orchard is sold. Act IV: the Cherry Orchard has been sold. As for the rest: life." (399)

Because the plot is largely inaction and most of its significant events occur offstage, character is heavily emphasized and interpretation requires imaginative filling in of the blanks. These qualities make *Cherry Orchard* ideal for applying the *Facebook* profile assignment.

The disconnect between what the characters appear to know and what gets posted on their social networking sites by their student impersonators also helps students appreciate a comic aspect of Chekhov's work. *Facebook* is a place where users construct identities for others to see, and students can relate that practice to the characters in *Cherry Orchard*, who also construct identities they want for themselves. Much of the comedy of the play—for example, in regard to Epikhodov and Yasha—arises because they are not very good at it. *Facebook* profiles and walls are also the perfect place to emphasize the often comic function of trifles, of what seems to be important to a particular character despite the larger issues that are happening beyond the immediately constructed space. As Moscow's great director Anatoly Efros sums it, "At the highest point of crucial conversations, it seems, extreme trifles burst in. And in the end, all the attention goes to these trifles" (65). When my drama students share their profiles of selected characters in class, they both offer and receive interpretive remarks of surprising insight, sometimes about small details that tend to be missed in more traditional assignments. This student-centered approach generates an understanding of internal motivation by imagining and mimicking ways characters make choices.

Asking students to impersonate Chekhov's characters in the task of making their *Facebook* profiles fits well with Stanislavsky's Method. *Facebook* is a comfortable venue for exercising their imagination, and building the profiles helps them move away from mechanical acting centered on the audience and into a system of realizing acting from the inside out. In chapter 3 of *An Actor Prepares*, Stanislavsky asks actors to open their minds to possibilities by using the word *if*. The word means that "nobody obliges you to believe or not believe anything. Everything is clear, honest, and above-board. You are given a question, and you are expected to answer it sincerely and definitely." The same is true of the *Facebook* exercise. By asking students to imagine what characters' profiles would be like *if* those characters had access to *Facebook*, students take the assignment, as Stanislavsky might have said, "only as a supposition" (44). If time allows, they might also read selections from *An Actor Prepares*. The beginning of chapter 2, "When Acting Is an Art," has a particularly helpful treatment of using the subconscious to reveal emotion (12–16). Chapter 3, "Action," introduces the notion of the "magic if," and its third section illustrates how the "magic if" frees the actor to invent action and motivation by playing with what the mind invents and using the body to reveal it (39–45).

When my drama students present their profile pages to the class, they must tell how and why they made their choices. In explicating what characters do and do not reveal of themselves, and in the sometimes indirect ways this explicating happens, students often discover and reflect on their own incorporation of subtext into these profile pages. They take risks and a tentative step into the actor's role, becoming their characters, who explain how they created the pages. Imitating Tortsov, the director in Stanislavsky's *An Actor Prepares*, I note when students' explanations appear real and natural, or, in contrast, when their explanations feel like a mechanical delivery that is only fulfilling the assignment. Like Tortsov's students, my students begin to recognize authentic moments.

I then have students block short scenes in groups and perform a read-through while they think about Stanislavsky's "magic ifs" (Stanislavsky, "From *The Actor*" 40). Students are surprised at how much time their characters spend onstage without speaking. In the first section of chapter 3, Tortsov teaches his students how to sit and wait (*Actor* 31–35); this lesson could be replicated in class to drive home for the students how important such moments are in the play. Students can then follow up with brief remarks about what they imagine their assigned character is thinking, both when speaking and when listening. I post these remarks on large sheets of paper in the classroom, which in effect has students writing in the voices of their characters on low-tech *Facebook* walls. The assignment thus makes them negotiate and block the literal space among their characters, while looking beyond the stage and inward to discover how and why characters experience certain thoughts and emotions. In this group theater exercise, students consider problematic performance elements of the play while relating to the characters with the students' own language and social mores. The resulting lively classroom discussion about relationships between men and women, family members, and social classes extends critical thinking beyond Chekhov's text.

When I piloted this exercise in my drama survey class, I worried that, on the one hand, the assignment stooped too low and would seem juvenile busywork or, on the other, that juxtaposing such radically alien culture milieus would be meaningless. But students appeared to understand what could come of the social networking and Method acting assignment better than I did. I had moved into their world and asked them to invite Chekhov's characters too. I hoped to enliven student thinking about a classic in the same way that Robert Brustein hoped to "revitalize familiar works wrapped in a cocoon of academic reverence or paralyzed by arthritic convention" with his call to modern directors to "freshen their thinking" (1). My assignment was thus analogous to adaptations that modernize or update a play by setting it in a later time and place. Brustein eventually reneged on his postmodern idea of "jollying up" classical plays, conceding that the "movement may have gone too far" (4), and there's no doubt that some of my students also went too far in imagining Chekhov's characters as their cultural contemporaries. But such excesses provoke valuable, animated discussion of what exactly too far is. What are the constraints on interpretation before we have left Chekhov altogether? My approach to *Cherry Orchard* does not obscure the play's meaning but rather arouses its spirited negotiation. After classroom discussion, students proceed to reflect in writing on their understandings of the play.

Stanislavsky was the kind of teacher we would today call a reflective practitioner. He "zealously kept journals and notebooks in which he entered his own commentaries on his work and his progress" (Hobgood 226). I ask my students to keep weekly journals as they respond to their assigned readings. Elizabeth M. Knutson claims, "Writing prompts students to think about, reread, and evaluate the texts they have read" (21). The *Facebook* profile assignment serves as a journal-homework prompt for the second class meeting devoted to the play, and students then reflect on the meeting (including the scene-blocking activity) in their next journal entry. I encourage students to write about the surface of Chekhov's dialogue and the character depth beneath that surface.

Thinking in terms of social networking profiles conveys new insight into the art of character construction generally speaking, because *Facebook* is all about the art of identity creation. Citing an article by Jean Reid in *English Teaching: Practice and Critique*, I remind students that "*Facebook* was originally created as a network for college students, but it was most often used as a place to chat about who's 'hot', what's 'cool' and where the 'hip' action is" (77). In creating social networking profiles for Chekhov's characters, students learn to see identity as something other than given, and they can coordinate character presentation and self-presentation with what is going on around them; this exercise historicizes Chekhov's characters and brings us to discuss how their notions of identity constructs are changing (or not) with changes in Russia. As students fill in gaps between characters' dialogue and characters' ideas of themselves, they come to understand, in the words of Lyudmila Parts, that "Chekhov, the poet of the present, does not engage the historicist perspective, but his audience does" (114).

This assignment answers Reid's call for teachers to "acknowledge learners' out-of-school literacy practices; understand how domains govern literacy practices and how technology changes communication; 'do' digital literacies rather than teach 'about' them; appreciate the diversity of language forms in digital spaces; enable critical practices in relation to writing" (78). Students find the *Facebook* forum an engaging and comfortable venue for understanding Chekhov's plays and his era, and also Stanislavsky's theatrical techniques; and, as I've been arguing, the kind of thinking that social media arouses can be quite fruitful in this project.

To keep up with technology and new possibilities for learning, I've revised my social networking assignment each semester, incorporating other *Facebook* elements and, more recently, other social networking sites, such as *Pinterest*, *Flickr*, *Tumblr*, and so on (should students choose to use them). My students have invented walls, likes, blogs, and *Twitter* pages. They may use any software they like to develop their presentations, which encourages them to make the project their own. The assignment's pedagogical value, however, has nothing to do with the level of technology employed, although some students are eager and proud to show off their fancy pages. The key to student success is their explanations of how and why they made the choices they did about specific characters. The explanations move them beyond a literal and superficial understanding of the text and into inferential and analytic reading, a reading that is developed further in their essays. The process parallels Thomas A. Angelo and K. Patricia Cross's "Invented Dialogues," in which students synthesize knowledge and invention (203). Seeing the choices students make also helps me respond immediately with feedback should a student misread. If more than one student makes a page for the same character, we often find that the students disagree—sometimes radically—regarding the choices their character might make. Constructing a social media persona thus gives rise to energetic discussion of the motives and goals of complex characters and supports dialectical thinking about differing perspectives.

The great Russian actor and director Yuri Zavadski said to his American cast, "Chekhov is close to us, especially today, because all his art is permeated with a faith in tomorrow's development of humanity" (Mitchell xxviii). The social networking assignment facilitates connectedness and builds such faith, even in the face of today's dramatically changing modes of communication. Students come to very personal understandings of *Cherry Orchard*'s characters and their humanity. As Stanislavsky wrote, "An artist must have full use of his own spiritual, human material because that is the only stuff from which he can fashion a living soul for his part. Even if his contribution is slight, it is the better because it is his own" (*Actor* 287–88). The social media and performance pedagogy approach gives students a chance to express creative ideas about characters using their current topical language, making their understanding of the play more true to themselves and thereby more meaningful.

Embracing technology in the classroom with activities like this social networking assignment will help us continue to transform ways we study classics as we work to connect with our quickly changing students and move into what we are beginning to call the digital humanities. Using contemporary social networking platforms to explore character analysis heightens our understanding of Chekhov's dramatic art. Students readily grasp the import of onstage inaction and offstage action by connecting theatrical conventions to their understanding of contemporary social networking's offstage identities. They see how the characteristic Chekhovian lack of plot is actually a portrayal of empty space and empty characters who cannot make contact with one another but instead are suspended by moments of time that are filled with the memories of their real or imagined lives. I close our class discussion by distilling the play to even fewer words than Barrault chose. As would have been called out after the last bid on the cherry orchard at the auction, we imagine the play as a series of Tweets, to which they can add hashtags and move into discussion forums on our electronic learning system while they prepare to write their analytic essays:

Act 1: going
Act 2: Going
Act 3: GOING
Act 4: gone

NOTE

[1] In "Student Learning through Social Media," Taylor et al. show that "[e]xtroverts prefer more social activity in the classroom, whereas introverts might find social networking unpleasant" (33).

Chekhov's *Seagull*: Teaching Poetics through Stage History

Olga Levitan

Accounts of the staging of Chekhov's plays include a number of contradictory narratives that are not always considered in critical discourse on Chekhov. Nevertheless, this complicated history, beginning with the very first Russian productions at the end of the nineteenth century in St. Petersburg and Moscow, may be read as reflecting the innovative character of Chekhov's drama. It can also serve well to teach his drama.

Key features of Chekhov's poetics may be fleshed out while students are introduced to the legendary failure of the first production of *The Seagull* at the Aleksandrinskii Theater in St. Petersburg (1896); to Chekhov's personal dissatisfaction with the extremely successful, subsequent (1898–1904) direction of his plays by Konstantin Stanislavsky and Vladimir Nemirovich-Danchenko in the Moscow Art Theater (MAT); and to the bipolar fluctuation of Chekhov's plays between failure and success in different countries over the first decades of the twentieth century. These are stories gripping enough as components of the playwright's creative biography, but the point of this essay is to show their usefulness in teaching his poetics. What follows is based on my experience in teaching the BA laboratory course Chekhov and the Art of Directing, in the Department of Theatre Studies at the Hebrew University in Jerusalem these past ten years.

My course involves students in a lively research process, in which they supplement their reading of the play with a number of extratextual documents (letters, diaries, memoirs, reviews, pictures, photos, etc.) and are tasked with discovering distinctive features of Chekhov's drama through the study of both its immanent features and its public reception. We discuss Chekhov's text in formalist as well as social historical terms, treating, for example, stage conventions, the creative influence on his vision by directors and performers, what critics had to say about the plays, and the reception of the plays by both the larger public and Chekhov and his correspondents. What emerges, always, is a somewhat incoherent picture assembled from contradictory pieces of evidence; it is the sort of picture that Thomas Postlewait describes as typical in theater historiography and that requires the scholar to adopt a broad perspective and integrate biographical, historical, and aesthetic methods of analysis (117–55). In the classroom, too, we are inevitably led to further analysis and exploration of the significant multipolarity of Chekhov's world and his place in it. Confronting a variety of historical, biographical, and artistic viewpoints on Chekhov in performance also exposes the aesthetic delicacy of his text.

In teaching Chekhov's *Seagull*, I focus on its first, notorious productions. Our material comprises the play itself, factual data concerning its stage productions, the critical response to those stagings, the directors' concepts of the play and ideas and methods for staging it, and Chekhov's response to the productions. This material may be delivered by lecture, but it can also be presented through interactive laboratory classes, where students are divided into groups, each one of which researches, discusses, and presents to the others one of the above-mentioned aspects, with the teacher monitoring and facilitating group work. In effect, evidence regarding the production, the theater text, is discussed as a kind of examination of the literary text (play), and key components of Chekhov's drama—namely, thematic concept and characters, dramatic structure and space—are understood as embodied in the artistic practice of directors, actors, and stage designers.

This nuanced, historicized treatment of *Seagull* and its stagings can be complemented by addressing a few filmed theatrical productions of it or even versions adapted for the screen. In the classroom, an instructor might pick one or two scenes and screen a few versions of them, while foregrounding the where and when of each production.[1]

Polarized Data: Failure versus Success

The performance history of *Seagull* started with two distinctly opposed events that were close in time, the play's respective premieres in the capital cities of St. Petersburg and Moscow. The premiere of the play at the prominent imperial Aleksandrinskii Theater (St. Petersburg, 17 Oct. 1896) was a failure. That subsequent performances there went much better does not fit into the conventional, polarized narrative of *Seagull*'s signal performances. In its second high-profile staging, two years later in Moscow (17 Dec. 1898), *Seagull* was performed by the novice MAT, and the result was a triumph. Both events were widely discussed by Chekhov's contemporaries, friends, colleagues, critics, and theater artists. In modern theater discourse, these two premieres remain famous, and they established a pattern of fabulous failure and fabulous success that requires an understanding of how the performances did or did not correlate to Chekhov's poetics of drama.

The Aleksandrinskii Theater was known for its perfect troupe. Evtikhii Karpov, the visionary director of *Seagull,* introduced an important repertoire reform there to demonstrate that theater can succeed without banal, popular plays. The best actors of the company were in the production of *Seagull.* However, all this did not prevent failure, which was described in great detail by newspapers, private letters, memoirs, and by Chekhov himself: "The play has fallen flat, and come down with a crash. There was an oppressive, strained feeling of disgrace and bewilderment in the theatre. The actors played more than stupidly. The moral of it is, one ought not to write plays" (*Letters on the Short Story* 147). Detailed descriptions of this production appear in Laurence Senelick's *The Chekhov Theatre* (28–37), Ernest Simmons's *Chekhov* (364–78), and elsewhere.

Two years later, when the premiere of *Seagull* was performed on the stage of the MAT, the audience not only applauded but also wept and shrieked in admiration (Stanislavsky, *My Life* [1952] 356; Magarshack 179–86). This time the play was performed by a company of young, unknown actors and directed by Nemirovich-Danchenko and Stanislavsky, beginners in the art of direction. The event was discussed by critics and described in private letters and memoirs as the beginning of a new theater era (*Moscow Art Theatre* 15–47; Edwards 72–80; Magarshack 181–86; Senelick, *Chekhov Theatre* 48–51).

The circumstances of this premiere were complicated. Chekhov barely agreed to allow the new production. In addition, his health had declined, and his sister warned the troupe that a second failure could be dangerous to him. At the same time, only one of the first five performances of the MAT had been successful, and the company, impatient, wanted a play that would cause an uproar. This double threat—for the theater as well as for the playwright—along with the impatience of the artists involved, gave the project the character of a risky, avant-garde creation. Stanislavsky portrayed the premiere of *Seagull* as a critical, existential moment, not just an event in the world of the arts: when the play was over, "it was said that we [actors] stood half-turned to the audience, our faces were fearful, no one thought to bow to the spectators and some of the actors were actually sitting." A few minutes later, "[a]ll were kissing each other. . . . One fell down in hysterics. A lot of us, including myself, were dancing a ferocious dance out of utmost joy and excitement" ("A. P. Chekhov" [Gitovich] 376; see also Stanislavsky, *My Life* [2008] 355–56; Benedetti 86; Magarshack 180).

A comparative analysis of the two productions was made by Sergei Balukhaty, who emphasized the causal relation between the innovative directing of Stanislavsky and the poetics of Chekhov's drama.

Contrasting the two theater events makes students curious and spurs them to look for the reasons behind the failure and success of the two productions. In my laboratory class, this phase of study includes both the teacher's descriptive introduction and the students' independent research. While collecting historical data and comparing narratives of the *Seagull*'s failure and success, students discover Chekhov's text as a living entity, one that has its own biography and expresses its character through its encounter with different artistic fates and personalities.

The Discourse of Theater Critics

In 1896, numerous reviews of *Seagull* were published in the Petersburg press, and they focused on Chekhov's play rather than on its performance. *Seagull* had been written without true knowledge of stage demands, and it was hardly understandable, they argued. But such criticism also revealed the innovative quality of Chekhov's drama. The most representative review was that of Aleksandr Kugel, an important St. Petersburg theater critic, known for his sharp eye and conservative thought:

> The problem is that Chekhov scarcely knows what he is telling all of this for. Why is the writer Trigorin living with the aged actress? How did he succeed in fascinating her? Why did the seagull fall in love with him? Why does the actress have a miserable character? Why is her son writing decadent plays? Why does the old man appear as a paralytic? Why are they playing lotto and drinking beer on the stage? Why is the doctor saying that a bottle with ether was smashed at the moment the suicide happened? Why is the young girl taking snuff and drinking vodka?

Kugel's satirical questions actually outline Chekhov's drama, in which the motivations of human actions are not clear, a direct connection between cause and effect does not exist, and the traditional spectator's desire to identify quickly with a character is not satisfied. Kugel's questions, stressing the absurdity of the play, anticipate future critical discourse regarding the distinctive features of Chekhov's poetics, which celebrated his fragmented, non-Aristotelian thinking and the complicated relations between the essential and the trivial in his writings (Chudakov, *Chekhov's Poetics*; Stepanov; Golomb).

In 1898, after the premiere of *Seagull* in the MAT, the tone of reviews changed radically. Although critics mostly discussed the same issues in Chekhov's drama as they had before, now they praised the play for exactly the reasons that previously had aroused ridicule. The fragmented and unclosed structure of *Seagull*, the conceptual features of Chekhov's art, and his refusal to dictate thoughts and feelings to the audience were described as an artistic method, as innovative drama (Chudakov, "Chaika"; Benedetti 77, 86; Senelick, *Chekhov Theatre* 48–51).

When students compare different critical reviews and extract the important ideas from them, they become aware, almost on their own, of the pioneering nature of Chekhov's poetics and of the uncertainty of his artistic fate (his work was so new, it was received in a way very different, even opposite, from what he intended). Studying such primary materials also has a way of liberating student thought, and it allows students to feel part of the research universe. One of my students wrote in a final paper, "As a researcher and a young artist I felt bewitched by different aspects of Chekhov's plays, especially by the problem of performing a thorny Chekhov's personage."

One point to be brought out is the obvious neglect of the direction in reviews of the St. Petersburg *Seagull* versus the obvious interest in the direction in many of the reviews of the Moscow *Seagull*. This difference in critical orientation is consistent with how the play was received in these two places, and it facilitates viewing it as a new type of dramatic text that requires a new kind of director.

The Directing

The rehearsal period for the Moscow production was complicated. At the beginning, the two directors, Stanislavsky and Nemirovich-Danchenko, worked separately. Stanislavsky went to his country estate and began writing what was later named "The Directing Score." He composed the mise-en-scènes and sent them by post, one after the other, to Nemirovich-Danchenko, who at that time was working with the actors and talking with them about the characters. The ideas of both directors were altogether experimental. Nemirovich-Danchenko, interpreting the play as an array of personal, inner tragedies, developed a polyphonic structure for the performance. Stanislavsky based his mise-en-scènes on the striking effect of multiple actions, which negated the conventional hierarchy of center over periphery. The two directors proposed the same idea of ensemble acting, using it as an instrument for decentralization and as an interpretive key for Chekhov's play. Photographs of their *Seagull* show a mise-en-scène with a number of characters, presenting a visual image of decentralization and ensemble at the same time: everyone is occupied with his or her own personal matters but at the same time connected to the whole.[2]

The directing ideas of Stanislavsky and Nemirovich-Danchenko included a symphonic performance structure, which was based on the simultaneous development of several different thematic lines and contrapuntal encounters among them. Access to Stanislavsky's "Score" allows the general audience, as well as scholars, to understand the theatrical image of opposing motifs: a dim light and the sounds of rural routine life in the beginning of the first act contrasted with Treplev's play; cheerful background sounds of music at the end of the first act contrasted with Masha's weeping (Balukhaty 121–67; D. Jones 21–32). Rehearsals of *Seagull* caused Stanislavsky to think about the phenomenon of intensive "inner action which Chekhov has in a greater degree than any other dramatist" and finally to suggest the idea of subtext in stage practice (*My Life* [1952] 353; see also 352–59).

It is important to note that the directors did not conceptualize their production and its theater stylistics under the influence of professional literary criticism of Chekhov's work. On the contrary, the complex connections that Stanislavsky and Nemirovich-Danchenko saw between the implicit and the explicit and the thematic importance they gave to structural elements preceded scholarly research into Chekhov's drama and in fact influenced future scholars (Skaftymov). Subsequent memoirs, analyses, criticism, and theater research describe a modernistic type of tragic situation that was developed in this performance. The main focus was on the inevitable encounter of ordinary people with the ruinous monotony of everyday life (Stroeva 616–30; Balukhaty; D. Jones). This model of tragedy represented Chekhov's dark humor: everyone could be a hero in life, but the role played would be tragic.

The MAT's *Seagull*, directed as a drama of ideas, offered a new type of relation between drama and stage: actors were asked not to perform but to live on the stage. Nonverbal action became meaningful, and performance became an art of thought, analysis, and interpretation. It was the beginning of a new theater era, in which the representation of a play's ideas and not the performance of its characters turned out to be the main point of a performance. Chekhov's play provoked the creation of this new approach, and the directing of Stanislavsky and Nemirovich-Danchenko revealed *Seagull* as a conceptual drama, where the audience was expected to interpret what took place on the stage. The specific conceptual character of Chekhov's play was discussed in the memoirs of both directors.[3]

In studying the MAT production, students engage in a multilevel, comparative analysis of written documents and photographic evidence, and they also incorporate ideas from current research in drama theory. This approach helps them discover the inner thought system of Chekhov's drama. Its effectiveness has been most apparent in increased student awareness of the power and meaningfulness of his poetics and its relation to the art of directing.

Chekhov's Response

Chekhov knew that his play was written contrary to stage conventions. In his letters to Suvorin, he wrote, "I sin frightfully against the conventions of the stage"; "Well, I have finished with the play. I began it forte and ended pianissimo—contrary to all the rules of dramatic art" (*Letters on the Short Story* 145 [21 Oct. 1895], 146 [21 Nov. 1895]). His letters regarding the first production of *Seagull* offer indirect evidence that he expected the essential mood of the play to be expressed in an innovative, or at least nonstereotypical, performance. It seems that the rhetorical manner of stage behavior, successful in many other cases and traditional for the Aleksandrinskii Theater, was unbearable for him. At the Aleksandrinskii's rehearsal, in fact, he asked the actors to avoid so-called cliché acting (Senelick, *Chekhov Theatre* 28–37). The only actor whose efforts he praised was Vera Komissarzhevskaya—after the first run he wrote that she "acts amazingly" (*Letters on the Short Story* 147). The second run made him angry: "One could not see the play at all through the loathsome acting" (148).

After a few days of thinking about the play's failure, he gave the following reasons: the scenery was worn, rehearsals had been too few, and the actors "didn't know their parts—and the result was a general panic and utter depression" (150).

Seagull performed by the MAT did not satisfy Chekhov either. This time his dissatisfaction related mostly to the stage direction, which he both liked and rejected at the same time. From the very beginnings of the MAT, he understood that the artistic secret and the power of its productions derived from the unique, intelligent directing of Stanislavsky and Nemirovich-Danchenko. He was touched by the stage success of his play, followed it carefully, and mentioned it often in his letters: "My *Seagull* is being performed in Moscow for the eighteenth time and I am told it is staged magnificently" (*Selected Letters* 237–38). Yet he disagreed in principle with a number of Stanislavsky's avant-garde staging ideas, including the use of nontheatrical, true-life sounds, the attempt to introduce the tempo of real life into the performance structure, and the reinforced, tragic atmosphere (Slonim 126–27; Benedetti 89; D. Jones 56-61).

In April, Chekhov came to Moscow, saw a practice run of the play and, according to Olga Knipper-Chekhova, "didn't agree with a lot of things," especially the slow tempo of acting. He got angry and even stopped the rehearsal, demanding that the play end with the third act and claiming that the piece performed on the stage was not his play (D. Jones 61). The naturalistic sound score of the performance elicited a sharply ironic response from Chekhov. At the rehearsal he asserted that theater conventions must differ from real life (Benedetti 79), and afterward he said that his next play would begin with the words, "How wonderful! How quiet! We hear no birds, no dogs, no cuckoos, no owls, no sleigh bells, no crickets" (Stanislavski, "A. P. Chekhov" [Gitovich] 411; Slonim 126).

Generally, Chekhov's attitude to the MAT production was ambivalent. In a letter, Chekhov said that he "hardly understood what was going on on the stage" and criticized Stanislavky's interpretation of Trigorin; but he ended with compliments and delight: "In general it was not bad and I was enraptured by the performance. Sometimes I even couldn't believe that I wrote this text" (*Selected Letters* 242). On one occasion he stated, regarding Stanislavsky, "When he is a director, he is an artist" (*Pis'ma* 8: 278 [to Olga Knipper, 4 Oct. 1899]), and he proposed publishing his plays with the mise-en-scènes of the MAT (200 [to Nemirovich-Danchenko, 16 June 1899]), but later he expressed dissatisfaction with the general tone of MAT productions, declaring that the exaggeratedly tragic accents of the directing deformed his plays (Benedetti 80; D. Jones 59).

Chekhov's complicated and contradictory responses to the masterpiece's productions, his apologetics for and sharp criticism of its staging, should not be dismissed as normal conflict between playwright and theater. They point toward important genre and thematic characteristics of his plays that Chekhov found unexpressed in the MAT productions, charactistics that can be fleshed out in discussion with students.

Studying the stage history of Chekhov's play allows us to approach his poetics through the dramatic encounter of different creative wills. Theater history becomes more than background knowledge or a story to be mastered: it reveals *Seagull* as a dynamic, sophisticated artistic phenomenon that influenced innovation in theater production. It can stress the value of interactive, creative reading; encourage students to explore and to think independently; and provide access to a rich, multilevel understanding of Chekhov's text. Students ask questions they might not have had when they began to learn about the Chekhov era in Russian theater. They understand the relation between the polyphonic structure and thematic motivations of Chekhov's drama and that relation's expression by the personages on stage. The historical approach brings students into close contact with Chekhov's artistic personality, and they come to understand his drama in connection with some compelling episodes in his life.

NOTES

Translations from the Russian are mine, unless otherwise indicated.

[1] For example, viewing Treplev's monologue about the need for new art forms and the performance of his play brings out the central role of art questions in *Seagull*. It connects Treplev's play with the stage history of *Seagull* and opens discussion of Chekhov's own literary identity and attitude toward convention and innovation. Students can be asked to register the behavior and responses of the stage audience for Treplev's play as a way of approaching both character psychology and the language of Chekhov's subtext. Comparing the filmed performance from the Williamstown Theatre Festival (directed by Psachoropoulos) with the *Seagull* of the Moscow Malyi Theater (directed by V. Dragunov) drives home the interpretive possibilities of different stagings and actor performances. The Williamstown treatment of the play within the play episode stresses the importance and irony of everyday life; the Malyi Theater emphasizes the ubiquitous desire to be an artist. Both productions reveal the internal energy of Chekhov's play, its multiple dimensions and amazing ability to correspond to different interpretations.

[2] Discussions of various aspects of the MAT production that might prove useful for students can be found in Allen 22–47; Benedetti 73–90; D. Jones 15–59; Gotlieb 18–20; and Edwards 72–79.

[3] Stanislavsky, *My Life* [Benedetti] 352–59; Nemirovich-Danchenko. See also Edwards 76–77; D. Jones 74–78.

Chekhov's *Seagull* in Postmodern Times: Boris Akunin and Tennessee Williams

Lyudmila Parts

The multiple literary and theatrical rewritings and reinterpretations of Chekhov's plays could by themselves constitute a subject of a university course. In undergraduate courses on Chekhov's drama, twentieth-century literature, or postmodernism, reading late-twentieth-century plays that enter into intertextual dialogue with Chekhov provides rich material for teaching both his continuing influence on world theater and literature and prominent contemporary literary trends. Reading two versions of *The Seagull*, one by Boris Akunin and the other by Tennessee Williams, opens such an investigation into the nature of postmodernism, especially its erasure of the line between high and low literature and between genres. This reading leads to very productive discussion of intertextuality as both a discursive tool of the postmodern skepticism toward cultural heritage and a defense mechanism of culture.

Akunin's *The Seagull* (2000; *Чайка*; *Chaika*) is an ideal test case for the study of such postmodernist concepts as parody, intertextuality, simulacra, palimpsest, pastiche, hypertext, and genre experiments.[1] Like works by all secondary writers, Akunin's text provides material for the study of relevant cultural trends in their pure form, uncomplicated by true artistic breakthroughs or the brilliant inconsistencies that one associates with pivotal works of art. Although Williams's *The Notebook of Trigorin* (1981–83) is neither a parody nor a postmodern experiment with Chekhov's text, his adaptation of *Seagull* to his audience's tastes and interpretative abilities results in changes that help an instructor flesh out significant aspects of Chekhov's original, including its style and genre.

Akunin's play, subtitled "A Comedy in Two Acts," begins where Chekhov's play ends. The curtain opens on "One of the living rooms in Sorin's house, converted by Konstantin Treplev into a study." The most striking thing onstage, however, is the collection of stuffed animals, a whole army of them, and "[i]n the most prominent place, as if at the head of the army, stands a large stuffed seagull with crushed wings." Under the seagull, Konstantin Treplev "is sitting alone at his desk. A large revolver lies nearby and he strokes it absentmindedly, as if it were a kitten" (116). In act 1, just as occurs at the end of Chekhov's last act, Treplev has a conversation with Nina, and a loud noise brings Doctor Dorn into the room, only to discover Treplev dead. The action doesn't stop there: on taking a second look, Dorn discovers that Konstantin did not commit suicide but was killed. The characters react to the news, and Dorn establishes the fact that the killer must be one of them. Act 2 consists of takes that begin with exactly the same action, each thus canceling out the preceding ones. In a succession of eight takes, each of the characters is forced to confess to murdering Konstantin Treplev, for reasons (variously) of jealousy, love, fear, professional curiosity, or revenge. Dorn (of the von Dorn, soon-to-become Fandorin, family)[2] takes charge of the investigation.

Akunin's play thus exhibits typically postmodern features: an openly intertextual and parodic stance, the erasure of the line between high and mass literature, a mixing up of genres, a nonlinear plot, emphasized theatricality, and metafictionalilty. Students should be asked to define these terms and concepts either while preparing for class discussion or in individual in-class presentations.

Discussing Postmodernism

Parody, like all forms of intertextual engagement, emphasizes the most recognizable features of the older text and reactivates accepted readings and interpretations. Akunin does not attempt to imitate or parody Chekhov's style or technique; instead he subjects Chekhov's characters to changes of genre and historical period. These changes dictate Akunin's style and technique: those of the contemporary detective story. Thus his play is a parody without an object; it is more a simulacrum of parody. In the same way a simulacrum is a copy that has no original, Akunin's *Seagull* doesn't engage Chekhov's *Seagull* beyond the most superficial level of plot but parodies something absent from Chekhov's text: the genre conventions of the detective story. As defined by Jean Baudrillard, simulacra and hyperreality characterize the inability of postmodern society to define reality outside the many versions of reality created in the technological world by various media. Akunin's graphic breaking up of the narrative flow to present eight versions of the "real ending" emphasizes the artificial, indeed staged, nature of all reality.

The surplus of motives for the same murder can be regarded as an ironic take on the postmodern rejection of the concept of truth, and its replacement by that of a multiplicity of truths. The different discourses, however, do not provide the protagonists with independent voices; on the contrary, while the play's structure is complex, the characters are stripped of all complexity. Chekhov's characters are variegated and their relationships are intricate, whereas in Akunin each character speaks and acts in strict accordance with his or her established personality and passion.

The multiple takes on the second act also exemplify postmodern pastiche, a lighthearted blend of traditional styles and forms characteristic of the postmodern condition, which Jean-François Lyotard famously defines "as incredulity toward metanarratives" (xxiv). Thus Akunin's parody is directed not toward a specific classic precursor but toward the canon itself, with its emulation of the classics as a primary metanarrative of Russian literature. Decanonizing the classic play redirects the parody from Chekhov's *Seagull* toward the clichés of its interpretations. When Dorn, having confessed to murdering Treplev, reaches for the stuffed seagull and shouts, "I took revenge for you, you poor seagull!"

(Akunin, *Seagull* 159), his anger might just as well be directed at the critics and theater directors who have treated and mistreated Chekhov's play over the last hundred years.

Yet the most productive application of the postmodern theoretical apparatus to Akunin's play is the blurring of the line between mass and high literature, which Akunin achieves through the mixture of genres. Chekhov subtitled *Seagull*, a play that ends in a suicide, as a comedy; he thereby emphasized the importance of the genre definition to understanding the play. The characters in Akunin offer a range of genres for their play: "to participate in this farce!" (131), protests Arkadina; similarly, Dorn announces repeatedly that "all the participants in this drama are in place" and warns Shamraev that "there is no time for melodrama" (147). Akunin's play has elements of all these; most notably, however, Akunin provides Chekhov's comedy with a sequel, in the form of a detective story.

Discussing Genre: Akunin's Postmodern Detective Mystery

A typical detective story will serve as a background to the examination of the generic features of Akunin's play. Agatha Christie's 1929 *Black Coffee*, for instance, has her favorite detective, Hercule Poirot, look for a thief in the usual setting of a country house full of relatives and guests, any one of whom could have been responsible. In the detective novel *The Poisoned Chocolates Case* (1929), by Anthony Berkeley, a group of amateur detectives formulate separate theories on a recent murder and suggest six different and equally plausible solutions to the mystery. These texts contain the stereotypes of the genre also present in Akunin: the secluded setting of a country house, a relatively large group of possible suspects, and the amateur but clever detective who figures out the murderer using only his powers of logic and keen observation. At least in theory, an attentive reader might be able to guess the meaning of the clues even before the detective. Most important, the answer to the question "Whodunit?" is always, inescapably, provided.

The generic detective story precludes the inclusion of the basic features of Chekhov's art: the subtlety of characterization and the insistence on raising questions instead of answering them. Throughout Akunin's play the characters keep to their fixed and hyperbolized mannerisms and to the conventions of the detective story. The dynamism of act 2 stems not from any psychological undercurrents; neither is there any mood or lyricism. Rather, the action is propelled by the relentless duplication of the same structure: Dorn checks his watch and asks "the participants of this drama to take their places" (132). At the end of each short take, a character confesses, and the scene ends with the stage direction "a peel of thunder, a flash of lighting, and the lights go out" (136, 141, 143, 147, 151, 153, 155). In Akunin, just like in a classical detective mystery, there is only one question, Whodunit?, and it receives not one but eight answers. The proverbial gun is conspicuously present throughout act 1 and is fired eight times in act 2, killing the writer over and over again.

Akunin establishes each character by caricaturing his or her most recognizable features. He inserts many stage remarks in Treplev's conversation with Nina, to emphasize his mental instability. The responsible estate manager Shamraev not only refuses to give Medvedenko horses but also grows increasingly upset about the valuable rug's having been stained by Treplev's blood. True to her self-obsessed nature, Arkadina is furious that her son chose to die on the day of her arrival and, moreover, that in dying he created a tasteless tableau of mixed colors: "It must be unbearable—red blood on the green rug. Why did he have to go and shoot himself on the green rug? His whole life consisted of pretensions and tastelessness" (125). In each take, she plays the grieving mother: "My poor, poor boy. I was such an awful mother to you. . . . My dear, untalented, unloved little boy . . ." (133), whereas Trigorin thinks exclusively of his work: "I have to finish work on a story. . . . Work, to bury myself in work . . ." (131); "that's what I ought to write about" (143).

Is there meaning to be drawn from Akunin's generic and stylistic experiment? Pavel Basinsky sees none: in his view, Akunin murders Chekhov according to "the iron law of the postmodernist game: before 'working' with a work of art you have to kill its 'soul,' erase its hidden meaning." Others see Akunin's play as a comment on the times. Elena Krasilnikova traces the transformation of Chekhov's themes in accordance with our modern culture: love becomes passion, jealousy, pity, or an offense; art becomes a game. Chekhov's motifs are both simplified and exaggerated: loneliness and the disintegration of family and, generally, of human connections are givens in Akunin (Kostova-Panajotova). Thus Akunin's play is seen as a serious comment on the disintegration of morality and on the dominance of the material and consumer culture of the late twentieth century.

Williams's American Soap Opera

Williams's plays, from the famous early ones to the less-known late ones, have been a staple at Russian theaters since the first productions of them in the mid-1970s. *The Notebook of Trigorin: A Free Adaptation of* The Seagull *by Anton Chekhov* (1981–83) was translated into Russian in 1999 and premiered at Moscow's Gogol Theater to favorable reviews in October 2000—several months after Akunin's *The Seagull* came out in the April issue of a major literary magazine, *Novy mir* (*Новый мир*; "New World"). While any Russian reader and theatergoer would be familiar with the plays of Williams, what matters to my investigation of his and Akunin's engagement with Chekhov is precisely that no dialogue takes place: neither between the two contemporary playwrights nor between them and Chekhov. Both Akunin and Williams treat Chekhov's play as the raw material out of which they fashion their own text.

Williams's *Notebook of Trigorin*, according to the "Interpreter's Note," is born out of genuine love and respect for Chekhov, an attitude one rarely associates with parody and postmodern experiment. This note is situated where a translator's note would usually be. The parallel is informative: if Akunin translates Chekhov's classic into the language of postmodernism and makes it relevant to postperestroika Russian society, Williams translates Chekhov into a language suiting the tastes and interpretive abilities of the late-twentieth-century American audience. In the "Interpreter's Note," he expresses his admiration for Chekhov's "first and greatest of modern plays" and his desire "to bring [Chekhov] more closely, more audibly to you than I've seen him brought to you in any American production." Because Chekhov is a writer "whose huge power was always held in restraint" while "[o]ur theater has to cry out to be heard at all" (4), Williams brings the hidden meaning and subtexts of *The Seagull* to the fore, sounding loud and clear—indeed, crying out.

In adapting to American dramatic tastes, Williams implements a change of genre; as Maria Ignatieva points out, he "transforms *The Seagull* into America's most popular television genre: the soap opera" (66). Just as Akunin's plot is determined by the genre conventions of the detective story, the genre of soap opera demands certain changes: in Williams's ending, for instance, Nina's child doesn't die (children do not die in soap operas) but is sent to America for adoption. This departure from Chekhov, Ignatieva notes, connects "the two plays and two traditions with embarrassing straightforwardness" (67).

What contemporary viewers associate with soap opera is its exaggerated emotional intensity and the predictability of plot twists. Even those students who never watch daytime television will know these typical features. The *SAGE Dictionary of Cultural Studies* defines *soap opera* as "open-ended narratives without the sense of closure" that put the emphasis on "inter-personal relationship . . . marriages, divorces, break-ups, new alliances, arguments, acts of revenge and acts of caring" (Barker). Any running daytime soap opera will serve to illustrate these typical features.[3] A parodic take on the soap opera can provide an illuminating example: consider, for instance, "Baby on Board," an episode in the prime-time TV comedy *Modern Family* that pokes fun at both the viewers of soaps and the genre's features.[4] In this episode, short enough to be shown in class, a gay character makes fun of his partner's fondness of daytime TV, and both find themselves in the midst of a Mexican soap opera plot when they arrive at a hospital to pick up their adopted baby.

Whether Williams was conscious of infusing his "free adaptation" with soap-opera-like features or whether this change was an unforeseen but inevitable result of making the play suitable for the viewing tastes of his American audience, the resulting difference between his *Notebook* and Chekhov's *Seagull* is striking. The liberties Williams takes with the text of Chekhov's play are in essence close to those taken by Akunin. Williams preserves the plot but changes the dialogue to the extent that the characters become one-dimensional, fully defined by their passions, and fixed in their expressions. Everything that is suggested in Chekhov is fully and explicitly developed. Arkadina actually takes the stage before Treplev's play begins, proving incapable of passing up any platform, however makeshift. Sorin's love for his nephew manifests itself in repeated appeals to Arkadina to give Treplev money. Masha is a drunk, and Dorn is a dirty old man trying to lure women into his doctor's office. Some of Dorn's lines, no longer appropriate to this version, are reassigned to Trigorin, who, as the title indicates, is the true protagonist of Williams's play.

Both Williams and Akunin express important aspects of their personalities in their plays—Williams as a gay man,[5] Akunin as a writer of detective fiction. But Trigorin becomes bisexual in both reworkings.[6] Williams's Trigorin is kind, soft, and somewhat effeminate. He cannot resist the grip of Arkadina, the aging diva, who in this version is well past her prime but refuses to admit it. His revolt is slight: he goes swimming after dark with Yakov, a worker on Sorin's estate, and accepts Nina's love, if only for a short while. In his speech to Nina about the writer's life, he alludes to his bisexuality and insists, "I think that a writer should have a bit of both sexes in him" (32). He continues writing in his notebook; he tears out a page to jot down the address of a Moscow hotel for Nina. When Arkadina implores him to leave the estate (and Nina), he remarks wistfully, "[I]t could be the most important romance I've ever written" (42). Arkadina responds by threatening to make public his homosexual encounters and by attempting to make him jealous. Trigorin submits to her ploys with a rather self-exculpatory "I am a coward—Morally flabby—soft—submissive" (44). Williams endows Trigorin with some of his own passions, concerns, and self-doubts (Hale xvi–xvii), just as Chekhov has endowed the writer with some of his own. Yet Williams's writer, a man of the late twentieth century, is much closer to Akunin's Trigorin than to Chekhov's.

Williams's play, like Akunin's, is emphatically theatrical: the stage for Treplev's play is actually constructed before the audience's eyes; at the end, as Treplev's body is carried onstage, Arkadina—"her face . . . a tragic farewell to her profession, her life, to her deeply loved son: her victim" (65)—faces the audience and takes a bow. Williams makes Trigorin's notebook the central symbol of the play, acknowledging, perhaps, that the symbolism of the seagull remains indecipherable. The loud cry of the bird that concludes Akunin's play seems to echo Williams's "cry out" approach to his adaptation. Paradoxically, however, Akunin's ironic treatment of the classic seems less a departure from Chekhov than Williams's earnest adaptation.

Although Williams declares his respect and admiration for Chekhov, he discards the essential features of Chekhov's art: subtlety, psychological complexity, subtext, and irony. That he keeps intact the skeleton of the action only emphasizes this loss. Akunin puts Chekhov's play aside altogether and engages in straightforward postmodernist jesting and genre experiments. But most important, while Akunin's translation into the postmodern invites the rereading of Chekhov, Williams's translation into the American does not. Rather, Williams's play performs an exhaustive interpretive rereading for the reader and viewer.

Intertextuality as an Invitation to Rereading

For a class discussion of the concept and practice of intertextuality, any critical take on Akunin's *Seagull* requires rereading Chekhov's. The primary function of intertextual engagement, to serve as a defense mechanism of cultural memory, is fully activated.

Critical opinions on the reasons for Akunin's success differ. Some emphasize his philological training: "[O]ne immediately sees the philological schooling. One immediately recognizes a person of one's own circle" (Remizova). Others stress good marketing: "[W]hat is justly associated with the name Akunin [is] a strong plot, a hyped literary brand, and the potential for success" (Filippov). Since the publication of his *Seagull*, Akunin has indeed established himself as a literary brand: he publishes under two additional pennames; creates multinovel literary projects—for example, Genres (Жанры);[7] incorporates elements of interactive computer games into his novels (*Quest*; *Квест*); and authors a popular blog. A number of his novels have been made into films featuring popular actors. He is thus an important cultural phenomenon, an engaging writer, an outspoken public persona; in other words, his name is well known and his endorsements matter. So when in 2002 Olma Press published Akunin's *Seagull* and Chekhov's *Seagull* in the same volume—reversible, in that the book can be started from either front cover or back, each beginning with one of the two plays—consumers ended up in possession of both Akunin's play and the classic. His fans are thus invited to reread, or tricked into rereading, Chekhov's *Seagull*.

By the late 1990s, Russian readers were accustomed to works engaged in intertextual dialogue with classical texts. The postperestroika period (late 1980s–1990s) was a time of passionate acquaintance and reacquaintance with texts of Russian and foreign cultures that had been, for various reasons, previously unavailable. Western mass culture ruled the day: street vendors sold poorly translated European and American detective mysteries and graphic love novels. Video stores offered subtitled copies of every foreign film imaginable; Mexican and Brazilian soap operas made their triumphant appearance on TV. It is remarkable that, despite the abundance of Western imports, the educated public's main preoccupation was with Russian texts: those that could not be published under the Soviet censorship and the classics that had been, it was widely felt, misinterpreted by Soviet ideology. Both the postmodern rejection of grand metanarratives, including that of "great Russian literature," and the postperestroika reevaluation of the literary canon, the widespread rethinking of classical texts and myths, helped address that ideological crisis and make sense of that cultural situation. In general, moments of ideological and political crisis, which threaten society with a rupture in continuity, activate intertextuality as a basic defense mechanism of cultural memory (see Parts).

Every instance of intertextuality, be it a small quotation or a complex network of allusions, signals that an older text is a vital part of culture. The recognition and the consequent creation of new meanings occur only if the reader and the writer carry the same cultural memory. Writers who employ an older text in the construction of their own, whatever their individual aims, rely on the reader's recognition of the referent text. Writers therefore exploit cultural memory and in so doing reconfirm and reinforce it. Akunin reintroduced Chekhov's play into the cultural scene whether he intended to or not. Thus Basinsky, in his scathing review of Akunin's play, is grateful to the author for one thing: making him reread Chekhov's *Seagull* "meticulously, almost with a magnifying glass."

The Williams play has been said to represent a new form of art, comprising "part adaptation, part interpretation" (Hale xx),[8] yet the work is not intertextual, because it is not in dialogue with its object. Akunin's play, however offensive its premise has been to many, brings Chekhov's play to the foreground of the reader's cultural memory and steps aside, as if inviting the reader to take a closer look.

NOTES

Translations are mine, unless otherwise indicated.

1 Boris Akunin is the penname of Grigory Chkhartishvili, a philologist, specialist on Japanese literature, and translator.

2 Fandorin is the protagonist of popular novels in The Adventures of Erast Fandorin series by Akunin.

3 Students may also be directed to such Web sources as *soapcentral.com*.

4 "Baby on Board" is episode 24, the finale of the third season (http://abc.go.com/shows/modern-family/episode-guide/season-03/324-baby-on-board).

5 "His awareness of Soviet policies regarding homosexuality, in addition to his frustrations regarding the treatment of homosexuals in the United States, led him to rewrite Trigorin as a bisexual character and . . . the alterations to [Trigorin's] sexuality mark an intentional act of defiance, on Williams's behalf, against the oppressive nature of both political systems" (Ross 260).

6 An American reviewer found this change offensive: "[O]nly a deep Russian freeze may keep [Chekhov] from spinning in his grave over Williams's transformation of the novelist Trigorin into a bisexual" (qtd. in Ross 256).

7 Novels in the project are, according to an interview with Akunin, " 'pure samples' of different genres of fiction; and each of the books is titled by the corresponding genre" (Akunin, "Ia nikogda").

8 On *The Notebook of Trigorin* as an adaptation, see also Ross.

Stagescapes, Scenescapes: *Uncle Vanya* on Film

Stanton B. Garner, Jr.

Performance and the Teaching of Chekhov's Plays

As anyone who has taught them will agree, Chekhov's plays are challenging to student readers. Lacking the narrative trajectories of conventional playwriting, they present cognitive obstacles to students trying to make sense of their incidents and exchanges. The Russian names, with their patronymics and nickname variants, certainly don't help. Chekhovian drama poses particular challenges for literature and other students who are not used to envisioning plays on stage. These students lack imaginative access to the very things that make Chekhov's plays remarkable: the multiple, shifting tensions between utterance and the unsaid; the actor-oriented mixture of depth performance and ensemble playing; the comedy, which is far more evident in performance than when the play is read; and the complex ecology of Chekhov's stage, with its material objects, sounds, and lighting, and its actors, who enter, exit, and move across the stage in an often elusive choreography.

Whether Chekhov is being taught in an introductory drama, modern drama, or multigenre literature course, it helps a great deal if students have the opportunity to see his plays in performance. Performance clarifies the structure of action and interaction, and it encourages the understanding that dramatic texts are open to interpretation by actors, directors, designers, and—through the mental staging that effective drama teaching can cultivate—readers. Since a play exists both as a work to be read and a script to be performed, students must appreciate that the written text is necessarily incomplete, that it finds its life through specific choices that realize its possibilities in real time and space through actual bodies. Given the limited number of live productions that university theaters are able to mount each year, though, and the fact that traditional plays constitute a diminishing percentage of these, films and made-for-television adaptations provide the medium through which most students will be exposed to performances of the plays they read. This limitation applies even for Chekhov, whose plays are second only to Shakespeare's in the frequency with which they are produced (Senelick, *Chekhov Theatre* 1). Fortunately, a number of strong film productions are available to support the teaching of Chekhov's plays. Teachers of *The Seagull* can work with Sidney Lumet's 1968 film, John Desmond's 1975 Great Performances television film, or Michael Lindsay-Hogg's 1978 BBC version; teachers of *The Cherry Orchard* can choose between Michael Elliott's 1962 BBC production and Richard Eyre's 1981 BBC production; and teachers of *The Three Sisters* can use Paul Bogart's 1966 film or two productions from 1970: Laurence Olivier and John Sichel's film version of Olivier's 1967 Royal National Theatre production and Cedric Messina's BBC television version.

With six easily available film and television productions, *Uncle Vanya* provides the richest opportunities to explore Chekhovian drama in performance.[1] These productions cover a period of forty years and represent a variety of performative styles:

John Goetz and Franchot Tone's 1957 American film, based on the 1956 off-Broadway production and featuring Tone in the role of Astrov. The 2010 DVD, which features a remastered version of this film, also includes the 1959 radio production of *Uncle Vanya* directed by Robert Culp and produced by the Theater Guild.

Stuart Burge's 1963 film, based on the highly acclaimed 1962 Chichester Festival Theatre production directed by Olivier and featuring Olivier, Michael Redgrave, Joan Plowright, and other luminaries of the mid-century British stage. The videotape of this film is widely available in university libraries, and its third act is included in the Films for the Humanities videotape *The Birth of Modern Theatre: Chekhov's* Uncle Vanya *in Performance*.

Christopher Morahan's 1970 BBC television film, with Anthony Hopkins as Astrov. This production is available on DVD in *The Anton Chekhov Collection*, which was released by BBC Video in 2008.

Andrei Konchalovsky's internationally acclaimed 1971 Russian film *Diadia Vania*. While this film lacks subtitles, it offers a powerful visual rethinking of Chekhov's play and is accessible in this way to non-Russian-speaking audiences. Konchalovsky's film was released on DVD in 2006.

Gregory Mosher's 1991 BBC film for television, featuring Ian Holm as Astrov and David Warner as Vanya. The DVD of this production, which is available in *The Anton Chekhov Collection*, includes the 1987 BBC program *A Visit from Vanya*, in which Moscow Art Theatre director Oleg Efremov conducts a master class on Chekhov's play with Russian, British, and American actors.

Louis Malle's 1994 film *Vanya on Forty-Second Street*, based on Andre Gregory's workshop production of *Uncle Vanya* and featuring Wallace Shawn, Julianne Moore, Larry Pine, and Brooke Smith. Considered by some to be the greatest of all Chekhov film adaptations, *Vanya on Forty-Second Street* was released on DVD in 2002.

Uncle Vanya has also inspired two feature-length films that adapt its story and characters to different geographic and social milieus:

Michael Blakemore's 1994 film *Country Life*, with Sam Neil and Gretta Scacchi, transposes *Uncle Vanya* to 1919 rural Australia. Blakemore's film uses Chekhov's story to explore early-twentieth-century Australia's attitudes toward Britain, Australia's involvement in the recently concluded Great War, and the continent's physical and demographic landscape, including its aboriginal population.

Also using Chekhov's play to explore the past, Anthony Hopkins's 1996 film *August* is set in North Wales in the 1890s. Starring Hopkins as Ieuan (the film's Vanya character), *August* explores the class structure of Victorian Welsh society, the hardships of working class life, and the fraught relationship between a landowning English class and a resentful Welsh population. Like *Country Life*, *August* is available on DVD.[2]

Theatrical versus Cinematic Performance

Approaching plays originally written for theater in cinematic terms presents its own pedagogical challenges and opportunities. Writing for the stage, Chekhov had little basis for envisioning his plays translated to a medium as young as film was in his time. Films were first shown in Moscow and St. Petersburg in 1896, and it was not until after Chekhov's death in 1904 that cinematic adaptations of his stories, and occasionally of his one-act plays, began to appear.[3] It would be many decades before one of the dramatist's full-length plays would be adapted for cinema: the 1957 American film of *Uncle Vanya* directed by Goetz and Tone was one of the first English-language adaptations, and the first Soviet film of one of the major plays was Samson Samsonov's *Three Sisters* in 1964. Though the decades since then have seen numerous adaptations of the full-length plays, the overall list of films made from Chekhov's fiction over the years outnumbers the list of those made from his drama. Such recent films as Michael Meredith's *Three Days of Rain* (2002, based on six Chekhov short stories) and Dover Kosashvili's *Anton Chekhov's* The Duel (2010) reinforce this predominance.

That film adaptation favors fiction over the plays may feel counterintuitive: after all, shouldn't plays already scripted for actors translate more easily to another actor-based medium than a narrative form like the short story? In truth, although theater and cinema are both performing arts, the representational conventions they observe differ in crucial, medium-specific ways. In most of its traditional and modern forms, theater is an art of fixed locales: performance areas are stationary, and spectators are restricted to specific viewing positions. The worlds represented by theater are grounded in three-dimensional space in which live bodies move through materialized environments. Audience members process events that transpire in the here and now, and they extend the visual scene to its offstage elsewheres through acts of imaginative projection. The perceptual density of stage actuality is intensified in theatrical realism, which seeks to replicate the observable world in its quotidian materiality. As Bert O. States, a theater phenomenologist, suggestively writes, "[W]hat the realist theater accomplishes, subliminally, is the imprisonment of the eye" (69).

Cinema, on the other hand, is an art of moving images. The immateriality that characterizes these images allows cinema's represented worlds a freedom from actuality that theater can never attain. Although cinematic spectators are traditionally bound to their seats, their perception of the unfolding narrative is liberated by the camera's eye—which identifies what is seen and what is not seen, adjusts angle and distance, and moves through the scene it records—and by editing and other postproduction processes that manipulate image and sound. The single-shot filming of Thomas Edison's 1894 kinetoscope motion pictures created a viewing experience relatively close to that of theater, but the early history of cinema shows rapid exploitation of the medium's nontheatrical dimensions. Film outdid realism by offering photographic representations of the world and by extending this representation across wider canvasses and opening it up to changing perspectives. At the same time, it could abandon the realist aesthetic altogether by exploring fantasy, dream, and the supernatural and by bringing its images into unstageable juxtapositions. With their similar freedom from theater's material constraints, novels and short stories are actually more intrinsically filmic than plays written for the stage.

Because theater and film tell stories in different ways, teaching plays through filmed or filmed-for-television adaptations must take into account the representational principles and spectatorial experiences intrinsic to these two mediums. That many cinematic adaptations of plays originate in theatrical productions calls attention to the act of translation by which cinema re-presents and thereby interprets theatrical narrative. Some adaptations—Mark Cullingham's 1982 made-for-television version of Sophocles's *Medea*, for example, which was filmed at the Eisenhower Theater of the Kennedy Center for the Performing Arts—stay close to a specific theatrical production, reproducing its stage and other production components while keeping its filmic interventions to a minimum. Other adaptations—such as the Soviet director Grigorii Kozintsev's 1971 *King Lear*, which locates Shakespeare's play on a vast cinematic landscape—reimagine a play in more purely filmic terms. Most television and film adaptations exist somewhere on a continuum between these two points, capturing what they can of a play's theatrical power while making use of film's unique resources to present offstage scenes that are only described in the play, to break up the theater's fixed distances and viewing angles, and to shift the optics through which the playwright's world is apprehended.

Morahan's 1970 television production of *Uncle Vanya* and Konchalovsky's 1971 film illustrate some of the contrasting ways that Chekhov's play has been reimagined cinematically. Filmed in a television studio, Morahan's *Uncle Vanya* uses the camera to open up and visually inhabit Chekhov's fixed settings. The intricate spatiality that this technique creates is particularly evident in act 2, where characters enter and exit what Chekhov's text indicates is a single drawing room. In keeping with other film adaptations, Morahan makes the entire house his setting, and his camera shifts from room to room, tracking the characters as they walk down corridors to different rooms. At several points during the act, a camera glides along the outside of the house, observing characters as they sit, read, occupy themselves, and gaze out windows. Characters are often framed by windows and doorways, sometimes in passing. Because the camera never provides a vantage point from which the overall relation between rooms and hallways can be determined, its moving lens creates a cinematic equivalent of Serebryakov's disorientation: "I don't like this house. It's a perfect labyrinth. Twenty-six enormous rooms, people wander off in all directions and you can never find anyone" (Chekhov, *Major Plays* 211). As characters converse throughout the play, Morahan uses the camera and lighting to direct the spectator's attention. Characters are brought in and out of focus at various points during conversations, isolated by close-ups, and foregrounded by the film's lighting design. By making the camera an active agent in the interpretation of Chekhov's text, the production's visual mobility goes a long way toward countering what I call the "BBC effect"—that boxed-in, mildly deadening quality that studio-filmed television adaptations of drama often fall victim to.[4]

Konchalovsky offers a more interventionist cinematic interpretation of *Uncle Vanya*. Liberally paring Chekhov's dialogue and eliminating the theatrical soliloquies that Vanya, Sonya, and Elena deliver in the play's second half, he expands the visual action in order to develop information stated or implied in the characters' words.[5] Before Vanya joins Elena, Sonya, and Serebryakov in act 2, for instance, he is seen sorting through a book filled with clippings and posters dealing with the professor's career. This addition underscores the rage and disillusionment that Vanya expresses toward his brother-in-law. Konchalovsky also uses cinema to foreground the play's political, social, and economic contexts. Interspersed among the film's opening credits are photographs of Chekhov among friends and actors, as well as photographs of the czar and his family, sick and dying children in impoverished areas of the country, the famines of 1891–92, and deforested, barren landscapes. Astrov looks at the photographs of human suffering and ecological destruction at several points in the play and shows them to Elena instead of the maps that Chekhov specifies in act 3. This backdrop of class inequality, poverty, illness, and death acts as a commentary on the self-preoccupation of the play's characters. When Sonya speaks in the film's closing moments about the sadness that she and Vanya feel, Konchalovsky departs from the practice of most directors, which is to film the two in medium close-up, by having the camera pan backward until the characters are framed in miniature through a series of doorways and Sonya's voice is barely audible. The film's final image is an aerial shot of the frozen and desolate Russian landscape, with no traces of human life. In another purely cinematic intervention, Konchalovsky switches throughout the film between a sepia-toned black and white and color, contrasting the monotony of the characters' lives with the promise (and fear) of something new.[6]

Teaching Uncle Vanya *on Film*

The wealth of available film adaptations constitutes a great resource for teaching *Uncle Vanya* in performance. Any one of the above-listed films provides an opportunity to look at specific scenes and the choices made by individual directors, actors, lighting designers, and postproduction teams. When the same scene is shown from different productions, students can make the kind of comparative observations that live performances of the same play also generate. It's remarkable how precise and sophisticated student insights into a play like *Uncle Vanya* become when they have the chance to work with and contrast interpretive choices. These insights can be carried in further productive directions when the issue of historical adaptation is involved, as it is in *Country Life* and *August*. Not only do these films establish fascinating interplays between different historical, geographic, and social milieu, they also follow Chekhov's script closely enough that they can be compared and contrasted with more directly faithful film versions.[7]

In my own introduction to drama and modern drama courses, I use Burge's 1963 *Uncle Vanya* and Malle's 1994 *Vanya on Forty-Second Street* to explore the performance aspects of Chekhov's play. Unlike the other productions considered here, these films openly address the theater-cinema relation and its implications for Chekhovian performance. Burge's film retains the stage setting of the Chichester production while "reading" it through the camera's point of view. Malle's film, which records a rehearsal of Gregory's workshop production in Manhattan's unrenovated New Amsterdam Theater, plays a cat-and-mouse game with the rehearsal's theatrical and cinematic settings. Both productions use the resources of film (such as close-ups and camera angles) to explore the inner states and communal relationships of *Uncle Vanya*, but each also insists on the theatrical grounding of the interactions represented. The result, in each case, is a hybrid performance field that negotiates the boundaries among the theatrical, the extratheatrical, and the cinematic. Discussing a scene from the Burge film in class and viewing the Malle film in its entirety in preparation for writing a paper on it, my students learn things about theatrical performance, but they also acquire a new way of thinking about cinematic performance and how the cinematic relates to, differs from, and manipulates the theatrical. At the heart of both sets of issues are the actor's craft, the text's complexities, and the guiding vision of the director as he or she draws theater and film into productive dialogue.

Of all the *Uncle Vanya* adaptations, Burge's film adheres most closely to the play's theatrical origins. After opening with an exterior shot of the Chichester Festival Theatre, the camera shows a series of interior views before resting on a shot of the theater's thrust stage seen from the back of the auditorium. Panning to the lighting equipment at the top of the auditorium, the camera stays still while the opening credits identify the film as "Laurence Olivier's production of *Uncle Vanya*" (Burge's name does not appear in these credits). When the camera returns to the stage, the seats are occupied with spectators waiting for the play to begin. The performance that follows uses a version of the theater's versatile wooden setting, which can serve as the interior or exterior walls of the Serebryakov estate, and its wooden furnishings. Lighting and sound are used theatrically rather than cinematically, and the actors retain a performance style more suited to theatrical projection than to the intimacies of film.

Viewing and discussing this production, students explore the theatrical energies of Chekhov's play and the ways they are directed through specific acting performances and staging choices. Students also come to see that Burge's camera makes a subtle but essential contribution to their reception of *Uncle Vanya*. Burge moves between long shots that capture characters in groups, close-ups that direct attention to a specific character (often a character other than the one who is speaking), and mixed shots where one character is positioned in the foreground and one or more characters are in the background. These alterations shift the film's focus between the ensemble dynamics so crucial to Chekhov's drama and the register of individual emotion on the part of characters who seem, at times, to inhabit their own, private plays. By directing audience attention in these ways, the camera choices emphasize certain points in Chekhov's multifocused dramatic world while downplaying others. When Serebryakov enters the stage in act 3 to speak to the household, Burge focuses the camera on Sonya, who absorbs the news she has just received that Astrov doesn't love her, and when the professor announces his plans to sell the estate, the camera focuses on Vanya's face as it slowly registers incomprehension and disbelief. When Vanya's anger builds and the buried emotions underlying this scene explode, Burge employs a longer-range camera to convey the bedlam that ensues. Because its theatrical energies are allowed to take the reins at this point, the scene is one of the funniest in all the *Vanya* films, though the comedy never distracts us from the emotion that Burge's close-ups have dwelt on.

Vanya on Forty-Second Street uncovers additional levels in the theater-film interaction. The film opens with shots of the play's actors and director making their way through a busy Forty-Second Street to the abandoned New Amsterdam Theater for a presentation of the *Uncle Vanya* workshop that they had been participating in for several years. As the actors engage in conversation with one another and with the guests who have joined them in the lobby and empty auditorium, Chekhov's opening lines emerge almost unnoticeably from their small talk. The actors perform in modern dress at a table, and throughout the play the makeshift staging space and the props they use—an I♥NY cup, for instance—playfully refuse dramatic verisimilitude. Their performance is conducted close to and in sight of the seated spectators, and the initial act breaks are marked by Gregory's explaining the time intervals while everyone moves around. The peeling walls of the run-down theater are visible, and the characters are filmed moving through its precarious spaces.

With its found setting and stripped-down performance style, Malle's film shows acting at its most fundamental, liberated from period costume and the other trappings of dramatic realism that traditional Chekhov productions employ. Because the actors do not fully submerge their real identities in the roles they play, their performances have a metatheatrical (and metacinematic) quality that makes their acting simultaneously exposed and intimate. Having already viewed act 3 of the Burge film and seen a different set of performances, my students offer nuanced observations on the particularities of character interpretation in Malle's film: Moore's giddy but bitterly disappointed Elena, Shawn's self-parodying Vanya, Smith's gentle, plainspoken Sonya. They also come up with remarkable insights about the film's extratheatrical world: the appropriateness of the dilapidated theater to the play's preoccupation with age, waste, and loss, for instance. The students have a lot to say about the relation of theater to film. Although Malle never appears as a character in this film, as Gregory does, his directorial interventions are evident throughout. The play's interactions are filmed with a cinematic sense of composition, and at one point—Elena's soliloquy near the start of act 3—Malle uses cinematic voice-over to convert words into unspoken thoughts. As the film moves increasingly inward, the production's audience disappears from view, and the opening exchanges of act 4 are filmed against the cavernous and empty theater interior. That several of the actors have reputations as film actors—and that Shawn and Gregory appeared together in Malle's 1981 film *My Dinner with Andre*—reinforces the film's cinematic self-reflexiveness. When Gregory and the offstage actors join Shawn, Smith, and the others in the film's closing shot to Joshua Redman's jazzy accompaniment, film and theater achieve a final harmony.

These and other productions enable students to think of *Uncle Vanya* performatively—to explore the choices made by directors, actors, and designers that give Chekhov's play its variable lives in production. In the finest of these films, students encounter a representational collaboration between theater and film, and they are invited to consider the medium-specific mechanisms whereby each clarifies the narrative and performative conventions of the other. More important, as these films work with and beyond what the theater can do, students gain an appreciation of Chekhov's complex drama, with its onstage and offstage worlds, its inner recesses and sometimes fraught sociality, and its signature play of direction and indirection. Students learn that although theater and cinema are different media, they bring surprisingly compatible ways of seeing to the carefully crafted world of performance.

NOTES

[1] An additional adaptation, Georgii Tovstonogov's 1986 Russian television film *Diadia Vania*, which was based on the director's 1982 Leningrad Bolshoi Drama Theatre production, was released in Russia on VHS in 1999, but is hard to find outside that country.

[2] For those who want their students to explore a looser cinematic use of *Uncle Vanya*, Chekhov's play provides an important background to Sophie Barthes's 2009 film *Cold Souls*. In this film, Paul Giamatti portrays an actor, loosely modeled on himself, who struggles with the role of Vanya. This film was released on DVD in 2010.

[3] According to Semen Ginzburg, a Soviet film historian, thirteen cinematic adaptations of Chekhov's shorter works were made between 1907 and 1912 (Youngblood 10). The

most notable of these adaptations was Kai Hansen's *Romance with Double Bass* (1911), based on Chekhov's short story of the same title. For further information on the development of Russian cinema during and immediately after Chekhov's life, see Leyda 17–53.

[4] Mosher's 1991 television film succumbs to this effect, unfortunately.

[5] Because the act of characters speaking aloud to themselves works more naturally in theatrical conventions than it does in film, the handling of these soliloquies in film adaptations of *Uncle Vanya* reveals much about their directors' attitudes toward the play's intrinsic staginess. More theatrically grounded adaptations retain the spoken soliloquies; more filmic productions eliminate them or present them in voice-over. The 1957 Goetz-Tone production employs the somewhat awkward device of having the characters deliver the opening but having the remainder of the soliloquy spoken as voice-over.

[6] For a brief but useful discussion of Konchalovsky's film, see Beumers.

[7] French discusses *Country Life* and *August* (158–59). For an engaging analysis of *Country Life*, see Burry.

Chekhov on the Screen: *Lady with a Little Dog* (1960) and *Vanya on Forty-Second Street* (1994)

John MacKay and Rita Safariants

The stories and plays of Anton Chekhov have been adapted for the cinema more often than the works of any other Russian author. As of June 2013, the *Internet Movie Database* lists, in what is surely an incomplete count, around 350 Chekhov adaptations for film or television worldwide, close to twice as many as devoted to the works of either Fyodor Dostoevsky or Leo Tolstoy. Only William Shakespeare's plays have been put on screen more frequently than Chekhov's. As for Chekhov's stories, the appeal they have exerted on filmmakers is no doubt due not only to the prestige factor but also to a combination of the multitude of dramatic situations they explore, the lucidity of their narrative construction, and the suggestive complexity of their treatment of character and theme.

This cinematic adaptability makes Chekhov's works pedagogically attractive, allowing the instructor to discuss narrative structure across artistic media and the student to access a visual reference point for the stories' characters and settings. The teaching opportunities offered by Chekhov on the screen, however, also carry a set of challenges that transcend the walls of the classroom and engage fundamental questions of cinematic adaptation and narrative fidelity. Both the instructor and the student must negotiate the extent to which either medium, the literary text or the film, is used to define or problematize the other, necessitating a discussion of the mechanisms of interpreting literary prose for the screen.

The purpose of this essay is twofold: to produce substantive readings of Chekhov's "Lady with a Little Dog" and *Uncle Vanya* as filtered through two striking cinematic adaptions and to provide the instructor with a practical outline of teaching methods that employ the medium of film to better understand the literary form. To begin, we propose the following questions as guidelines for discussing literature through film:

What are some possible limitations of both cinematic and literary forms relating to narrative structure? And what are the advantages of each?

What aspects of a literary narrative might be particularly challenging to reproduce in a cinematic adaptation? What aspects of a cinematic narrative might be challenging to reproduce in a literary adaptation?

How do literature, theater, and film represent time and space differently?

Many of Chekhov's works have traditionally been dramatized. How does cinema differ from drama in terms of rhetorical/narrative devices? What are some parallels between the two mediums?

Both drama and cinema rely on the individual textual interpretations of actors. Does this have a significant effect on the original literary work's historical legacy? If so, how?

Given the remarkable onscreen dissemination of Chekhov's work, it would be counterintuitive to argue that the work somehow resists translation to the screen. But it is interesting to consider what has made the work so irresistible to the cinematic imagination. Not that success has been surefire: we can all name plenty of Chekhov adaptations that flopped because they trivialized, failed to enter imaginatively into Chekhov's text, overburdened their source with poorly assimilated agendas, or were simply boring. A preliminary identification of the challenges Chekhov's work presents to cinematic adaptation would be useful—because meeting them has led to the creation of some richly conceived and brilliantly realized films that deepen our understanding of his writing.[1]

There is, first of all, the question of the iconographic expectations of the audience, surely shared to some extent by filmmakers and important for adaptation more generally, not least as conventions to be undone: a sense of how Gurov or Anna Sergeevna (of "Lady with a Little Dog") or Vanya (of *Uncle Vanya*) should look and sound, how the world in which they move should look and sound. Some of these expectations come as much from book illustrations and period photographs as from stage productions or explicit descriptions given in Chekhov's writings, although it is worth considering the possibility that the centrality in Chekhov's oeuvre of drama might encourage filmmakers to regard his short stories, too, as narratives to be embodied, as photoplays in embryo.

When we watch a film of "Lady with Lapdog," even if we are presented with onscreen representations of Chekhov's actual verbal text, we need to confront a specific body and voice inhabiting the space of Anna Sergeevna, or, rather, there must be a conversion of Anna Sergeevna into a specific body and voice. Familiar problems of believability are exacerbated here, because the performance has to be plausible not only as a performance but also in relation to what we already believe about Chekhov's story and its protagonists. There is nothing predictable about what might or might not work in putting a story onscreen, even if responses to and evaluations of a given reworking are conditioned by only a few factors: the degree to which the story invites visualization and tries to set limits to it; extraliterary conventions of visual embodiment (stage, illustration, photograph); the formal and thematic preoccupations of the filmmaker and his or her cocreators; the occasion for and timing of the adaptation's creation and release; the residual associations brought to the adaptation by the director and actors from their previous work, particularly if they are famous; the unpredictable effects of translation from Chekhov's Russian; and the expectations of a given historically situated audience in regard to both story and film—if Russian audiences enjoy a broad and detailed, if complexly inflected, knowledge of Chekhov's work, we shouldn't forget that avid New York and London theatergoers know their *Uncle Vanya* too.

Then there are problems of narration specific to Chekhov. Iosif Kheifits noted how, when adapting "Lady with a Little Dog," he had to execute a kind of narrative dilation, a stretching of the story into a film, rather than the usual paring down and compression (217). Not all of Chekhov's stories present this problem—"A Boring Story" comes to mind—but Kheifits's predicament suggests that, for viewers familiar with the source text, there are many times involved in the encounter with an adaptation: the time of watching, the time of the narrative, and the difference in time between the source story or play and the film.

We also need to consider the ironic temporalities of Chekhov's stories. Think, for instance, of how the central melodramatic narrative of Anna's revolt in "Anna on the Neck," harking back to models like Nikolai Karamzin's "Poor Liza" (1792; "Бедная Лиза"; "Bednaia Liza"), is in fact counterpoised throughout to a story about the emergence of her love of attention and spectacle. Think of how the mythographic tale of age-old Russian misery in the first part of "The Student" remains essentially the same but is transfigured or reevaluated in the second part, or how the story of Startsev's disappointment in love and attendant embourgeoisement in "Ionych" can also be read as the story of the banal triumph of sheer physical inertia and appetite. Ricardo Piglia, a contemporary Argentine writer, points to these temporal striations with unusual precision:

> In one of his notebooks, Chekhov recorded the following anecdote: "A man in Monte Carlo goes to the casino, wins a million, returns home, commits suicide." The classic form of the short story is condensed within the nucleus of that future, unwritten story. Contrary to the predictable and conventional direction (gamble–lose–commit suicide), the story is presented as a paradox. The anecdote disconnects the story of the gambling and the story of the suicide. That rupture is the key to defining the double character of the story's form. . . . The classic short story . . . narrates Story One (the tale of the gambling) in the foreground, and constructs Story Two (the story of the suicide) in secret. The art of the short story writer consists in knowing how to encode Story Two inside of Story One. A visible story hides a secret tale, narrated in an elliptical and fragmentary manner. . . . Each of the two stories is told in a different manner. Working with two stories means working with two different systems of causality. The same events enter simultaneously into two antagonistic narrative logics. (63)

Cinema has its own powerful means of temporally complicating the overwhelming here-and-now-ness of moving image and sound, of producing "crystals of time," as Gilles Deleuze called them:[2] through the weaving together of plot and subplot; narrative repetition (e.g., the two halves of Alfred Hitchcock's *Vertigo*); superimposition, often used to materialize visually memory or future-directed fantasy; insertion of anachronistic, often "documentary" footage;

voice-over and music; the period indices or allusions generated by costume, set, gesture, intonation, and cinematography. As Dudley Andrew recently stressed, registrations of sound and image are always traces of some former event or object as well; with the right inflection, they can generate a "delayed action" effect that not only drifts between past and present but also opens a space for mental projections into the future.[3] In the concluding scene of Kheifits's *Lady with a Little Dog* (*Dama*), the director orchestrates unobtrusive collisions between the lovers' naive absorption in their present meeting, the "vulgar" time of the world of society and its "lackeys" (as when Gurov orders tea), and the slow passing of chronological and biological time, aurally marked by the irritant of the fast-running clock in Anna Sergeevna's room more than by Gurov's oblique encounter with his own physical decay in the mirror (Chekhov, "Lady" [Pevear and Volokhonsky] 375).

One way to frame these problems of temporality for students is to ask them to list key details or images that reappear in the original and compare them to the visual motifs of the film adaptation. Although the examples may be too bountiful to cohere to one reading, the exercise will prove valuable in beginning a discussion of the advantages and disadvantages of the print and cinematic media.

The weight of Chekhovian iconography is greater in Chekhov's plays than in his stories, mainly because, as Laurence Senelick has noted, "a consensus of what is Chekhovian has congealed over the last century," and audiences often "[expect] to be sucked into a plausible and *gemütlich* world of bygone gentility" (*Chekhov Theatre* 2). Therefore resistance to innovation in performance style and mise-en-scène, even among actors and directors, is often fierce. It may be, as Christian Metz observed (9–12), that cinema also generates a stronger expectation of scenic realism than does the stage: if in the theater the separation of the play world from the audience is a matter of convention and suspension of disbelief, in the movie theater spectators look onto a world that is truly separate from their own and therefore is expected, paradoxically, to look as weighty and believable as the real world.

The tight association of Chekhov's plays with the Stanislavsky approach to acting generates especially interesting problems for screen adaptations. The Method famously attempts to find ways to keep performances fresh and mutable, to resist "the tyranny of ingrained actor's habits," to conceptualize performance as the authentic and believable expression of "living feeling" and "inner life" (Stanislavsky, *My Life* [2008] 255, 260). It is equally well known that the challenges presented by Chekhov's plays—their muting of conventional dramatic eventfulness, their hedging or blurring of subjective motivation, the way their discrete dramatis personae seem to precipitate out of a rigorous ensemble polyphony—were central to Stanislavsky's post-1905 development of his highly psychological, collective, and organicist approach to training actors (192–97).

Yet film ossifies of necessity, capturing (as Henri Bergson might say) only momentary slices of the mutable dynamic among body, consciousness, and unconscious (the role), reconfiguring those slices, then offering them as representative: indeed, cinema is arguably not a performance art at all.[4] The theater director Andre Gregory has described Chekhov's dramatic art as centrally about "what it feels like to be here as we travel across the ocean of life" and Chekhov performance as ideally mutable in accord with the affective and cognitive tenor of the ensemble on a given night (*Like Life*). If one takes this version of the theatrical Chekhov seriously, it would seem that his transfer to the screen could lead only to drastic reduction, something a shade better than production stills.

In this essay, we explore responses to these different if related issues in Chekhov adaptation: the problem of representing the multiple layers of time that striate Chekhov's prose and the problem of acknowledging the temporality of theatrical representation in terms of the very different temporality (or even ontology) of film. In discussing these problems of cinematic adaptation, we hope to provide useful tools that might be applied in a variety of classroom settings, from literature seminars to film and interdisciplinary media courses. We confine ourselves to two particularly successful adaptations that offer sensitive responses to these issues—Kheifits's 1960 *Lady with a Little Dog* (*Дама с собочкой*; *Dama s sobachkoi*) and Louis Malle's 1994 *Vanya on Forty-Second Street* (a film of Gregory's staging of David Mamet's 1988 adaptation of *Uncle Vanya*.[5]

Lady with a Little Dog

Kheifits (1905–95), the director of *Lady with a Little Dog*, in a shamefully understudied career made early classics of socialist realism like *Baltic Deputy* (1936; *Депутат Балтики*; *Deputat Baltiki*), occasional documentaries (e.g., the Stalin Prize–winning *Defeat of Japan* [1945; *Разгром Японии*; *Razgrom Iaponii*]), and, after World War II, a host of adaptations of literary works by writers as diverse as Iurii German, Ivan Turgenev, Aleksandr Kuprin, and Chekhov.[6]

Lady with a Little Dog appeared in the midst of the Khrushchev thaw (1956–64), a time of significant cultural liberalization that stands, along with the years 1924–36 and 1986–89, as one of the three great periods of Soviet cinema. The thaw was marked by important films about World War II (Mikhail Kalatozov's *The Cranes are Flying* [1957; *Летят журавли*; *Letiat zhuravli*], Grigorii Chukhrai's *Ballad of a Soldier* [1959; *Баллада о солдате*; *Ballada o soldate*], and Andrei Tarkovskii's *Ivan's Childhood* [1962; *Иваново детство*; *Ivanovo detstvo*]) and by remarkable screen adaptations of literary classics. The year 1960 alone saw the release of Leonid Trauberg's *Dead Souls* (*Мертвые души*; *Mertvye dushi*); Ivan Pyr'ev's *White Nights* (*Белые ночи*; *Belye nochi*); Roman Tikhomirov's *Queen of Spades*, the Tchaikovsky opera (*Пиковая дама*; *Pikovaia dama*); and, as part of the Chekhov centenary, Iakov Bazelian's *House with the Mezzanine* (*Дом с мезонином*; *Dom s mezoninom*), the omnibus *Three Tales of Chekhov* (*Три рассказа Чехова*; *Tri rasskaza Chekhova*), Mark Kovalev's popular short *A Work of Art* (*Произведение искусства*; *Proizvedenie iskusstva*), and Kheifits's masterpiece.[7]

In the summer of 1959, Georgii Berdnikov, a literary scholar who was then head of the script department at Lenfilm, suggested "Lady with a Little Dog" to Kheifits.[8] Although Kheifits had already adapted a number of literary works, he felt unprepared for the challenges presented by that story: the need to come up with effective visual equivalents for its paucity of dialogue, use of free indirect discourse, and abundance of verbal description of inner states, especially Gurov's. Kheifits did not want to use voice-over narration, one of the main default solutions to these problems.

But Kheifits did not entirely exclude Chekhov's language from the adaptation. He found elegant ways to incorporate descriptions of interior reflection into dialogue, such as this famous passage:

> Sitting beside the young woman, who looked so beautiful in the dawn, appeased and enchanted by the view of this magical décor—sea, mountains, clouds, the open sky—Gurov reflected that, essentially, if you thought of it, everything was beautiful in this world, everything except for what we ourselves think and do when we forget the higher goals of being and our human dignity. ("Lady" [Pevear and Volokhonsky] 367)

In the film, the couple sits silently, looking over the sea (as in the story), when Anna Sergeevna asks Gurov to "say something . . . anything at all." Gurov then pronounces the above reflection (from "essentially" to "human dignity"), which Anna Sergeevna not unreasonably takes as a rather cruel innuendo, a hint that he (as Chekhov's Anna Sergeevna would remark later in the story, through the third-person narrator) "did not respect her, did not love her at all" (367). Kheifits uses Gurov's indulgent meditation on nature as an occasion to sharpen our impression of the dynamics of the lovers' relationship, inflecting the lines to demonstrate Gurov's complacent sense of superiority and Anna Sergeevna's perceptiveness and quiet strength.

A similar tactic is used for the story's self-cancelling final paragraph: "And it seemed that, just a little more—and the solution would be found, and then a new, beautiful life would begin; and it was clear to both of them that the end was still far, far off, and that the most complicated and difficult part was just beginning" (376). Kheifits gives the first half of the sentence to Gurov, the second—changed into the slightly less contradictory "I believe it, but the most complicated and difficult part is just beginning"—to Anna Sergeevna. Letting her have the film's final word not only imparts to her greater weight in the relationship but also endows her with the authority of a commentator. Kheifits also seems to incorporate space for the audience to recollect Chekhov's story on a number of occasions. Gurov, shivering next to the "gray fence" and listening to Anna Sergeevna playing the piano, smiles bitterly in close-up, as though thinking (to quote the text again) "with vexation that Anna Sergeevna had forgotten him, and was perhaps amusing herself with another man" (371).[9]

Fig. 1. From *Lady with a Little Dog*. "Everyday vulgarity."

Kheifits caps the mute humiliation of Gurov here by having him struck from behind with a snowball, a visualization that demonstrates the director's brilliance as an adapter. In creating *Lady*, Kheifits found that his early silent film experience came in handy, because it had trained him to work with objects, faces, and gestures instead of words as vehicles of communication. Like many filmmakers and writers of his generation, he was strongly influenced by the Hungarian film theorist Béla Balázs's 1924 *Visible Man* (translated into Russian in 1925), which argued that cinema returned to human beings their primordial nonverbal expressivity (17–51). This expressivity is conveyed, in Kheifits's words, by "eyes, gestures . . . international and comprehensible to all, regardless of the native language" (124–25). A good example is the downward tilt to the empty bottle floating in the Black Sea at the very beginning of the film (fig. 1), a camera movement that immediately sets up a contrast between the sublime, eternal expanse of the sea and the mindless ephemerality of commodity culture: Kheifits thought of the bottle as a metaphor for "everyday vulgarity" that would drift throughout the film (Basina and Khravchuk).[10] He was able to zero in on and interweave details of this type because of the film's moderate scenic density: although he used old photographs of Yalta, illustrations from early Chekhov editions, and his own childhood memories of ships and holidaying along the shores of the Dnieper to re-create (together with the designers Kaplan and Manevich) the look of late-nineteenth-century Yalta and Moscow, he took pains not to overburden the film with realistic detail, thereby making it easier to pull psychologically and thematically significant details out of the mise-en-scène.

Fig. 2. Past traversing present through superimposition: Gurov (Aleksei Batalov) and Anna Sergeevna (Iya Savvina).

Kheifits regarded the use of things rather than dialogue as a way of "creating space for [the spectator's] visual associations, for the awakening of fantasy [and] cocreation," and in this respect he was faithful to the complexities and ambiguities of Chekhov's text (127). "Lady with a Little Dog" provides fertile ground for Kheifits's materialist approach, especially as present and past, gaze and memory, and perception and imagination intertwine in Gurov's growing obsession: "In the evenings [Anna Sergeevna] gazed at [Gurov] from the bookcase, the fireplace, the corner, he could hear her breathing, the gentle rustle of her skirts. In the street he followed women with his eyes, looking for one who resembled her . . ." ("Lady" [Pevear and Volokhonsky] 369).

Kheifits creates chains of apparently chance visual associations—the brief high-angle shot from Gurov's point of view of the horses pulling the Moscow trolley in winter, an involuntary memory of the coach that transported the lovers along the coastline; the inserted sequence during which Gurov pursues not women in the street but a little white dog he believes to be Anna Sergeevna's Ralph—to illustrate how his consciousness is continually ambushed by the past. On one occasion, the director resorts to the classic technique of superimposition when Gurov, listlessly playing the piano for guests at his wife's salon, is pulled mentally back to Anna Sergeevna by a candle burning in front of his eyes (fig. 2).[11]

We find this ambiguity even in the eyes, in the slow dance of the actors' gazes. The gaze of Iya Savvina (Anna Sergeevna) has a particular complexity, as we are often uncertain, because of the way Kheifits blocks Aleksei Batalov

Fig. 3. The ambiguous gaze of Anna Sergeevna (played by Iya Savvina).

(Gurov) in relation to her, whether her intense look is directed at him, whether she is evading him, or whether her glance expresses anxious reflection on past or future (fig. 3).

Kheifits also wanted to give the film a "polyrhythmic" character and to establish a contrast between the pace defined by "the hearts of the [central] characters" and that of the "stagnation" that surrounds them (216). This contrast is marked by the use of nondiegetic music—for example, the mournful repetition of the A-flat minor triad in the opening Yalta sequence, punctuated by bottles popping and the vulgar discourse of Gurov's friends from Moscow, which momentarily turns into a brief, yearning melody for strings when Gurov gazes for the first time at the strolling Anna Sergeevna in the distance, then again when Anna Sergeevna herself stops to turn and look in some unspecified direction.

The contrast of rhythms and worlds is established most forcefully by Kheifits's main narrative innovation in the film, the direct representation of the fallen social world surrounding the lovers in Yalta, Moscow, and Saratov. The wealthy, wasteful Muscovite friends of Gurov are inventions of Kheifits—the unnamed vulgarian who first mentions Anna Sergeevna to Gurov, the rich, depressed, alcoholic Aleksei Stepanovich, with whose wife Gurov is clearly carrying on a flirtation at the outset of the film. These characters are first seen in Yalta and later in the Moscow clubs, cafés, restaurants, and salons frequented by Gurov.[12] In Saratov, meanwhile, Anna Sergeevna's husband, the lackey-like von Dideritz, is shown (before the performance of *The Geisha*) to be engaged in an incipient flirtation with the governor's daughter (another invention).[13] The lovers are shown explicitly as the objects of gossip and malicious looks, and the gazes of others become increasingly oppressive over the course of the film, justifying Kheifits's decision to have Anna Sergeevna suddenly close Gurov's eyes in the final scene—a desperate effort to hide not only from traces of mortality visible in the mirror but from the social world of "apparent" life as well (374).[14]

Gurov's early cynicism is indicated primarily by his involvement in the socialite world, rather than (as in Chekhov) through side remarks about women as an "inferior race" or comparisons of the lace on his former lovers' underwear with "scales" (362, 365; phrases not included in Kheifits's film).[15] Gurov never extracts himself entirely from this world. Responding to the question from him, already obsessed, about the nature of love, a cool scoffer at the Doctor's Club replies that love's main precondition is a separate apartment, adequately if cruelly presaging the arrangement to come.

Perhaps the most remarkable polyrhythmic effect is created through the contrast between the bustle and idle talk of the Moscow bourgeoisie and the longueurs characteristic of Gurov's scenes of solitude. These stretches of frustrated yearning are presaged by the unusually long (almost one and a half minutes) sequence following Anna Sergeevna's departure, as we see Gurov walking away from the platform, finally hanging an abandoned glove on a fence in a quietly raffish gesture of closure—or so it would have seemed if his departure from the platform had not been so very slow. Later we are treated to a full two minutes of his shuffling return to his apartment, captured largely in a single, perfectly executed rightward dolly shot that leads only to his pathetic embrace of a stone pillar in the apartment, in an almost childlike expression of desire for silence and escape. The four-minute sequence of his pacing along the gray fence is followed by an even emptier minute-long scene in the hotel room, where his frustration and "vexation" (371) find expression in his sitting on the bed, smoking, blowing dust off a headless statuette, overhearing muffled shouts, and finally moving listlessly to the window (where he sees the ad for *The Geisha*).

This kind of eventlessness was highly unusual in Soviet (and non-Soviet) cinema at the time, and it links *Lady with a Little Dog* stylistically not only to Chekhov's protomodernist subduing of dramatic anecdote—"At least half an hour passed in silence" (365)—but also to the new, narratively open or antidramatic cinema emerging in Europe then, in works like Roberto Rossellini's *Journey to Italy* (1954) and Michelangelo Antonioni's *L'avventura* (1960).[16] *Lady with a Little Dog*, despite its apparent classicism, is actually multitemporal or polyrhythmic in terms of film history, in the way it weaves together silent film practice, mid-century melodrama, hints of socialist realism, and what Deleuze called the modernist or "time-image" art cinema in its remarkably successful effort to render Chekhov's elusive text. For purposes of the classroom, Kheifits's film offers an excellent meditation on the problematics of the verbal (or literary) image and the narrative structure of the Chekhovian psychological ambiguities that appear throughout his oeuvre. It may be particularly useful to center discussions of *Lady* on the dynamics of the wordless cinematic image in contrast to the inflections of dialogue and descriptive exposition.

Vanya on Forty-Second Street

In Malle's *Vanya on Forty-Second Street* we have an American rendering of the Russian play directed by a cosmopolitan Frenchman, with a jazz score by Joshua Redman and equally jazzy title and without sets or period costumes. The film nonetheless yields the ultimate Stanislavsky Method version of Chekhov's *Vanya.* But this description leaves out most of what's extraordinary about Malle's film and its production. His adaptation is an absolute must in any Chekhov classroom that seeks to explore the intersections of literary, dramatic, and visual interpretations of the original text.

Vanya is a film not of a play exactly but of a run-through, a rehearsal by a remarkable group of actors who had first assembled years earlier (in 1989) expressly to explore and rehearse *Uncle Vanya.*[17] Gregory, a celebrated director, was the convener, and for several years on and off, as schedules allowed, the cast of eight under his guidance collectively explored Chekhov's text and themselves as actors in various spaces in New York, without costumes, lights, sets, or audiences.[18] The *Vanya* laboratory was a central experience for all involved, and when scheduling made it impossible to continue the explorations, Gregory proposed running through the entire script four times a week for six weeks for a small invited audience, as a kind of farewell to the project (London). Malle was one of the friends invited to see the production—he had, of course, worked with Gregory and Wallace Shawn (playing Vanya) on *My Dinner with André* (1981)—and, after some hiatuses due mainly to funding and health issues (*Vanya* was to be Malle's final work), he set to work directing a film on Gregory's urging (London).

Malle, like Kheifits, was a veteran by the time he came to make *Vanya*, having created New Wave–era classics like *The Lovers* (1958) and *The Fire Within* (1963), documentaries like *Calcutta* (1969), and major early United States indie features like *Atlantic City* (1981). As Steven Vineberg has noted, Malle's work in both fiction and documentary film—and in films like *My Dinner with Andre* that blurred the boundaries between those modes—along with his talent for directing actors and his experience with Gregory and Shawn made Malle an obvious choice to direct this film.[19]

Initially, Gregory asked Malle simply to document one of the run-throughs on film (London), but *Vanya*, though modest in budget and scope—shot on Super 16mm (rather than the standard and much more expensive 35mm) with a single camera, in street clothes, very minimally staged in the then abandoned and decrepit New Amsterdam Theater[20]—is far from what might be called filmed theater. The scenes were all professionally lit and edited together from a number of long (about ten-minute) single-camera takes. The film's intense sense of continuity is constructed out of these many takes captured over the course of about two weeks. Malle carefully blocked the actors' movements—in stark contrast to the physical openness of the earlier run-throughs[21]—that he might then reconstruct a continuous texture in the editing room, incorporating numerous shot and reverse shot patterns, close-ups of significant expressions (particularly in the meeting scene in act 3), and dramatic cuts to visually and emotionally expressive features (such as the sudden medium close-up of Elena (played by Julianne Moore), haloed by that shock of red hair, after Serebryakov (played by George Gaynes) rejects her sexually near the beginning of act 2).

The main problem confronting Malle must have been how to preserve a sense of the fundamental mutability of the run-throughs, their intrinsically nonfinalized quality, in a film. Gregory has said that he wants the emotional and dramatic "river" of a production to flow in various directions on various evenings: indeed, this kind of endlessly mutating actorly exploration was the whole point of the *Uncle Vanya* enterprise to begin with (*Like Life*). But filming seems inimical to this approach, requiring as it usually does some degree of predictable organization of bodies, objects, and light before the camera and yielding as it always does a fixed, constructed, and singular redaction. The paradox is obvious: Either one produces a straightforward record (or, better, numerous straightforward records) of *Vanya* performances in a more or less point-and-shoot fashion, which would be of interest to no one except theater historians, or one brings all the formal and technical resources of cinema to bear on the project, to create an effective film that, by being effective, betrays the workshop's raison d'être of open exploration.

Put in these terms, of course, the problem has no solution; but Malle found ways not to solve the problem, exactly, but to acknowledge it in the deep texture of the film. Although actors' movements were blocked out in advance, he and Declan Quinn, the cinematographer, used newly available handheld video cameras to make initial documentary explorations of the actors and their space in order to find an effective and unobtrusive shooting plan. Malle limited the number of cameras to one hand-held unit in order to achieve greater intimacy and intensity, to avoid shifting the balance of on-set attention to, in Quinn's words, "the filming [rather than] the performance" (Wasson).

Unable to incorporate living performance as such, Malle devised at least two allegories for performance to be read at a metacinematic level. First, he staged a version of the invited-guests-at-a-rehearsal scenario, representing the invitees in the film's prologue sequence, very occasionally during the first two acts, and in an intermission dinner between acts 2 and 3, where the actors are shown bantering with these audience members around a table.[22] The inclusion of this audience has intriguing cross-media implications, because apart from the prologue and the dinner interlude, they are entirely silent and in no way interact (as is normal in the theater) with the performances they are watching: that is to say, they become effectively a cinematic audience, being outside the physical time-space of the spectacle they observe. This impression increases as the film progresses: by the end of the film, even the theater has largely disappeared from view—its sudden reappearance at the top of act 4 comes as a small shock—and the performances seem to be happening, to quote Quinn again, in "a neutral space . . . [a] void" (Wasson).

Second, in the film's famous documentary prologue on the streets around the New Amsterdam, Malle constructs an elegant allegory for the production's dependence on the real bodies and real emotions of the performers. He tracks six of the eight actors as they arrive at the theater, already, though unbeknownst to us, in costume and to an extent in character. We see Shawn nibbling on a knish with a kind of glum Vanya-esque anxiety; we see Lynn Cohen (playing Maman) emerging from the subway, looking for all the world like part of New York's professional intelligentsia; we see Brooke Smith (Sonya) and Moore (Elena) arriving together, happily chatting, a hint at the later centrality of that character dyad; we see Larry Pine (Astrov) taking a backward glance at a passing attractive woman; and we see Gaynes (Serebryakov) conspicuously arriving later than the other actors and sporting an equally conspicuous wide-brimmed white hat that he will still be wearing when he makes his first entrance.

At the cusp of the transition from prologue to play—a transition maximally blurred by Malle—both Pine (in dialogue with Phoebe Brand) and Shawn (in dialogue with Mrs. Chao, one of the rehearsal guests: she is in fact none other than the celebrity chef Madhur Jaffrey) talk about how exhausted they are (Pine through overwork, Shawn through insomnia), offering discreet dialogue hooks that will soon link up with the text of the play. The prologue is then terminated twice, in effect: once theatrically, when Smith shakes the bells that will sound again at the end of the fourth act at the departures of the Professor and Elena, and later of Astrov ("they're gone"), then more cinematically, with a close-up of Shawn incongruously lying down to take a snooze (that is, to adopt Vanya's initial recumbent position), the close-up dollying left to Pine and Brand, who are apparently continuing their conversation but in fact speaking the opening lines of the play. Not until a minute and fifteen seconds into their chat (and after three cuts) do we fully realize that the performance is on, and we are given a from-behind-the-actors view of the invited audience. This blurring of reality and theater might have come off as a bit corny, but Malle executes it with such rhythmic sureness and quiet verve that it remains striking even twenty years after the picture's release.[23]

Most important, Malle finds ways to acknowledge the difference between theatrical and cinematic modes and relations of representation in the film's mise-en-scène and cinematography. Consider those moments when the camera pulls or cuts back from the intense, tightly shot scenes of emotional interaction to reveal the theatrical conventionality of the set and positioning of the actors. Two beautiful examples occur near the top of the fourth act, when Sonya descends onto the set from her barely noticeable perch in the theater, only to be

Fig. 4. The monologue of Vanya (Wallace Shawn).

fully integrated immediately into the cinematic dynamic of close-ups and shot and reverse shot patterns that have predominated up to that moment; then shortly afterward, when Elena arrives to tell Vanya to speak with Serebryakov, the camera moving backward from a medium close-up of Sonya and Vanya at the table to a medium shot of Astrov, Vanya, Sonya, and Elena together on the set, with Astrov conspicuously (and very stagily) standing with his back turned to everyone else, until his final dialogue with Elena, his final attempt to seduce her, commences.

Especially fascinating are three set pieces that Malle builds around the play's three major monologues—Vanya's and Sonya's in act 2 and Elena's in act 3—to illustrate the tension (or dialectic) between theatrical intimacy-immediacy on the one hand and cinematic constructedness on the other. Vanya's speech begins right after Elena has left, telling Vanya that he "disgusts" her: we see him as though from the position of the audience members seated on the other side of the table—we witnessed them take their places at the top of the act—but as the camera slowly dollies forward across the table (fig. 4), we come to realize that we are party to a specifically cinematic intimacy with and proximity to the actor, inasmuch as this kind of forward movement of the gaze is impossible in the theater (especially this bare-bones theater). Indeed, we might sense that our vision has been freed up rather than constricted by cinema, now that we can see, very much in the Balázs spirit, the drama of the face in a way we previously could not.

Near the end of the act, we get an equally brilliant but subtler representation of theater inside cinema with Sonya's monologue after Astrov's departure. We watch Sonya more or less from Astrov's former position, that of an interlocutor,

Fig. 5. Sonya's monologue, Elena approaching (Brooke Smith and Julianne Moore).

as she reflects aloud on her love for the doctor. But the moment she asks, "Oh Lord, why did you make me so plain?," the camera begins to track almost imperceptibly to the right, creating a space into which Sonya's rival, the beautiful Elena, will presently step (fig. 5). In *Vanya on Forty-Second Street,* cinema envelops theater completely but envelops it like a glove or container that expands or contracts—now looser, to allow the actor's art the time to be captured by the camera; now tighter, to insert the actors and set back into Malle's cinematic dramaturgy.

The glove is tightest, though paradoxically so, in the final monologue, that of Elena just before her interrogation of Astrov. The monologue is delivered as a voiceover, a specifically cinematic technique that is possible, though rare, onstage and certainly not employed in Gregory's original *Vanya* run-throughs. Again, as with Vanya's monologue, we are suddenly party to a character's inner life, but again through the intervention of cinematic technology, here very conspicuous (fig. 6). As the physical closeness we would enjoy in the theater is replaced by a different kind of proximity, the realism of the staging is slightly altered as well, when the white noise that vaguely murmurs across the course of most of the film—the distant rumble of Forty-Second Street—is suddenly turned off, only to become distantly audible again as Elena's monologue reaches its conclusion. It is in moments like these that *Vanya on Forty-Second Street* offers a powerful meditation not only on the relation between theater and film but also on the fundamental themes—the desire for intimacy and the reality of and need for distance; the longing for the possibility of change and the recognition of the end of that possibility—that lie at the core of Chekhov's *Uncle Vanya* itself.

Fig. 6. Elena's voice-over monologue (Julianne Moore).

NOTES

All translations are ours, unless otherwise indicated.

1 For an overview of major issues in literature-to-film adaptation, complete with an excellent bibliography, see Stam.

2 "What the crystal [of time] reveals or makes visible is the hidden ground of time, that is, its differentiation into two flows, that of presents which pass and that of pasts which are preserved. Time simultaneously makes the present pass and preserves the past in itself" (Deleuze 98).

3 "Innumerable . . . constellations of image-oppositions," writes Andrew, "can compete on the movie screen" (16–17).

4 For the philosopher's critique of cinema's mimicry of real movement and change, see Bergson 301–15.

5 We do not engage in detailed comparison of Mamet's version of Chekhov's play with the original Russian or with the alterations made in *Vanya on Forty-Second Street*—excisions almost exclusively—to Mamet's text: our focus is on play to film.

6 The Chekhov adaptations are *Dama s sobachkoi* (1960; *Дама с собочкой*; *Lady with a Little Dog*); *V gorode S.* (1967; *В городе С.*; *In the City of S.* [based on "Ionych"]), and *Plokhoi khoroshii chelovek* (1973; *Плохой хороший человек*; *A Bad Good Man* [based on "The Duel"]). All three can be watched online (*YouTube*) though without subtitles, alas.

7 *Three Tales of Chekhov* included adaptations of "Vanka," "Anyuta," and "Vengeance," directed by Eduard Bocharov, Veniamin Dorman, and Meri Andzhaparidze, respectively. Kheifits was of course one of the grand old men of Soviet cinema by 1960, having begun his career in 1930 at the cusp of the transition to sound. Famous for his skill as an actors' director, he had already worked three times with the actor-director Aleksei Batalov (Gurov) since 1954 and discovered the twenty-four-year-old Iya Savvina, who debuted onscreen as the lady in *Lady*.

[8] Berdnikov wrote at least two studies of Chekhov, including a slim 1976 volume devoted to "Lady with a Little Dog."

[9] Kheifits also occasionally calls attention to Chekhov's verbal motifs: "lackey," for example, is used initially by Anna Sergeevna to refer to her husband (as her expression is captured by an unusual and rapid forward dolly), then later by Aleksei Stepanovich to describe the toadies who surround him. (Aleksei Stepanovich, Gurov's rich friend, does not appear in Chekhov's story.)

[10] He also claimed that the bottle was an unplanned detail, discovered when they were filming the shore: one of the cameramen was going to remove it when Kheifits asked that it remain in the shot (Basina and Khravchuk).

11 A detail in Chekhov's text, "the solitary candle burning on the table [that] barely lit up [Anna Sergeevna's] face," motivates this association (365). On superimposition as a means of "visualizing thought, memory, mind" in fiction film, see Vernet 64–85.

12 The main salon is that of Gurov's wife, another and quite plausible Kheifits invention.

13 This modification could be read as a slight bowdlerization, in that it mitigates the adultery of Anna Sergeevna by making her a victim of adultery.

14 Adding to the sense of social polyrhythmy, the film incorporates brief gestures toward working class and non-Russian people: the veiled woman and begging child in Yalta, the peddler who attempts to sell a white lapdog look-alike to Gurov in order to buy coffee, the peasant carter with whom the drunken Gurov briefly speaks on his way home from the club, and so on. These details, in part responding to the exigencies of Soviet ideology, add yet another layer of social signification extraneous to the lovers but do not really relativize their centrality or freight the film with an ideological message.

15 Kheifits intensifies our impression of Gurov's vanity by having Gurov comb his hair while giving Anna Sergeevna a consoling embrace.

[16] *L'avventura* and *Lady with a Little Dog* were competitors at the 1960 Cannes Festival (where the Palme d'Or was taken by Fellini's *La dolce vita*). Savvina won a special acting prize. For a superb essay on the cinematic modernism emerging then, see Mulvey 104–22.

[17] The version used Mamet's text, which was first performed in 1988. Shawn made alterations to this text as the run-throughs progressed, though the film hews quite closely to Mamet.

[18] Besides Gregory, the participants were Shawn (Vanya), Julianne Moore (Elena), Brooke Smith (Sonya), Larry Pine (Astrov), George Gaynes (Serebryakov), Lynn Cohen (Maman), Ruth Nelson (Marina, the nanny), and Jerry Mayer (Waffles). Nelson died before the film was made and was replaced by another Group Theatre veteran, Phoebe Brand.

[19] Malle was an expert literary adapter as well, having directed such films as *The Lovers* (1958; based on a novel by Dominique Vivant), *Zazie in the Metro* (1960; based on a novel by Raymond Queneau), and *The Fire Within* (1963; from Pierre Drieu La Rochelle).

[20] The theater, at 214 West 42nd Street in Manhattan, between Seventh and Eighth Avenues, was built in 1903; it was purchased during the *Vanya* shoot by Disney Theatrical Productions and reopened in 1997 after restoration as a flagship venue for big Disney productions like *Aladdin*. The staging, done by Gregory's long-time collaborator Eugene Lee, placed the main action in the orchestra pit and front-row seating area, because of

the danger of working on the stage of the deteriorating theater. Malle evidently selected the New Amsterdam as, in the words of the cinematographer Declan Quinn, "a decadent space for a play about decadent attitudes" (Wasson).

[21] As confirmed by the remarks of both Larry Pine and Brooke Smith in *Like Life*.

[22] Dinners were incorporated into the original invitation-only performances of *Vanya* as well (London).

[23] Malle wisely chose not to repeat such overt metacinematic gestures throughout the film, thus avoiding heavy-handedness.

CROSS-CURRICULAR APPROACHES

History, Voice, Money, and Trees: "Rothschild's Fiddle" and the Jews

Benjamin Knelman and Gabriella Safran

Yakov, the hero of Chekhov's "Rothschild's Fiddle" (1894), is a coffin maker who hates it when people from his town die away from home; he tots up as a loss his missed opportunity to earn money by making their coffins. As a sideline, he plays the fiddle with some Jews whom he dislikes (he is an ethnic Russian and a Christian). We see him count his losses, watch his wife die, criticize his and his community's misuse of their natural resources, and then die himself, passing his fiddle on to Rothschild, the flautist in the Jewish band, who achieves fame by playing Yakov's sad melody. When situated inside the landscape and soundscape of Russian-Jewish interactions in the late-imperial period, the story offers students an opportunity to exercise a cultural studies approach to literary criticism: they can consider Chekhov as an observer of his complex time, analyze his mature prose style, and experiment with economic and environmental approaches to literature. We provide background material on Russian-Jewish history and geography as well as suggestions and exercises for four classroom approaches to the story. Some teachers might decide to use all four in a single session (the four are linked); others might choose only one or two.

Jewish Spaces and Sounds in the Russian Empire

Yakov's work with Jewish musicians and his contempt for them will prompt students to inquire into the historical position of Jews in Chekhov's Russia. According to the authoritative 1897 census, the Russian Empire contained a Jewish population of about five million, four percent of the country's total (Stanislawski).

Fig. 1. The Pale of Settlement, late-imperial Russia. Map by William L. Nelson.

The ancestors of most of these Jews had been absorbed into the empire with the partitions of the Kingdom of Poland of 1772–95, following which the czarist government, nervous about allowing their Christian subjects contact with Jews, restricted Jewish residence to the formerly Polish lands, called the Pale of Jewish Settlement. In 1897, ninety-four percent of the empire's Jews lived in the Pale (exceptions included Jewish army veterans, high-guild merchants, college students, and members of certain professions). Because the small town where "Rothschild's Fiddle" is set contains a Jewish orchestra, it is probably a shtetl, the Yiddish term for a market town with a large Jewish population located in the Pale. (The Russian term for shtetl is *mestechko* (*местечко*), but Yakov thinks of his town as a *gorodok* (*городок*; "little town"; "Skripka" 297].)[1] A map of the Russian Empire that distinguishes the Pale will help students grasp its geographic scope (fig. 1).

The interactions between Jews and Christians in the late-imperial shtetl fit in many ways the patterns that had been established in the Kingdom of Poland. Jews differed from Christians not only in their religion but also in their language (they spoke Yiddish and used Hebrew and Aramaic for liturgy and study), their clothing, the construction of their houses, and their occupations. Jews ran hotels and taverns and worked as craftsmen (tailors, shoemakers, carpenters) and musicians. Their relatively high literacy and numeracy qualified them as merchants: they bought produce from Christian peasants and sold it at weekly markets, and they used the languages they shared with Jews in other countries to import and export goods. They managed estates for the nobility, but the laws that prevented them from owning land made it hard for them to run their own farms. Jewish and Christian occupants of the shtetl interacted inside a framework of restrictions. While Christians ate in Jewish taverns, Jewish dietary laws kept Jews from eating in Christian houses. Churches and Jewish prayer houses were often located close together on the market square, but Jews and Christians usually did not enter each other's houses of worship. Sound, which carries, defies spatial separations, so Jews and Christians heard each other pray, sing, and speak. Many Jews knew the peasants' languages (Ukrainian, Belarusian, Moldovan), and some Christians spoke Yiddish. As Chekhov's story reminds us, Jewish musicians, like Gypsies, were hired to perform at Christian weddings, while Jews would invite Christian musicians to play during a celebration that lasted through the Sabbath, when Jews were forbidden to play instruments (Freeze 24). To help students understand how Jews were heard as producing a distinctive voice in the Russian imperial soundscape, one could have them listen to the sixth movement of Modest Mussorgsky's 1874 piano suite *Pictures from an Exhibition*: " 'Samuel Goldenburg' and 'Shmuyle' " or "Two Polish Jews, Rich and Poor."

During Chekhov's lifetime, tensions grew between Jews and Christians. In the wake of the emancipation of the serfs in 1861, some former peasants moved into small towns and began to work as petty craftsmen, leading to economic competition with the Jews already occupying that niche; Yakov, as a carpenter, experiences this competition. The assassination of Czar Alexander II in 1881 by a group of conspirators that included a Jewish woman triggered a wave of pogroms, episodes of violence against Jews and destruction of their property. In May 1882, Czar Alexander III issued the May Laws, which further restricted Jewish settlement and land purchase. Anti-Jewish legislation in the Russian Empire was motivated by the same fear that triggered the rise of anti-Semitism in Germany in the 1880s: that Jews were insufficiently loyal to the state and that they used their access to capital to the advantage only of other Jews, to whom they were linked through an array of more or less conspiratorial organizations. The Rothschilds, a family of wealthy and influential European bankers, provided a focal point for this anxiety. Despite the stereotype of Jewish wealth, the population boom among Eastern European Jews in the second half of the nineteenth century contributed to a decline in craftsmen's wages in the Pale and fueled resentment among Jews about the laws that restricted their settlement beyond it. They moved out of the Pale without the needed permission to the big cities of European Russia, but at times, most notoriously in Moscow on the eve of Passover in March 1891, they were rounded up and expelled. Economic pressures along with the threat of violence and their worsening legal status prompted Russian Jews to migrate to Western Europe, the Americas, and elsewhere.

Born in Taganrog, inside the Pale of Settlement, Chekhov interacted with Jews often and regularly wrote about Jewish characters. In an era when some intellectuals and journals could be identified as anti-Jewish and others as pro-Jewish, his Jewish politics were difficult to pin down. In his mid twenties in 1886, he had a romantic relationship with Dunya Efros, a Jewish friend of his sister, and in the apparently unhappy wake of its dissolution he wrote the 1887 story "Mire," depicting a wealthy, vampiric Jewish woman. The story was published in *New Times* (*Новое время*; *Novoe vremia*), edited by his friend, the anti-Jewish Aleksei Suvorin, and it was read as an anti-Jewish statement. A decade later, in 1898, Chekhov would quarrel with Suvorin over the Dreyfus affair, indicating his willingness to situate himself against anti-Semitism at that moment. In his letters, he freely used terms that sounded derogatory to Jews, especially *zhid* (*жид*; "Yid"), which sounds like the most common Polish term for Jew (*żyd*, etymologically linked to the term *Judea*) but felt crude and offensive to Russian-speaking Jews, who preferred *evrei* (*еврей*, etymologically closer to "Hebrew"). Note that Soviet editors of Chekhov's works systematically removed his uses of *zhid*. The first publication of "Rothschild's Fiddle" uses *evrei*, possibly because of the sensitivities of Chekhov's editors at the liberal journal *Russian News* (*Русские ведемости*; *Russkie vedomosti*). In subsequent publications, Chekhov had his narrator, voicing Yakov's thoughts, apply *zhid* to the Jews in the band, and he gave Rothschild's speech the Western Slavic sounds commonly used in the late-imperial period to represent a Jewish accent—replacing *s* with *sh* in *shvad'ba* (*швадьба* for *свадьба* [*svad'ba*; "wedding"]), *ch* with *ts* in *tseloveka* (*целовека* for *человека* [*cheloveka*; "person"]), and *y* with *i* in *vi* (*ви* for *вы* [*vy*; "you"]) ("Skripka" 305, 305, 302). Whether or not they know Russian, students can be asked to consider the dilemma that dialect and ethnic slurs pose for translators; they might compare various translators' depiction of Rothschild's speech and what the translators chose to do with *zhid* (Pevear and Volokhonsky use "Jew").

"Rothschild's Fiddle," written after "Mire," before the Dreyfus affair, and three years after the 1891 expulsion of the Moscow Jews, is sometimes read as a statement against the oppression of the Jews, an apology of sorts for Chekhov's earlier negative portrayals.[2] We believe that this approach is unproductive for the classroom. Instead of urging students to locate the story along a spectrum of more or less politically correct attitudes toward Jews, we suggest that they be asked to identify the ways in which the story both constructs and blurs the boundaries between Christians and Jews. Students might notice that the Jewish character with the name of the famously powerful Rothschild is depicted as poor and weak; the story's title draws attention to the irony of this name. Meanwhile, stereotypically Jewish attributes such as literacy, numeracy, and an obsession with money and profit are assigned to the Christian Yakov, who is also given an Old Testament name (Yakov is the Russian form of Jacob). If the teacher distributes the text of Psalm 137, "By the rivers of Babylon," the students will find many echoes of it in Yakov's words: the river, the willow, the string instrument, the tears, and the themes of memory, loss, death, and destruction. (There are beautiful musical settings to this psalm; one might be played in class, or students could be asked to listen to one in advance.) The psalm, numbered 136 in the Orthodox Psalter, is part of the church liturgy, so Chekhov, a former choirboy, knew it well. (Students of Russian can be given the Church Slavonic version of the psalm; even though the language will be difficult, they will be able to puzzle out enough to notice the words that appear in Chekhov's story.)

Psalm 137 (King James Bible)

By the rivers of Babylon, there we sat down, yea, we wept,
When we remembered Zion.
We hanged our harps
Upon the willows in the midst thereof.
For there they that carried us away captive required of us a song;
And they that wasted us required of us mirth,
Saying, "Sing us one of the songs of Zion."
How shall we sing the LORD's song
In a strange land?
If I forget thee, O Jerusalem,
Let my right hand forget her cunning.
If I do not remember thee,
Let my tongue cleave to the roof of my mouth;
If I prefer not Jerusalem above my chief joy.
Remember, O LORD, the children of Edom in the day of Jerusalem;
Who said, "Raze it, raze it, even to the foundation thereof."
O daughter of Babylon, who art to be destroyed;
Happy shall he be, that rewardeth thee
As thou hast served us.
Happy shall he be, that taketh
And dasheth thy little ones against the stones.

Students can be asked, given what they now know about Russian-Jewish history, to make sense of the blurring of the boundaries between the Russian Christian Yakov and the Jewish Rothschild. What are its implications for Chekhov's construction of Russianness? What does Chekhov accomplish by depicting a shtetl where physical spaces remain sharply divided between Christians and Jews (as when Rothschild fears to approach Yakov's door) but sounds break down this boundary? How does the treatment of Jews affect the representations of music and listening in the story? How does the episode in which Rothschild inherits Yakov's fiddle and begins playing his sad tune shed light on Chekhov's understanding of creativity and originality in art, a theme to which Chekhov returns in other stories, such as "Holy Night" (1886) and "Student" (1894)? The Jewish themes in "Rothschild's Fiddle" lend themselves to a variety of historically inflected readings, and these readings demonstrate that for Chekhov, as for some of his contemporaries, depictions of Jews offered a way to reflect on issues that concerned Russians.

Free Indirect Discourse

The story's foregrounding of people making and listening to sounds will help students think more carefully about narrative voice in relation to issues of Russian-Jewish interaction. "Rothschild's Fiddle" exemplifies free indirect discourse, in which the third-person narration is suffused with the attitudes of one of the characters. Alexander Chudakov, a Soviet expert in Chekhov's prose, calls this style "objective narration," meaning that it avoids the subjective evaluation of an omniscient narrator (*Chekhov's Poetics* 62); he notes that while it is most common in Chekhov's middle period, from 1888 to 1895, it tends to be identified with Chekhovian style in general. The teacher can challenge students to identify the markers of Yakov's grumpy perspective in the narration, starting with the first sentence, "The town was small, worse than a village, and in it lived almost none but old people, who died so rarely it was even annoying" ("Rothschild's Fiddle" 253). Students could be asked to reflect on the effect of this style.

Free indirect discourse creates the shifts in tone as Yakov mourns his wife's death and then succumbs to the illness that killed her. Grief and then fever affect his perception and his evaluations of what he sees and does. "Rothschild's Fiddle" could be compared with two other well-known middle period works, "Sleepy" (1888) and "Gusev" (1890), both also narrated from the perspective of a character whose perceptions are distorted for physical reasons: the young nursemaid Varka in "Sleepy" is exhausted; the soldier Gusev is dying of tuberculosis. In those two stories, the character's mental decline and its tragic outcome, Varka's murder of the baby in her care and Gusev's death, can be blamed on a social system that allows those in authority to abuse the powerless: Varka's masters insist that she work day and night, and Gusev's commanding officers put Gusev onto a boat crossing the Indian Ocean even though they should be able to see that he will not survive the difficult voyage. The effect is a dramatic irony that allows these stories to be read easily as social criticism. Because they are told from the limited perspective of characters who do not understand the reasons behind their difficult situation, readers must deduce the reasons. In "Rothschild's Fiddle," what does Chekhov accomplish by narrating from the point of view of a character who voices his opinions about the Jews and other topics but whose perceptions and judgments become confused and inconsistent over the course of the story as he moves closer to death?

Opportunity Costs

A central concern of "Rothschild's Fiddle" is the compulsion of Yakov to count the losses he constantly senses around him. His nickname, Bronze, a metal used in Roman currency, points to his obsession with money. For him and other Russians of his time, this preoccupation with money—the attitude that success requires awareness of the monetary value of things and the accumulation of as much of that value as possible—was experienced as a disturbing new development, brought about by the emancipation of the serfs, the rise of industrialization and urbanization, and the dissolution of the old feudal system whereby rural people, serfs and landowners alike, had rarely needed to use money. The rise of money was associated in Russians' minds with Jews, as with Western Europeans and other non-Russian groups who traded goods and invested in new industries; thinking in monetary terms, for Russians, meant thinking like Jews, something that felt immoral and wrong. Thus the anxiety of the fictional Yakov and his real-life counterparts about Jews and money could serve as a proxy for larger concerns about money and modernity. Given this background, students can use approaches from economics as well as history and literature to think about Yakov's concern with his losses in the context of his comments about Jews. Indeed, the story can show students how to bring together tools offered by the humanities and social sciences for answering questions about the human experience. They can be urged to pay close attention to how Yakov's relation to his losses changes over the course of the story; they can be asked to reflect on the extent to which the reader trusts Yakov's accounting of his lost opportunities in life.

Free indirect discourse leaves it up to the readers to decide if the losses of Yakov are what he believes them to be. Opportunity cost, a foundational concept from microeconomics, provides one way for students to consider his point of view. Although this notion was named only in the early twentieth century, it was developed in a famous 1850 essay, "Ce qu'on voit et ce qu'on ne voit pas" ("What Is Seen and What Is Unseen"), by Frédéric Bastiat, a French economist. This essay could have been accessible in French or German to Chekhov or those in his circles. Interest in Bastiat is demonstrated by the first publication of "What Is Seen" in Russian in 1896, two years after "Rothschild's Fiddle" (Say and Bastiat).[3] As Bastiat explained, we face opportunity cost in any decision we make: it is the value of the best alternative thing we chose not to do. One can explain this principle to students by asking them to imagine what they could have done, in a parallel universe, if they had not acted as they did. If students decide to travel this summer, for example, they will incur the direct costs of transportation, food, lodging, museum passes, and so on, but they will also be giving up the opportunity to work (say, at the library). That is the opportunity cost of their choice. Conversely, if they choose to work at the library this summer, the opportunity cost of that job is their inability to travel with their friends.

Sometimes the opportunity cost of a decision can be much greater than the direct costs involved, and the discipline of economics strives to teach its students to recognize the costs that are invisible, that people often ignore or mistake. Having outlined the concept of opportunity costs, a teacher could ask students to find the weaknesses in Yakov's mental accounting of the balance sheet of his life. When does Yakov correctly identify the opportunity costs of his choices, and when is his calculus mistaken? Should the lost income he tallies around him be included in the total of his life's sufferings? If we imagine Yakov as—like Chekhov himself—the urbanized descendant of a serf, can we theorize about how the difference between the opportunities available to serfs and those available to small-town craftsmen might affect his calculations? As the story progresses and Yakov nears his death, how does his view of the opportunity costs in his life change? Where do Chekhov's views appear to align with the narrator's voice, and where is there perhaps separation? How does interpreting the story from the perspective of economics and economic history shed light on Yakov's interest in Jews? Conversely, how does his obsession with Jews make readers see differently his interest in economic questions?

Trees

Observers of Christians and Jews in the Russian Empire tended to distinguish between the ways in which these two groups used natural resources. Both Christian observers of the Jews and Jews who wished their own people to modernize asserted that the Jews had little appreciation for nature and preferred book learning to an understanding of the natural world. It is often remarked that the Yiddish terms for plants and animals are borrowed from Slavic languages; this linguistic phenomenon can be seen as confirmation of Jews' lack of interest in nature. Such criticism may have applied to elite Jewish males, who traditionally devoted their time to the study of rabbinic texts, but there were many Jews in the Russian Empire who worked as lumber merchants, mill operators, and estate managers. A particular opportunity cost that Chekhov highlights in "Rothschild's Fiddle" emerges from the shtetl dwellers' use of the natural resources around them. When Yakov goes to the river, he recalls what it was like long ago. Back then, before the surrounding forests had been cut to supply the timber used by him and the other carpenters in the town (among others), fowl were plentiful and there was a bustling barge industry. He senses waste and loss in what happened to the land. Yet he also deplores the opportunities that he and others missed in using the natural resources around him. When he asks himself in dismay, "Why was the common left unused?" (260), is he speaking for Chekhov? Overuse of the common land, termed "tragedy of the commons" in economic literature, is an archetypal example of the way environmental degradation can result in worse economic outcomes for everyone involved. Should Chekhov therefore be considered an environmentalist? a conservationist?

Students could be asked to confront the tensions in this text or across Chekhov's works in his seeming support for the very activities (fishing, fowl catching, lumber barges) that result in consequences he condemns (environmental and economic loss when the forest is gone). How do we make sense of his complex views on natural resource use? In what ways can we use those views to illustrate how perspectives have changed since his time? In what ways do his views still resonate with environmentalism today? How do they mirror—or challenge—traditional (and still regnant) Russian views of a natural world limitless in its vastness? Can his concern with the use of natural resources be understood more clearly in the light of his hostility to Jews, or of the gift eventually given to Rothschild?

Among all Chekhov's stories, "Rothschild's Fiddle" offers the most complex and nuanced engagement with what his era called the Jewish Question. As this story demonstrates, depictions of Jews could provide late-imperial Russian artists with a lens through which many compelling issues of the age—about space and voice, passivity and agency, money and the environment—could come into new focus. Scholars of history, literature, economics, and environmental studies examine how people make the choices that determine the outcomes of their own personal narratives. All four of these disciplines help students consider what is truly at stake in Yakov's choices, which are so closely linked to his opinions about Jews, and thereby reflect on larger questions about the interactions between choice and circumstance in lives today. In "Man in a Box" (1898), Chekhov explicitly links a character who avoids risk to the coffin that awaits him. The less overtly didactic "Rothschild's Fiddle" focuses instead on an array of wooden objects and the shifting roles they play for the characters: Yakov's coffins, Rothschild's fiddle, the lumber that provides the raw material for both, the forests that once gave a home to birds, the remaining willow tree that stimulates memory and evokes the biblical psalm. In the conclusion to a class focusing on this text, students can be asked to bring these different woods together. What does wood mean for Yakov, whose nickname, after a metal, would seem to distance him from the material of his craft? What does wood mean for Rothschild, or for Chekhov? Can the construction of fiddles or coffins from wood be seen as a metaphor for the construction of a story? How do the tools that this essay offers students—historical background about the position of Jews in the Russian Empire, Chudakov's notion of free indirect discourse, the economic concept of opportunity costs, and the environmental perspective on the use of resources—lead toward similar or different interpretations of the repeating image of wood? How do these interpretive strategies confine readers, as a coffin confines; how do they open opportunities for communication and creativity, as a fiddle does? How can these interpretive approaches shed light on the interactions—monetary, musical, verbal—among Jews and Christians in Chekhov's Russia?

NOTES

[1] In this essay, citations of the story refer to the English rendering of Pevear and Volokhonsky ("Rothschild's Fiddle") and, where appropriate, to the Russian ("Skripka Rotshil'da"). Although this translation is the best to use for teaching, it does have limitations and inaccuracies.

[2] A classic and beautifully written example of this approach is Robert Louis Jackson's "'If I Forget Thee, O Jerusalem': An Essay on Chekhov's 'Rothschild's Fiddle.'" Jackson reads Chekhov's references to Psalm 137, words that are sacred to both Christians and Jews, as an optimistic gesture by Chekhov that indicates the possibility of Jewish-Christian reconciliation. Later, in his "Chekhov's 'Rothschild's Fiddle': 'By the Rivers of Babylon' in Eastern Orthodox Liturgy," Jackson offers a somewhat darker interpretation of the story, indicating that Rothschild stands in for the Christ image that permits Yakov to repent—a solitary repentance that offers little possibility of change for the Jews in the story or in the world.

[3] Interested students can easily find the parable of the broken window in Bastiat's essay, which is widely available in English.

"A Talent for Humanity": Teaching Chekhov and the Medical Humanities

Cathy Popkin

This essay offers classroom strategies for teaching Chekhov's literary prose in the context of his medical training and practice. Focusing on the genre of the medical case history as framed by Chekhov's contemporaries as well as on his 1889 story "A Nervous Breakdown" ("Припадок"; "Pripadok"), I call attention to what links medical and literary writing: their shared concern with access to the pain of others. For Chekhov, the correlation between narrative prose and diagnostic discourse is fundamental; an awareness of this connection contributes to a richer understanding of his artistic goals.

Chekhov is a natural choice for both the literary training of medical professionals (narrative medicine) and the medical turn in literary and cultural studies (medical humanities).[1] As a writer who was also a practicing physician, he cautioned prospective editors that medical emergencies would take precedence over publication deadlines.[2] His capacity to "think medically" (*Pis'ma* 3: 37 [to Aleksei Suvorin, 18 Oct. 1888]) never deserted him, even as he composed fictions, and he wrote doctors into innumerable stories and most of his plays.

While his portraits of doctors run the gamut from grotesquely caricatured to reasonably plausible, many of his fictional colleagues exhibit such deplorable bedside manners that it's been suggested that his stories be assigned to aspiring doctors as object lessons in how not to practice medicine.[3] Yet if Chekhov's debt to medicine is most brilliantly discharged by his fiction, the terms of that transaction are best discerned not by monitoring best (and worst) practices of characters but by considering how the author's several practices interact with and shape each other.

In letters to colleagues, Chekhov emphasized the complementarity and synergy of disciplines: If I know the theory of circulation *and* can recite poetry, I'm that much richer, he wrote to Suvorin (*Pis'ma* 3: 216 [15 May 1889]). Declining to fret about his divided professional loyalties, he played up the benefits of serving both medicine and literature: When I get tired of one, he liked to say, I spend the night with the other.[4] Creative multitasking aside, the most defining by-product of his devotion to more than one mode of inquiry is an enduring concern with how one comes to know things, a fascination with inquiry per se; his work probes the very process of making sense.

The most pressing issue, in other words, is epistemological, medicine representing just one of many modes of acquiring knowledge. Chekhov's literary forays lay bare the possibilities and pitfalls of diagnosis and deposition, library and laboratory, microscopy and metaphysics, painting and politics. Chekhov deployed an equally impressive array of approaches on his 1890 research expedition to Sakhalin, the bleak island in the Sea of Japan to which Russia exiled thousands of prisoners in the nineteenth century. In keeping with the multidisciplinary imperatives of medical geography, he surveyed the hygienic conditions of the penal colony by collecting the data of an ethnographer, geographer, meteorologist, demographer, cartographer, sociologist, statistician, and physician.

At the same time, Chekhov had misgivings about the presumption of expertise in any field. Trained in medical science, he maintained a positivist's faith in the evidence of the physical world, but as a refugee from his family's religious dogmatism he shunned certainty. His famous dictum that writers should pose questions instead of answering them reflects not only an artistic preference but also an epistemological position; in his correspondence, he points with emphasis to Socrates, whose greatest wisdom consisted in knowing what he did not (and could not) know (*Pis'ma* 3: 45–46; 2: 280–81 [to Suvorin, 27 Oct. and 30 May 1888]). It doesn't take students long, once they begin to read Chekhov's stories, to pick up on his reluctance to draw definitive conclusions. As a medical textbook, then, his fiction conveys modesty more than mastery—and properly so, since both literature and medicine take on one of the greatest cognitive challenges of all: somebody else's pain.

Chekhov's sense of obligation to those who suffer exceeded the requirements of the medical oath he took in 1884.[5] Alertness to the pain of others was a human rather than a professional responsibility. "I haven't even left [for Sakhalin] yet," he fulminated to Suvorin, "but thanks to the books I've had to read, I've learned about things that everyone should know on pain of forty lashes and that I had the ignorance not to know before":

> You write, for instance, that Sakhalin is of no use or interest to anyone. Is that really so? Sakhalin could be of no use or interest only to a society that doesn't deport thousands of people to it and doesn't spend millions on it. . . . Sakhalin is a place of unbearable suffering, the sort of suffering only man, whether free or subjugated, is capable of. The people who work near it or on it have been trying to solve problems involving frightening responsibility; they are still trying. I'm sorry I'm not sentimental or I'd say that we ought to make pilgrimages to places like Sakhalin the way the Turks go to Mecca. . . . From the books I've read and am now reading, it is evident that we have let *millions* of people rot in jails, we have let them rot to no purpose, unthinkingly and barbarously. We have driven people through the cold, in chains, across tens of thousands of versts, we have infected them with syphilis, debauched them, bred criminals and blamed it all on red-nosed wardens. Now all educated Europe knows that all of us, not the wardens, are to blame, but it's still none of our business; it's of no interest to us. The much-glorified sixties did *nothing* for the sick and the people in prison and thereby violated the chief commandment of Christian civilization. In our time a few things are being done for the sick, but nothing at all for the prisoners. . . . No, I assure you, Sakhalin is of great use and interest, and the only sad part of it all is that I'm the one who's going and

not someone more conversant with the problems and capable of arousing public interest. (*Anton Chekhov's Life* 159–60 [9 Mar. 1890])

While characteristically modest about his own contribution to the effort, Chekhov pulls no punches about the fundamental problem: What access do we have to the pain of others? Sakhalin, an entire continent away, presents even greater difficulties. What hope can there be of understanding human suffering at such a remove? Is a pilgrimage required? Do you have to see pain with your own eyes to grasp it? And even if you do, if you don't feel it with your own nerves, can you take it in? Must pilgrimage include reenactment? Supposing you are able to fathom it, can you then communicate it to someone else, produce a written (or dramatic or artistic or musical) account that provides remote access? What form might that communication take? Vivid letters? Documentary prose? Fiction? What kind of sense making might such an account entail, and what kind of sensibility would it require of the reader?

When I teach Chekhov, we ask all these questions as we read his letters, documentary prose, and fiction, whether he comes up in a course on medical humanities or medical humanities informs a course on him. (For a course on Chekhov, see the appendix to this essay for reading suggestions.) The fiction includes, predictably, stories about doctors and patients. But the treatment of these characters is unpredictable: in "Enemies," the pain that stymies the doctor is somebody else's heartache; the snapshot of the absurd medic in "Rothschild's Fiddle" pales in comparison to the account of the coffin maker who can't bear to contemplate the sorrow of a Jewish musician; the interpretation or misinterpretation of pain in "The Student" involves no medical personnel at all. "A Medical Case" is explicitly the report of a doctor's visit, but all of Chekhov's stories are case histories of sorts, struggles—and opportunities—to make sense of the human condition.

I often begin by asking students to consider this epistemological challenge: Is it possible to understand another person's pain? To grasp what it feels like, to know how to respond? To help focus the discussion, I like to work from (and work with the class to refine) a rudimentary visual that gives us a schematic way to think about the relationships involved.[6] Its simplest form is:

S(elf) O(ther)

S indicates the position of the inquiring subject, and O represents the target of the self's inquiry, the suffering other. The vacant space between the two is illustrative, waiting to be populated by whatever operation, practice, or talent might give S access to O's pain.

A useful refinement of the S/O dyad is the familiar sequence borrowed from grammar. We add V, a verb to specify the terms of the interaction:

S(ubject) V(erb) O(bject)[7]

Whether we make S a surgeon or Shakespeare or Shakespeare's reader (and we plug in lots of candidates), Chekhov draws our attention to the central variable, the verb that names the investigatory strategy adopted by the subject in the hope of gaining access to the elusive pain of the other. Think of the med student drawing ribs on Anyuta's body with a piece of charcoal (S marks up O?); consider "On Official Business," where the doctor never even removes the sheet from the corpse he's meant to autopsy (S avoids O?). I ask students to consider as well what Chekhov achieves by casting the human body so often as the object of knowledge. Infinitely desirable but irretrievably other, available to the gaze but stubbornly opaque, the body nicely encapsulates the challenge of comprehending the other's distress and the need for epistemic modesty.

But what does it mean to understand someone else's pain? Are we talking about empathy (as in "I feel your pain," when in fact we cannot)? Do we mean professional competence (as in "I see the problem; take two pills and call me in the morning")? Or does arriving at an understanding of pain consist of making metaphysical-religious sense ("It's your comeuppance," or "It's God's will," or "Grin and bear it")? Here I turn the discussion to "Ward 6." Even if students do not know Chekhov's forceful letter about Sakhalin, this story suggests that explaining suffering away is not an option. Dr. Ragin, whose ability to empathize has dried up, identifies his indifference as an occupational hazard and justifies it on the basis of Stoic philosophy: S closes his eyes to the suffering O; the remove between them is complete. Ragin understands pain only at the eleventh hour, when he is suddenly subjected to it himself (S feels his own pain). At the opposite extreme lies his patient, Ivan Gromov, whose wholesale identification with suffering others (S = O) is psychosis, a certifiable persecution complex.[8]

Keeping the field of verbs (and the potential for intercourse) between knower and sufferer in mind (and on the board), I find Chekhov's earlier story "A Nervous Breakdown" a productive focus for several reasons. Chekhov wrote it for a memorial volume for Vsevolod Garshin, a fellow writer whose sense of responsibility for the suffering of humankind was acute. It presents us with both the hero's protracted efforts to understand and remediate a formidable social ill (prostitution) and our own daunting task of making sense of that character's debilitating distress when he fails. It invokes the relatively well-defined genre of the medical case history while it also reflects the need to develop a mode of discourse to account for *mental* illness. Moreover, while the story introduces a med student in its opening breath, we realize by the end of the sentence that two other young scholars and a whole course catalog of fields—painting, sculpture, architecture, law (and, though we don't find out till later, natural science)—have been similarly mobilized for this research expedition.[9] The story is emphatically about how to formulate the right questions.

Given the object of their research (fallen women), the knowledge that these scholars seek is hardly cerebral. Yet the story brings us insistently back to epistemological frameworks. It's useful, for instance, to ask students what they think the second paragraph is for. In it, Chekhov foregrounds the mediated nature of the law student's knowledge of prostitutes, the distance of the inquiring subject from the object of his inquiry, by presenting his knowledge of prostitutes as a litany of clichés garnered from rumor, sentimental fiction, popular culture, the rhetoric of social determinism, legal jargon, and Christian writ. The point may be to separate received wisdom from the hands-on personal experience that the trio seeks. But for all the voyeuristic potential of the brothel sequence, Chekhov presents us chiefly with the spectacle of Vasiliev's trying to make intellectual sense of prostitution as a phenomenon. Eros is supplanted by this young man's "burning desire to find out."[10] His desire is to establish "how to formulate the proper question" (*Sochineniia* 7: 207) when confronted with that supreme epistemological challenge, the pain of others, embodied here in the young women who have fallen prey to prostitution. But despite—or perhaps because of—his well-documented proficiency in scientific reasoning, his interdisciplinary training, and the cultural discourses he draws on, he remains cut off from the object of his inquiry. He can whistle as many arias, amass as many advanced degrees, and recall as many brothel narratives as he wants, but he gains no firsthand knowledge of prostitutes. He also fails miserably to find a cure for the broader affliction.

As Chekhov emphasized repeatedly in his correspondence about the piece, "I have quite a lot to say about the problem of prostitution here, but I don't offer any solutions" (*Pis'ma* 3: 67, 76 [to Suvorin, 11 Nov. 1888; to E. M. Lintvareva, 23 Nov. 1888]). For Vasiliev, the inability to find a solution is crushing, and Chekhov describes the young man's emotional and physical prostration. Note that Vasiliev's response is visceral. His profound sentience diverges sharply from the late-nineteenth-century cult of objectivity. Moreover, his emotional responsiveness is adduced as a "talent":

> One of Vasiliev's friends once said that he is a talented person. Talent comes in many forms—literary, dramatic, and artistic—but his is of a very special sort: a talent for *humanity*. He possesses a fantastically keen sensitivity to pain in general. As a good actor reflects in himself the movements and voices of others, Vasiliev is able to reflect in his own soul another person's pain [чужую боль; chuzhuiu bol']. Seeing someone's tears, he cries; if he's around a sick person, he himself becomes ill and groans; if he sees violence, it seems to him that the violence is being inflicted on him; he gets scared and runs for help. Someone else's pain irritates him, arouses him, and produces in him a state of ecstasy, and so on.
>
> (*Sochineniia* 7: 216–17)

The narrator goes on to concede, "Whether that friend was right, I don't know." But he is undeniably correct that Vasiliev assumes other people's pain. When a woman in the brothel is slapped around, Vasiliev becomes upset, certain that people are trying to beat him. When he is beating his head against the wall over the solution to prostitution, it is because he has imagined that he is the brother of a fallen woman, then the woman's father, and finally that he is the fallen woman herself—which makes the problem he sets out to solve "not someone else's, but his very own" (215). So much for making sense of the suffering of others; our S has internalized any O right out of existence. (I erase O from the board.)

Where the friend goes wrong is in touting Vasiliev's propensity to appropriate other people's pain as a talent.[11] The upshot of Vasiliev's identification with the victim is a nervous breakdown, which suggests that this quality in him is pathological, precisely the kind of persecution mania that gets Gromov institutionalized in "Ward 6." For all his vaunted feeling (чувство; chuvstvo), Vasiliev exhibits not a shred of empathy. He doesn't come close to understanding the experience of a single prostitute. Rather, he usurps the prostitutes' subjectivity, makes their pain his own; it's a form of solipsism, a suggestion that the self can know only the self.

Where does Vasiliev's epistemological misadventure of cognitive failure and resultant collapse leave us? With the interesting possibility that the story is also concerned with the reverse sequence: collapse, followed by a concerted effort to make sense of that distress. The object of desired knowledge, in other words, is not just prostitution but also mental illness; the story gives us both Vasiliev's attempt to understand and an attempt to understand Vasiliev. There are two pathologies to investigate here, two forms of stranger pain to comprehend. We've seen that Vasiliev's mental constructs and emotional responses fail to account for, save, or even get to know prostitutes. The story evinces an equally pressing need to account for and describe, perhaps cure, the pain of emotional disturbance, to find a way, narratively, even clinically, of reassembling pieces of mind.

Three points of reference will help us here. One is the promising line of investigation first articulated by Vasiliev (207–09): The question to answer: how did they—the musicians, the servants, the patrons, and the women themselves—wind up here? How did innocent girls come to be prostitutes? "How?" (как?), he wonders. "From where?" (откуда?), "On account of what?" (от чего?), "For the sake of what?" (ради чего?), "To what end?" (зачем?). These are the most fruitful questions. What, they ask, is the connection between the present and what preceded it? What is the story? Etiology is a narrative epistemology. If Vasiliev fails to account for the how, whence, and wherefore of prostitution, it may be because, in appropriating the women's suffering, he renders the women speechless, affectless, and storyless. The prostitutes cannot be grammatical, emotional, anatomical or storied subjects any more than they are legal ones—which makes Vasiliev as guilty of endangering prostitutes as his sexually active friends are.

This brings us to the second point, for which we go back to the drawing board, this time with the radical proposal to fill the vacancy left by the erasure of O with another full-fledged S. If Vasiliev is the S when he plays the analyst, he (and any other sufferer of mental illness) must remain a subject in the role of analysand. What's envisioned is an encounter between one S and another S.

The third point of reference is the genre of the psychiatric case history as Chekhov knew it from his reading of *Vrach* (*Врач*; *The Physician*) and the newly minted Russian psychiatric journals of the 1880s (Shereshevskii 160–67).

Chekhov's story gives us a glimpse of the format of this diagnostic discourse in a developing field with agendas of its own.

The medical case history as developed in Western Europe and used in Russia had assumed a fairly standardized form by the early nineteenth century, and the sequence of elements, still more or less intact, had been codified by century's end:

> Medical history (*anamnesis*), elicited from the patient or relative in response to specific questions posed by the physician. This information includes:
> - identifying facts (name, age, height, weight)
> - chief complaint (and its duration)
> - history, with details, of the present illness
> - past medical history (major or chronic illnesses, childhood diseases)
> - system review
> - family medical history
> - social history (occupation, living arrangements, marital status, number of children, economic factors, use of alcohol, etc.)
>
> Present condition (*status praesens*), determined by clinical examination conducted by the physician at time of initial observation
>
> Treatment (*decursus morbi*): plan for treatment, ongoing record of results, progression of illness

The case history, as it has been taught since the 1890s, distinguishes clearly between the medical history, which is subjective in that it records the patient's perception of the illness (the symptoms), and the objective manifestations of the illness as ascertained by the physician through direct physical examination (the signs). Symptoms make sense within the patient's own associative system. The self is a source of knowledge, and the subject of the medical history is emphatically to remain an S.

Moreover, not only must the history of the present illness use the patient's own words, but it must be written in full sentences. Facts and findings can be jotted down, but history requires syntax. Above all, the history is narrative (Epstein 32–33); selves, as Jean-Jacques Rousseau has shown, are inherently narratable (Kiceluk 341). *Anamnesis* relies on the patient's recall and reconstruction of a series of events; it relies on the patient to pick out relevant information and organize it temporally into a version that makes sense of the symptoms. It addresses Vasiliev's question, How did they—or you—wind up here? What's the story?

In the psychiatric arena, the relation between the story of the patient's symptoms and the clinical picture that emerges from direct medical observation is more complex but also more crucial, and psychiatrists across Europe struggled to work out this diagnostic puzzle well into the twentieth century.[12] The case histories by Russian psychiatrists that began to appear in the 1880s were often devoted to patients suffering from hysterical symptoms, which further complicated the relation between subjective sensations and physical signs.

The end of the nineteenth century was a moment of transition in the study of hysteria, a paradigm shift from the neurological understanding of the disease as brain and nerve dysfunction to a psychological paradigm that attributed hysterical symptoms to emotional disturbance rather than to physiological causes. The Russian psychiatric community still leaned heavily toward the neurological model, but Russian psychiatrists were beginning to recognize the etiological force of emotional trauma and its translation into physical pain. Hysterical fits and nervous breakdowns were conceived as "expressions"—signs—of suffering (Pasternatskii 49). Significant for us, and for Chekhov, is how the clinicians read those expressions and how they chose to write them.

The Russian case histories, which placed an inordinately high premium on objectivity, came in the same three sections as their European counterparts: *anamnesis*, the medical history, an "act of remembering"; *status praesens*, which enumerated the patient's physical symptoms and recorded in detail the results of the initial examination (reflexes, measurement of skull, quantity of urine passed, sensitivity of skin, and so forth); and *decursus morbi*, the record of treatments and responses. As for the *anamnesis*, acts of remembering notwithstanding, there is little reminiscing or recovery of a personal past discernible in most of these patients' medical histories.

Anamnesis, it turns out, was important to the Russian practitioners principally in establishing heredity: were there any discernible signs among the patient's forebears that point to a genetic predisposition to nervous disorders? The section was diachronic insofar as it proceeded in chronological order, but it made little effort to establish the patient's progression from one state to another, to craft connections between episodes, to link then and now, to draw correlations between an earlier trauma and present symptoms. Moreover, although a patient's symptoms are by definition subjective responses and no professional can be the expert on them, the voices of the patients themselves were never heard. The hysterical self was thus doubly effaced and silenced, first by the disease and its fits and aphasias, second by the discourses that diagnosed it. The elimination of the patient's subjectivity made a travesty of *anamnesis*.

The clinical report of the patient's physical condition, the second section, did not proceed from what the doctor actually observed any more than the *anamnesis* answered the question, How did this come about? Hysteria, not the hysterical patient, drove the *status praesens*. The protocol for the examination was set not by what the patient exhibited but by what the disease stipulated, and what was recorded was only the presence or absence in the patient of each classic symptom. This section considered not how well a patient was but how well the person fit the profile: Was the patient a bona fide hysteric or not? Connections were severed here not only between signs and story but also between signs and self.

Russian psychiatrists, like their predecessor, Jean-Martin Charcot,[13] focused on the visible, clinical signs that made knowledge about the patient a matter of seeing the patient from the outside at a particular moment and snapping a clinical picture; they were not interested in the more narratological procedure that elicits in words what has befallen the patient over a period of time, bridging the gap between then and now and reconstituting a clinical story (Kiceluk 332–35, 362–63). The narratological method, which privileges plot over image, views the patient as a subject with a coherent story to tell and demands knowledge of—and from—that individual, not just a classificatory grid.

As for the *decursus morbi*, the progression of the illness during the course of treatment, the less said about the jets of cold water aimed at parts of the body, the better. The prescriptions recorded in this section bore little relation to the patient's symptoms, let alone to the suffering that produced them. Nor was there much narrative in the chronicle of successive days of treatment, since significant improvement was rare.[14]

As a detailed exploration of Vasiliev's pain in terms of Vasiliev's own experience, Chekhov's story may be seen as a response to prevailing psychiatric practice and as a kind of corrective to the genre—the poetics, as it were—of the psychiatric case history. Case history format is openly lampooned in Chekhov's concluding scene, set up as interview (*anamnesis*), examination (*status praesens*), and treatment (*decursus morbi*) in the psychiatrist's office. The doctor sets the tone in his welcome: Come on in, I've heard so much about—your illness (*Sochineniia* 7: 219); in good classificatory form, he's focused on the syndrome, not on the sufferer. The taking of the medical history (referred to explicitly as *anamnesis*) is a caricatured witch hunt for neurasthenic relatives. And although the doctor is posing questions, they are uniformly useless ones; also, he directs them to Vasiliev's friend rather than to Vasiliev. The psychiatrist learns nothing about Vasiliev's pain but writes down a lot.

Still, the psychiatrist is an easy target, and the coda in his office is only the coup de grace. From the very beginning, the story itself presents a case history that achieves what the ones in the journals did not, for although the authors of the case histories Chekhov read posited the expressiveness of hysterical symptoms, seeing them as signs of emotional trauma, they had been largely unable to operationalize that insight by reconstructing and telling patients' stories. Yet narrative, belletristic or otherwise, is the only way to address the question that Vasiliev had formulated as his own problem to solve: How did they wind up here?

Vasiliev admits that he's terrible at eliciting the stories of the fallen women. The best *anamnesis* he can put together is a chronology of breakfast, lunch, and dinner at the brothel, and the only point of origin he can adduce is geographic, not emotional. The authors of the case histories exhibit the same failing in their determined severing of present symptoms from past suffering; we don't see how a single breakdown came about.

In "Breakdown," Chekhov attempts to rectify this shortcoming in the psychiatric case study by harnessing narrative himself, offering his story as a form of inquiry, analysis, and diagnosis of how and why Vasiliev had a great fall and what it felt like to him instead of what it looked like from the outside: "It seems to me, as a physician, that I have depicted emotional suffering [psychological pain] properly, in accordance with the protocols of psychiatry" (*Pis'ma* 3: 68 [to Aleksei Pleshcheev, 13 Nov. 1888]).

Chekhov produces a viable and valuable account by starting well before the attack itself, which doesn't materialize until the penultimate scene, but the title, "Breakdown," hovers over us the whole time and forces us to consider the origins and development of the breakdown as we go along. The self unfolds—or degenerates—before our eyes, producing thereby a substantive *anamnesis*. We hear Vasiliev's voice, we feel his pain—in short, Chekhov makes the symptoms expressive and the attack intelligible by returning to the patient his subjectivity, by writing a history of the present illness that is rooted in his subjective experience. Chekhov thus succeeds where Vasiliev fails with his fallen women, where the psychiatrist fails with Vasiliev, and where the case histories of psychiatric disorders foundered in reading and describing the pain of others. As revisionary case history, the story attempts to reestablish the connections effaced by the discourses it draws on: the link between past and present, mind and body, observable sign and story of origins. It also brings together the belletristic and the clinical. Finally, as successful case history, it establishes a viable epistemological connection between the inquiring subject (S) and the suffering subject (another S) by making sense of the latter's pain without appropriating it wholesale.

"Breakdown" is thus richly suggestive for Chekhov's poetics and hermeneutics in several respects. First, it advances the proposition that narration and representation are not alternatives to medical science but essential to it. Diagnosis, exploratory and interpretive, entails careful scrutiny and analysis to make sense of, account for, figure out the relevance of the symptom, the import of the problem, the meaning of the pain. It is not surprising that this kind of diagnosis calls to mind the work of the careful reader.

Second, in its sustained scrutiny of narrative form in particular, the story foregrounds its commitment to a temporality that is not just chronological but also logical, composed not only of sequences but also of consequences. Narrative provides an explanation because it reconstructs how the past led to the present.

Finally, the story is suggestive in its predication on connection—between past and present and between afflicted other and self (whether the self is clinician, storyteller, or reader). Chekhov's penchant for narrative continuity and progression makes the psychiatric case study as crafted by his contemporaries a logical target for a critique of both how suffering is read and how accounts of it are written. The story also links the treatment of psychopathology and the reading of fiction: both forms of interpretation represent hermeneutic efforts to articulate the connections repressed or muddled by the text (or by its troubled characters), to put together what's not said, reconstructing a coherent and compelling *anamnesis*, making logical and psychological sense, restoring health by restorying illness.

NOTES

Translations are mine unless otherwise indicated.

[1] The two fields are somewhat less distinct in practice, and universities often use the mirror-image designations interchangeably. The proliferation of literature curricula in medical schools in the past several decades reflects broad agreement that training in the workings of narrative gives practitioners a more nuanced understanding of what's at stake in their patients' stories and enlarges their capacity for empathy; that it exercises their moral imagination and strengthens their ability to confront difficult ethical issues; and that it gives them a keener awareness of their own unexamined assumptions (Hawkins and McEntyre 5–6). The growing number of undergraduate programs in medical humanities is best seen in the context of the academy's wholehearted embrace of interdisciplinary inquiry.

[2] Though Chekhov's literary career gradually eclipsed his work as a doctor, medical emergencies would always trump everything else; during the 1891 famine and the ensuing cholera epidemic of 1892 Chekhov spent nearly all his time treating the sick, organizing clinics, and raising money for supplies. He closed his medical practice only in 1897 when his own health failed, and he continued to provide medical assistance even then.

[3] Robert Coles, a writer who spent precious time during his own medical training with doctor-poet William Carlos Williams, recalls Williams's insistence that Coles read Chekhov's "Anyuta" (1886) for the best possible account of the worst possible practices, that "it wouldn't hurt all the medical students over there at Columbia to read 'Anyuta,'" and that they wouldn't encounter a more important reading in any medical text (Coles and Finke 272).

[4] The punch line of Chekhov's often cited quip, "Medicine is my lawfully wedded wife, literature is my mistress" (*Pis'ma* 2: 236 [to Suvorin, 11 Sept. 1888]).

[5] For the text of the "Medical Oath of the Graduating Physician," see Frieden 326–27.

[6] This schematic exercise is a group blackboard activity, not a *PowerPoint* presentation. Students are welcome to pick up the chalk at any time.

[7] The epistemological proposition formulated by analytic philosophers—S(ubject) knows that *p*—renders the SVO sentence diagram more specific. Here S is the knowing subject, the verb *knows* is supplied, and the knowable proposition, the desired object of knowledge, is *p*, the role of which, in our context, is played by pain.

[8] See Knapp's suggestive discussion of Chekhov's attempt to provoke a viable response to suffering on the part of the readers of this story by arousing their pity and fear (rather than abject identification) through the representation of suffering, far less debilitating (and voyeuristic) than witnessing the thing itself. Lenin's famous reaction to Chekhov's story ("I felt as if I, too, had been incarcerated in Ward 6") suggests that productive forms of imaginative identification are possible and that recognition of suffering can be aroused by a writer's account of it—and a fictional account at that (Knapp 146–47).

[9] This inclusiveness is in keeping with Chekhov's equal-opportunity employment practices. Interestingly, in his trio of med student, art student, and law student, Chekhov has

resurrected the three young scholars who made similarly edifying use of Anyuta's body in that story's original version.

[10] Eros is supplanted not because Vasiliev is high-minded but because the garish costumes and tasteless settings fail to arouse him.

[11] The word *talent* is a curious choice here but not a random one: "My holy of holies is the human body, health, intelligence, talent, inspiration, love, and the most absolute freedom imaginable, freedom from violence and lies, no matter what form the latter two take," Chekhov wrote to Pleshcheev within days of beginning this story (*Pis'ma* 3: 11 [4 Oct. 1888]). A talent for humanity would be an excellent thing, but what Vasiliev has is not that.

[12] Kiceluk provides an excellent account of this aspect of the study and representation of mental illness.

[13] Charcot (1825–93) was a French neurologist whose famous *Iconographie photographique de la Salpêtrière* (1876–80; *Photographic Iconography of the Salpêtrière*) captured the visual signs ("stigmata") he used to diagnose and classify cases of hysteria (107, 113–16).

[14] For excerpts (in translation) from a number of these case histories, see Popkin, "Hysterical Episodes." For a translation of a case history that Chekhov wrote himself as a medical student, see Harrigan 51–59.

APPENDIX
SUGGESTED COURSE READINGS

Primary Literature

- "Anyuta" (1883)
- "Enemies" (1887)
- "A Nervous Breakdown" (1889)
- "Ward 6" (1892)
- "Rothschild's Fiddle" (1894)
- "The Student" (1894)
- "A Medical Case" (1898)
- "On Official Business" (1899)

Secondary Literature

Epstein, Julia. "Historiography, Diagnosis, and Poetics."

Kiceluk, Stephanie. "The Patient as Sign and Story: Disease Pictures, Life Histories, and the First Psychoanalytic Case History."

Reading the Environmental Chekhov

Jane Costlow

Chekhov's stories and plays offer a wide range of opportunities to explore environmental themes. His interest in documenting the changing geophysical landscape of Russia is certainly connected to his training in the natural sciences and to his friendships with natural scientists. Landscape and the natural world figure in his works, however, not as objects of scientific knowledge but as part of the human drama, inextricably bound up with human perception, aspiration, and imperfection.

There are many moments in Chekhov's stories and plays where environmental problems come into play, along with nascent awareness of them and efforts to address them. The 1899 story "In the Ravine," for example, begins with a description of a heavily polluted village, where "there was always a smell of factory waste and the acetic acid used in the treatment of the cotton" (383). And *Uncle Vanya*, written two years earlier, includes an extended monologue that catalogs the devastating effects of deforestation on wildlife, agriculture, and climate ([*Major Plays*] 207–08). By the time Chekhov was writing, there was broad awareness of the threat of deforestation, growing concern over soil erosion and the loss of topsoil, and better understanding of the harmful consequences on human health of industrial development (see Costlow, ch. 3). Works like "The Reed Pipe" and *Uncle Vanya* led Simon Karlinsky, over forty years ago, to note Chekhov's appeal for an audience concerned with "the threatened environment and industrial pollution" (28). Chekhov's stories and plays register environmental degradation often in startlingly casual ways. But his narratives reward environmental reflection not only because of their documentary value. There is something in his approach to the issue that resonates with the mixture of longing, idealism, and near-apocalyptic malaise of our own century. My students (and not only students of environmental studies) are eager for answers but skeptical of what seem like unrealistic programs of action. They want to know what should be done but often respond to visionary proposals by saying, That's not realistic. They are aware of the scale of impending disasters, and they see deeply entrenched interests that resist solutions. They live in a time in which banality and catastrophe rapidly replace each other. Chekhov, with his profoundly unsentimental vision, opens up imaginative and discursive space in which to reflect on the impetus of ideals and the drag of inertia in our lives. Do dreams of a better life prompt us to transformation, or do they blind us to the world in which we are situated? How can art work toward moments of recognition and the building of conscience? Chekhov is an excellent catalyst for all these questions, each of which I see as central to teaching both about human nature and our responsibilities to the "more than human" world.[1]

There are other reasons why Chekhov's stories repay environmental consideration. Alongside their documentary impulse (squalid villages, inert landowners, corrupt officials allowing factories to remain open) we find in them evidence of a meticulous and loving attention to the variety and detail of the natural world. Even in the stories that remind us of the brutality of human lives and the myriad ways in which people despoil and destroy, we discover moments of great natural beauty, moments that intensify our sense of the acute suffering of the world, the physical suffering of an environment increasingly stressed by human actions as well as the spiritual and mental suffering of human beings who realize how far their lives are from the beauty and health of nature. In Chekhov's stories and plays, rarely (if ever) is action taken to ameliorate a situation: the only kind of activism in them is the steady, dreary laboring in one's own garden, a Chekhovian form of Voltaire's famous response to the violence of the world. *Uncle Vanya* ends not with grand resolve to end deforestation (although the Russian state had instituted new regulations on woodlands in 1888) but with the undramatic decision to continue barely visible labors: Sonya's insisting that in some future world those labors will be rewarded ([*Major Plays*] 230–31). That final passage sounds the frequent Chekhovian motif of future generations. In environmental ethics today, *future generations* refers to our duty to keep in mind the long-range consequences of our actions, but Chekhov's characters reverse temporality and evade responsibility: future generations, not we, will solve the problem.

Part of the task of teaching an environmental Chekhov, then, is encouraging students to experience and respond to a difficult, almost heartrending, duality: a world that is still beautiful but in the process of being destroyed, a world in which Chekhov is always reminding us—through his use of irony, humor, contrast, and deflation—of human fallibility. He situates the environmental challenges of late-imperial Russia in narratives and dramas of human longing and choice where the best intentions are so often no match for the forces of inertia, both social and psychological.

In this essay, I suggest a series of specific strategies for reading and teaching Chekhov through an environmental framework. By *environmental* I mean several things: these are narratives in which landscape functions not merely as background, as setting for human action, but also in ways that Laurence Buell has identified as central to "environmentally oriented work," ways in which "human history is implicated in natural history" or questions are raised about human accountability to the environment as part of the text's "ethical orientation" (7). I also have in mind Greg Garrard's fruitful exploration of environmental texts in terms of tropes—pastoral, apocalypse, pollution—that help us see literature as part of larger fields of discourse and cultural imagination.

Landscape and Perception

Our experience of the natural world arguably begins with place or landscape: bounded spaces that have been shaped for human use or spatial expanses that human beings frame, both through perceptual organization and in their technologies of building, order, and use. Lucy Lippard suggests that landscapes are places viewed from a distance; "place," on the other hand, is the locus of desire, attachment, what is known not from a distance but from inside (8). Her distinction is useful to us, since Chekhov is deeply attentive to the human perceiver and how things look to a particular person:

> . . . now the wheat, too, has flashed by. Again the scorched plain, the sunburnt hills, the torrid sky stretch out, again a kite skims over the ground. The windmill beats its wings in the distance, as before, and still looks like a little man waving his arms. You get sick of looking at it, and it seems you will never reach it, that it is running away from the britzka.
>
> ("Steppe" 9)

The landscapes of his stories are as varied as Russia itself: from the vast steppe to the disappearing forests of "The Reed Pipe" to his gardens and orchards, of which the orchard in *The Cherry Orchard* is the most famous. These gardens, orchards, estates, and dachas ask to be considered in multiple ways: as meaningful places for his characters; as evidence of human interactions with the natural world; as reflective of cultural value, botanical or agronomic knowledge; as arenas of work, vision, and desire.

In "The Steppe," Chekhov gives us a closely observed, almost mythic journey through one of Russia's iconic landscapes, tied closely to the perception of a young boy leaving home. The story can be approached as a narrative that is both experiential and philosophical. This story is an excellent example of what nature writing has been in Russia: instead of taking the form of a nonfiction essay in the Thoreauvian manner, with an educated, often quixotic first-person narrator who is not that different (in social class or level of education) from the reader, it is primarily fiction. We experience and perceive the natural world through a counterpoint of differently situated perspectives.

The landscape of "Steppe" breathes wildness and profound health. "The Black Monk" offers a stark and intriguing contrast to its vision of unconstraint and vitality, giving instead a detailed and disturbing description of a garden that is both enormously productive and bizarrely, even violently, molded: "What whims, refined monstrosities, and mockeries of nature there were here! There were espaliered fruit trees, a pear tree that had the form of a Lombardy poplar, spherical oaks and lindens, an umbrella-shaped apple tree, arches, monograms, candelabras, and even an 1862 of plum trees . . ." (*Selected Stories* [Pevear and Volokhonsky] 224). An overwrought intellectual, Kovrin, retires to the countryside, where he lives with an acquaintance and his daughter, whose lives revolve entirely around the cultivation of extensive orchards and vast, exhaustively tended gardens. This pastoral retreat ends not in health, however, but in madness, as Kovrin is visited by a mysterious black monk who seems to arise from a noxious mix of insomnia, exhaustion, and erudition. The reader finishes this gothic tale of madness, love, and death pondering the connections in the story between the aggressive forcing of natural forms into artificial and the theme of sickness. Just what is health or healing? Is the garden healthy? Is the story working toward some insight about the harm of human forcing? What is the relation in this narrative between nature and madness?[2]

Chekhov's landscapes invite consideration in broader cultural terms as well. "Steppe," along with his stories of forests, estates, and gardens, can be productively paired with painting and poetry of the nineteenth century, as a way of establishing these landscapes' emotional, intellectual, and political resonance. These landscapes are in some sense "ethnoscapes," evocatively imagined and associated with national identity and the memories of a people (Smith 151). Historical and geographic contexts can help students grasp the cultural associations with these landscapes, moving from there to a consideration of how Chekhov's treatment of a given landscape may be idiosyncratic, ironic, or irreverent.[3] Given the powerful resonance of prairies as American ethnoscapes, one might compare steppe texts and prairie texts. How, for example, does Willa Cather's Nebraska differ from Chekhov's steppe?

Hunters' Tales and the Naturalist's Eye

That nature writing in Russia grows out of hunting sketches is most obviously true in the work of Ivan Turgenev, whose stories combine a naturalist's attention to detail, diversity, and change with vividly rendered human encounters as the hunter wanders the central Russian countryside. These stories create a distinctively Russian form of nature essay, in which human beings are always part of a landscape that is less wild than hybrid, long inhabited and deeply shaped by human history. The landscapes of these stories are working landscapes, geographies onto which are written two cultures: the culture of a landed gentry that was European in education and orientation and the culture of a peasantry that was agrarian, settled, and deeply dependent on knowledge of nature and place for its survival. The most brilliant of these narratives play on the tensions between the two in one landscape. The hunters tromping through Chekhov's trilogy of interlinked stories, which includes "Gooseberries" (along with "On Love" and "The Man in a Case"), seem to have wandered out of Turgenev's collection, and reading either those trilogy stories or "The Reed Pipe" along with Turgenev would help students consider how narrative strategy, tone, and diction take us into different worlds. The shepherd's lament in Chekhov's "The Reed Pipe" seems to echo the opening pages of Turgenev's "Khor and Kalinych" when the narrator complains that all the wildfowl in that part of Russia will soon be gone (15–28). In Turgenev's "Kasyan from the Beautiful Lands," a peasant who rebukes the gentry hunter for killing wild birds (132) suggests a growing awareness of the kind of loss that also appears in *Uncle Vanya*. The narrative dynamics of Turgenev's and Chekhov's stories are strikingly different, however, giving students something to ponder in terms of irony and authorial intention: does Chekhov expect us to take his oddly named hunter and shepherd interlocutor at their word, or does the apocalyptic tone of their exchange undermine the sense that it is real?

Gooseberry Pastoral and Spiritual Death

"The Black Monk" begins with an intellectual's retreat to the countryside. It's a classic pastoral moment, harking back to any number of retreats in Russian and world literature (Ivan Turgenev references Vergil's *Arcadia* in his 1861 *Fathers and Sons* [*Отцы и дети*; *Ottsy i deti*]). One way to think of a story like this is to ask how Chekhov challenges our assumptions about the countryside as a place of leisure, rest, and health. The pastoral theme appears in numerous other stories by Chekhov, including "Gooseberries," in which a civil servant finally attains his life's dream of owning a small plot of land and growing gooseberries. Chekhov's narrative undermines any sense that getting back to the land is a dream that will bring deep human fulfillment. But what is wrong with going back to the land? In moments in the story Chekhov seems to take issue with Tolstoy, his contemporary, in particular Tolstoy's "How Much Land Does a Man Need?" In that story, a fable whose moral is explicit and uncomplicated, a grasping landowner cuts a deal with Bashkir herders, who agree to sell him the amount of land he can pace out in a day. The exercise leads to overreach, exhaustion, and death. There's no such dramatic ending in "Gooseberries," but Chekhov does give us a depressing tale of a man regressing into a lethargic, unchallenged death in life on his country estate, "which is just the same as those three arshins of land" (*Selected Stories* [Pevear and Volokhonsky] 71). Henry Thoreau might be an interesting match for these "back to the land" narratives, particularly given the way the hermit of Concord downplayed his frequent converse with town.[4]

Russian Peasants and the Devils of Modernity

The factories of Chekhov's stories remind us that his Russia is in the process of sweeping change, much of it the result of the emancipation of 1861, when the millions of peasants who had been serfs were freed. That emancipation came, however, without land and began a seemingly inexorable process of modernization that involved the gradual erosion of agrarian traditions, increasing urbanization, and a shift toward a more industrial economy. The Russian intelligentsia—radicals, liberals, agrarian populists, and anarchists of various stripes—debated through the 1870s and 1880s whether Russia must necessarily follow the Western, capitalist, and industrial model of development. There were powerful voices (Alexander Herzen and Peter Kropotkin among them) who held that Russian peasant culture contained the embryo of agrarian socialist development.[5] Far to the right of men like Herzen and Kropotkin, Slavophiles and pan-Slavists had argued for decades that the Russian peasantry was deeply conservative, endowed with natural links to soil and Russian Orthodoxy.

The future of the peasantry and of agriculture was the future of Russia, and to participate in discussions and representations of the peasants was to participate in a debate about modernity and all its attendant virtues (or vices).[6] Chekhov's writing about peasants, agriculture, village life, and the coming of industrialization can often be productively viewed as addressed to this question of Russia's future. The modernizing Russia that Chekhov describes is often tragically corrupt and benighted. The ravine of "In the Ravine" is a geographic and moral pit of human and environmental abuse and corruption—the story might be paired with fiction and essays from other traditions that address the hopes and perils of modernization. His refusal to idealize indigenous traditions and peasant knowledge resonates with postcolonial or native writers in whose work the tension between science and traditional knowledge is differently conceived and resolved.[7]

Learning to Write, Learning to See the World

Chekhov wrote this advice to writers:

> I think descriptions of nature should be very short and to the point. Commonplaces such as, "The setting sun bathing in the waves of the darkening sea poured out a flood of crimson gold," etc. . . . should be eliminated. In describing nature, focus on minute details and group them in such a way that when the reader will have finished reading he will be able to close his eyes and see a complete picture. You can produce the impression of a moonlit night, for example, by writing that the broken bottle glass twinkled like stars on the milldam, and that the black shadow of a dog or a wolf rolled by, and so on. (qtd. in Brunello and Lenček 30)

Students who consider Chekhov's depictions of the natural world should be asked to think about why those depictions work so well and about how writers can learn from them. I have my students practice the highest form of praise, imitation. In our classes in reading, we ask students to write in different modes, both analytic and creative; in our classes on environment and literature, or on nature and writing, we should ask them to describe the world around them. I therefore have my students take a passage from any one of the Chekhov stories discussed here and use it as a model to work toward a description of the world they know. A colleague of mine begins a class in environmental writing by asking students to describe a tree in such a way that the reader will be able to identify it. No street or building names are allowed. The challenge is to see the tree vividly and clearly, to pay attention to it, and then to find the words to describe it. This process is not quite what Chekhov advised, but it's a preliminary step: first see the world well, then you can select the details that will render it best.

Energy, Ecocriticism, and the Man with the Hammer

In a wonderful early essay on ecocriticism, William Rueckert suggests that the ecological function of poetry (and by extension fiction) is to store energy: the classroom becomes, in our best moments, a place that can release it in narrative or poetry, recycling it into the world (108). I find his notion marvelous, even if I'm unsure just how to make it happen. It's a suggestion that surely would have intrigued a natural scientist who also happened to write for the stage—a genre in which the latent and potential meanings of a text are always dependent on the collaborative efforts of director, actors, and audience. For Rueckert, the energies of reading circulate through the classroom but finally move beyond whatever text we have at hand into a broader world. Chekhov would have agreed: his stories give us constellations of human lives, places, and energies, to all of which we must bring our own. There's always that moment when we step outside Chekhov's story and ask what it means to us. This involvement of self is deeply relevant for environmental questions and is made nicely manifest in "A Medical Case" (*Selected Stories* [Pevear and Volokhonsky] 321–31), where we're left with the question of what the doctor should have said to his enormously privileged, protected, and unhappy patient. There is a very small step from that question to "Are we like the unhappy heiress, living both entrapped and enabled by that devilish factory just outside the door?" What should a doctor say to a patient? What should a teacher say to a student? What is demanded not merely by professional ethics but also by human compassion and environmental concern? What's the relation between privilege and the world of the factory in which a person is ill? These are questions we might address historically, but we might also see Chekhov's narrative as creating a space in which we can adapt his story for our own time.

Chekhov is a wonderful writer to teach in an environmental studies course—not because he has answers but because he doesn't. "At the door of every contented, happy man somebody should stand with a little hammer, constantly tapping, to remind him that unhappy people exist, that however happy he may be, sooner or later life will show him its claws, some calamity will befall him—illness, poverty, loss . . ." (*Selected Stories* [Pevear and Volokhonsky] 318). This statement from "Gooseberries" suggests the need for someone who will wield the hammer of discomfort, who will keep us awake. It's a desire I hear voiced in my classes with remarkable regularity. Our students are maturing and entering a world in which there are precious few answers and lots of change, and they wonder whether they (or someone else) will wield that hammer. Teaching the environmental Chekhov invites both teacher and students to think about what is to be done—given human frailties and foibles, our deep and often deluded connections to place, and the relentless forces of development and modernization whose meanings for our lives we must continue to struggle with.

NOTES

[1] The phrase "more than human" comes from Abram.

[2] In using these terms I'm thinking in part of Paul Shepard, the ecologist and psychotherapist whose *Nature and Madness* poses an inquiry into the motives for destructive relation between human beings and their environment.

[3] See Costlow; and Milner-Gulland's discussion of "wooden Russia" (28–36).

[4] Chekhov sent Vladimir Korolenko, the writer, the first chapter of *Walden*, clipped from Suvorin's *New Times*, in 1887. Chekhov wrote that the first chapter "was very promising; it's filled with thought, fresh perspectives and originality, but it's hard to read. The architecture and construction are impossible" (*Pis'ma* 2: 130 [17 Oct. 1887]).

[5] For a helpful introduction to some of these currents, and their international legacies, see Marks.

[6] For a useful overview of representations and politics of the peasantry in nineteenth-century Russia, see Frierson.

[7] Two works of fiction that I have used to make this comparison are Kamala Markandaya's *Nectar in a Sieve*, which gives an idyllic view of Indian village life and the gradual degradation of the environment with the arrival of an ever-growing tannery, and Leslie Marmon Silko's *Ceremony*, which represents a complex web of human and environmental abuse among Pueblo Indians in the post-WWII era. *Ceremony* includes a series of doctors and medicine men who attempt to heal the central character, who suffers ongoing trauma from the war.

Teaching Chekhov as Environmental History: *Sakhalin Island* and Cold Climates

Conevery Bolton Valencius

Anton Chekhov was not only a writer and social critic; he was also a physician and a scientific and medical thinker. But his most substantial scientific publication, *Sakhalin Island* (*Остров Сахалин*; *Ostrov Sakhalin*), has proved hard to read and to teach. One way to draw students into this nonfiction work is to show how it represents Chekhov's engagement in nineteenth-century science and medicine (see Finke, *Seeing*). *Sakhalin Island* is a report on the connections between health and environment in a relatively unknown island penal colony. In particular, Chekhov crafted this report as a contribution to a nineteenth-century branch of environmental sciences known as medical geography, which studied the interconnections between people and their environments in order to improve human health (Valencius, "Chekhov's *Sakhalin Island*"). This was an older approach that still held salience in Chekhov's era despite the exciting new developments of germ theory: medical environmentalism was a powerful framework for understanding human well-being. Teaching *Sakhalin Island* in the context of science and medicine of Chekhov's time can help draw students into this often neglected aspect of his writings.

Reading Sakhalin Island

Two strategies work well for approaching such a long piece of nonfiction: encourage students to read with explicit prompts about the science and medicine of Chekhov's time and assign reading strategies that are intentionally different from those typically used to make arguments for fiction or shorter nonfiction. *Sakhalin Island* can serve as an excellent exercise in group reading and note-taking.

First, introduce the work as a project in the history of scientific exploration and nineteenth-century environmental medicine. Focusing questions could include:

> Why does Chekhov make this journey? What does he aim to accomplish?
> What forms of evidence does he present? Quantitative? Qualitative?
> What made Sakhalin's residents sick and unhappy—aspects of their environment or aspects of the penal system? Both?
> What does Chekhov point to as consequences of unhealthful environments?
> What is scientific about his observations? How do they differ from those that scientists might make today?
> What portions of the book are most keen or convincing?
> What does Chekhov want to see happen with the colony at Sakhalin? What kinds of reform would make the penal colony better managed or more healthful?

From a thirty- or forty page selection of *Sakhalin Island*, students can gain insights, see structure, and learn much of this long book's tone and ideas. This strategy goes against our usual notion of how to read literature, but it accords with what pedagogical specialists teach us about the importance of different kinds of reading for different tasks.

For *Sakhalin Island*, I suggest two alternative reading strategies:

Have everyone read the same brief excerpts. Chapter 1 of the translation by Brian Reeve (Chekhov, *Journey*) provides a brief, compelling introduction to the book; chapter 3 describes Chekhov's interviews; chapter 7 sums up his arguments about climate; chapter 16 deals with women; chapter 18 encapsulates his environmental critique.

Have everyone to read chapter 1 as a common base for discussion, after which groups choose which further chapters to read (perhaps four).

In the second assignment, instructors use class discussion to create a map of the entire book (students called this "charting chapters"). Students break into small groups for discussion of the sections they read, then everyone reconvenes with each group responsible for outlining the main arguments of its reading.

Students at the University of Massachusetts, Boston, were highly satisfied with this approach to discussing similar long works. White boards or chalk boards allowed groups to outline their chapters. No one student was put on the spot; rather, a group scribe stood at the board, writing the outline that the group had prepared during the breakout period, and the scribe was assisted by suggestions or questions from the whole room. As conversation went from group to group, people from the first groups would get up to add notes to their board—comments like, "This argument is different from the one in part 2" or "Foreshadows chapter 12"—or they would simply draw an arrow pointing from a section in an earlier chapter to a section in a later one. At the end of the session, someone would transcribe the boards for posting or take a photograph of each chapter or section outline and upload it as an image file on the class Web site (smartboards would make this recording easier, but the physicality of a chalkboard helps everyone in the room see all sections simultaneously, which facilitates cross-conversation and the making of additional notes). This approach allowed students to take intellectual ownership of their notes and to tackle a large and daunting book without feeling that they as individuals had to account for every detail. Instructors who assign long and complex nonfiction are accustomed to hearing groans. It is lovely instead to hear, "Hey prof, can we read that in groups like we did last time?" "Can we chart chapters on the board again?"

Sakhalin Island may be paired with one of Chekhov's many short stories that explicitly address the context of medicine at the time, such as "Anyuta," "Ward No. 6," or "The Fidget." Such pairing shows how both his intellect and professional identity shaped his writing. Alternatively, an instructor might assign a story dealing with peasant life and criminality, such as "In the Ravine" or the heartbreaking "Sleepy" (for students recently out of high school, the teenage protagonist may be particularly sympathetic).

In his travels across Siberia to Sakhalin, Chekhov encounters some exiles, people who were not formally prisoners but victims of the czarist penal system: students might compare *Sakhalin Island* with excerpts from George Kennan's contemporaneous report on the Siberian exile system or with excerpts from Fyodor Dostoevsky's fictionalized memoir of his time in a czarist Siberian prison, *Notes from the House of the Dead*. The rich literature on the Soviet gulag provides analogous context: one might assign excerpts from Aleksandr Solzhenitsyn's *Gulag Archipelago*, from his novel *One Day in the Life of Ivan Denisovich*, or from the *Kolyma Tales* of Varlam Shalamov.[1]

Chekhov's *Sakhalin Island* offers linkage with other fields. In courses on Russian history, *Sakhalin Island* is a way to engage with the long story of Russian eastern frontier development and the use of penal colonization. In Russian environmental history, Chekhov represents an early example of an environmentally based critique of the Russian state (for background, see Josephson, Dronin, Mnatsakanian, Cherp, Efremenko, and Larin; Weiner, *Little Corner* and *Models*). In a survey of the history of medicine, brief excerpts from *Sakhalin Island* could demonstrate that even during the triumphs of germ theory, educated thinkers believed in the environmental underpinnings of human health (see Barnes).

Chekhov and Sakhalin Island

Sakhalin Island is massive and seems to go in many directions, and its heft and style are far from the precision and economy of the rest of Chekhov's prose. Many enthusiastic and even expert readers of Chekhov know little of his work on Sakhalin Island. Step 1 of introducing students to that work is for the instructor to know about both book and island.

In 1890, Chekhov traveled to northern Sakhalin Island and spent two months researching the system of penal justice that led people to be condemned to agricultural labor there. He interviewed the men, women, children, prison administrators, and guards who made up Sakhalin's society. In *Sakhalin Island*, he takes readers along on this journey of exploration. He shows them the considerable challenge of reaching the island and the mire of its culture and geography.

The result is a book that is messy by twenty-first-century standards, full of observations and tables that give facts about rainfall and literacy, crop yield and the education of children. Chekhov seems to be as much indignant journalist as clear-eyed playwright. In *Sakhalin Island*, his activism is not unlike that of such heavy-handed American contemporaries as Jacob Riis, Nellie Bly, and Upton Sinclair. This tone surprises us when we approach his work as literature (Popkin, "Chekhov") but makes sense when we read it as a piece of late-nineteenth-century environmental science.

In his 1893 report, Chekhov sought to bring the land and people of this desolate, distant penal colony into broader Russian knowledge. Sakhalin Island, desirable today because of its extensive oil reserves, was first developed in the mid–nineteenth century as a source of coal for the Russian navy. It soon became part of the czarist penal system of forced servitude or *katorga* (каторга). By the time Chekhov visited it, the entire island was a penal colony.

Sakhalin forms part of an island arc once connected by land bridge to the island of Hokkaido, and Japan has repeatedly claimed Sakhalin. Russia established competing territorial claims through the nineteenth century in part through penal settlement (neither country recognized the preexisting claims of the native Ainu). In 1875, Russia formally acquired the island from Japan, only to cede back portions after the Russo-Japanese War of 1904–05. For the first half of the century, administration was split between the two nations. After World War II, control shifted again to the Soviet Union. (In 1983, a South Korean passenger flight was shot down over the island by the USSR as a spy plane, killing almost three hundred people.) A long and narrow island (950 km long and between 25 and 170 km wide), Sakhalin is cold and humid. Annual precipitation varies between 600 and 1200 mm, and winter temperatures range between 10 °C and 24° C below zero (14° to -11° F). Even summer temperatures stay below 13–15° C (54–59° F). Northern reaches are flat, but the south is cut into low, steep mountains. As Chekhov documented, the island was not hospitable to nineteenth-century agricultural settlement.

When Chekhov visited, Sakhalin Island was largely unknown to Russian science. It had been found to be an island rather than a peninsula of the mainland only in 1809. Between the 1840s and the 1870s, Russian scientific expeditions explored the island, but the prison colony Chekhov visited was colonizing frontier areas little known to the Russian state (Bonhomme 69–70).[2] Chekhov thus framed the island for the broader reading public in factual as well as moral terms. He was part of the late-nineteenth-century scientific endeavor to understand the cold eastern edges of Russian expansion.

Nineteenth-Century Medicine: Medical Geography and Germ Theory

Sakhalin Island represents a major contribution to the field of medical geography, which sought to observe, study, and quantify the effects of environment on human health. Drawing on ancient ideas, medical geography became fully articulated in the late eighteenth century. The field was sprawling and diffuse, involving experts in meteorology, practicing physicians, and writers on economics and demography as well as on diseases and climates. Yet it was united by central intellectual commitments clearly expressed in Chekhov's Sakhalin report (Valencius, "Histories"; see also Barrett, *Disease*; Mitman and Numbers, esp. 392–93; Paul; Rupke).

Medical geography held that environment comprised a web of influences. These ranged from winds and waters to topography and elevation but also encompassed a variety of other factors, such as the kinds of foods available, the underlying geology and available minerals, the arability of soil, the past history of human beings on the land, and prevailing diseases. Older medical geographies looked to identify harmful miasmas or foul airs that conveyed disease. (The notion of miasmas dates back at least to Hippocrates.) By Chekhov's time, the ancient concept of miasma had fallen out of favor as backward-looking and old-fashioned, but medical professionals, like ordinary people, remained suspicious of the baleful influences of muck and marshes.

For those writing in the tradition of medical geography, unlike for people today, environment was the product of human endeavor—food supplies, trading networks, current medical treatments—in addition to natural circumstances, like geology, atmospheric chemistry, or watershed. It was a matrix of interacting forces that reached from weather patterns to governmental organization.

Medical geography was a main current of research in Europe and North America for much of the nineteenth century. In the 1850s, Daniel Drake, a doctor in Cincinnati, published a compendium parallel to Chekhov's work on Sakhalin, entitled *A Systematic Treatise, Historical, Etiological and Practical, on the Principal Diseases of the Interior Valley of North America, As They Appear in the Caucasian, African, Indian, and Esquimaux Varieties of Its Population*. Both books are structured as travelogues, having personal conversation interspersed with reported and tabulated quantitative data. Both books addressed governmental systems and human societies, as well as what we would now think of as more strictly medical facts.[3]

Such a holistic understanding of health was later undercut by the rise of what we now call germ theory. This revolution in medical and scientific thought was propelled by discoveries in the 1860s and 1870s, especially in the laboratories of Louis Pasteur in France and Robert Koch in Germany. In a few exciting years, European researchers led the world in arguing that invisible microorganisms, isolatable in a lab, were responsible for humanity's chief diseases. The transformation in scientific and medical thinking was astounding. Cholera, tuberculosis, diphtheria, plague—much of what killed human beings—could be isolated from the wider environment and combated through hygiene, vaccines, and specific treatments. Chekhov traveled to Sakhalin Island during what one historian of medicine has termed the "twenty-one golden years between 1879 and 1900," when scientists were discovering the microorganisms responsible for many of humanity's major diseases at a rate of one a year (Porter 442).

Yet this bacteriological revolution, exciting and powerful as it was, remained incomplete. Though the magic bullets of vaccines and antitoxins could perform remarkable cures—preventing deaths from diphtheria and rabies, in particularly dramatic and well-publicized cases—no one in the nineteenth century could cure tuberculosis, even though researchers identified the bacillus in a microscope. (Students may be interested to know that while antibiotics of the mid–twentieth century brought about the miracle of a cure for TB, subsequent overuse of those antibiotics has created a resurgence of antibiotic-resistant TB in our own day.)

Older ideas still held currency. When Chekhov was in medical school, the notion of environmental miasma was old-fashioned, but no one had a better explanation for what caused malaria, one of the chief killers of people in hot, humid climates. Further, an explanation does not always mean a cure: though scientists in 1890 were able to identify the plasmodium, or microscopic parasite, that mosquitos inject to cause malaria, the disease is still a main killer of children in regions of Africa today. In Chekhov's time, many scientific and medical practitioners, particularly in Russia, were interested, despite germ theory, in the broader environmental matrix as conceived in medical geography.[4]

When Chekhov traveled to Sakhalin, he shared this contemporary concern to understand what caused ill health. He read widely in scientific and geographic literature and prepared extensive statistical information to ground his investigations (Valencius, "Chekhov's *Sakhalin Island*" 306). Once on the island, he talked with officials, bureaucrats, and guards and consulted official logs and reports, which he excoriated for their carelessness and inaccuracy (*Journey* 311).

Chekhov also traveled widely among the convicts and families who made up the colony's population. He undertook in-depth interviews with hundreds of the inhabitants and filled out thousands of informational census cards. In the book, he is both precise and compassionate. He records the condition of women regarded as sexual workhorses, whose unofficial marriages are arranged in the same way that one would buy a bottle of vodka. "Describing their everyday life to me," he writes, "three women burst into tears" (120). He paid particular attention to the island's children, born to makeshift families that composed the frayed social fabric of the place.

Chekhov took care to record the widespread ill health on the island. Even in official statistics, he reports, more than ten percent of the population was too feeble to engage in any labor (310). Chapter 23 of *Sakhalin Island* is a devastating inventory of the epidemics that periodically swept the colony, as well as the endemic diseases and debility of people with too little to eat. Of a typhoid-like fever characteristic of Sakhalin, he reports that "the major role in the aetiology of this sickness is played by the chilly climate; those who fall ill are the ones working in cold, damp weather in the taiga [northern scrub forest], and who spend the night in the open air" (313). The very place, he argues, ages and destroys its people: "[I]nhabitants of Sakhalin grow old and decrepit early," he observes, "and for the most part, a convict or settled exile of forty already looks like an old man" (316).

Chekhov's dismal analysis of the organization and prospects of Sakhalin Island is a form of environmental activism, advocating change in this penal colony on grounds not only of social justice but also of environmental appropriateness. Because no one is using environmental data to plan crops, people suffer. In the district of Aleksandrovsk, even according to the official record keeping, "the amount of warmth sufficient for the full ripening of oats and wheat has not been observed in one single year" (Chekhov, *Journey* 110). Southern Sakhalin possessed a more promising climate but remained unsettled. The vast prison failed to adapt agriculture to environmental constraints, failed even to place settlements where they could capitalize more on the abundant fish stocks: the penal colony imported forms of agriculture that did not work environmentally, ignoring the riches of the sea.[5] The fundamental truths of geography and resources are ignored in the administration of the colony, at the cost of lives and futures.

Sakhalin Island, runs the argument in Chekhov's book, will continue to fail as a penal colony because its climate is unsuited for the forms of agriculture the Russian state sought to promote and was deeply unhealthy for the people living there. In one penned-in village in a steep valley, Chekhov observes "no hay meadows at all." The arable plots were far too small to allow for agriculture to support the ever-growing population:

> And since the valley is narrow here, and on both sides press mountains on which nothing flourishes, and since the administration will not pause to take anything whatsoever into consideration when they have to get people off their hands, and will certainly settle scores of new householders on plots here every year, the cultivatable plots will remain just as they are now, that is one-eighth, one-quarter and half a desyatin, or very likely even less [elsewhere, Chekhov writes that people on Sakhalin would need to cultivate at least four desyatins to survive (252)]. I do not know who chose the spot for Krasny Yar, but it is obvious from everything that the task was entrusted to incompetent people who have never stayed in the country, and most of all, people for whom an agricultural colony was the very last subject they had ever thought about. There is not even any decent water here. When I asked where they got their drinking water from, they pointed out a ditch to me. (116)

This is a place where challenging topography has been combined with almost willful bureaucratic neglect, where potential resources have been ignored and squandered, to the destruction of the lives and spirits of those condemned to live there.

Throughout, Chekhov combines the quantitative with the impressionistic to paint a portrait of devastation. At one village, he calculates the amount of cultivated land, demonstrating its insufficiency, and concludes, "The settlement bears no resemblance whatever to an agricultural village. The inhabitants here are a disorderly rabble of Russians, Poles, Russian ethnic Finns and Georgians, hungry and ragged, who have come together not by their own will but by chance, as if after a shipwreck" (142). Sakhalin is no carefully planned colony but an accident in which souls have been crushed by the lack of productive options and the brutal conditions of life.

Chekhov evaluated Sakhalin as part of the Russian frontier. He found its resources sorely lacking to the goals placed on it, and he argued from an environmental and scientific perspective that the Russian state should use this resource differently. His pessimism is a useful reminder that in an expanding late-nineteenth-century world, educated thinkers like him had reason to be wary of expansion, worried about environmental limits, and pessimistic about frontiers (see Valencius, *Health*, ch. 6).

For Chekhov, the evaluation of Sakhalin Island was no side pursuit but a main part of his intellectual legacy. He wanted *Sakhalin Island* to be received as a serious scientific work, and he was hopeful that it might effect some reform.[6] He meant it as part of a contribution to Russian medical and environmental history and as part of emerging Russian science of the far frontier.

Examining *Sakhalin Island* allows us to recapture some of what Chekhov meant in his time as a person qualified to speak on matters scientific and medical as well as literary. He argued that poor environmental information took a toll on human health. Recognizing that such beliefs fitted the medical and scientific thinking of Chekhov's time can help modern students understand the scientific passion animating this dense volume of social and geographic commentary.

NOTES

1 On the gulag, see Pallot; see also Appelbaum, esp. the introduction.

2 On the politics of the science of cold regions, see Bocking; on Sakhalin history, Gentes; on the environmental background, Ivanov.

3 Levine is more available than Drake for classroom excerpts. On Drake, see Barrett, "Daniel Drake's Medical Geography" and *Disease* 241–54; Dorn. On Drake's larger context, see Valencius, "*Health*."

4 See Barrett, *Disease*, chs. 12 and 13; Markovin, "Historical Sketch" and *Razvitie*; and Valencius, "Chekhov's *Sakhalin Island*." August Hirsch is a major European example of such a practitioner. On Hirsch, see Barrett, *Disease* 297–305 and "August Hirsch."

5 On the oceanic history of the region, see Ryan Jones, esp. 356–57.

6 On Chekhov's intentions, see his letters to Suvorin, 9 March 1890, in Moscow, and 11 September 1890, on the steamer *Baikal* in the Tatar Strait (Chekhov, *Journey* 370, 387); Valencius, "Chekhov's *Sakhalin Island*" 307–10.

Beauty in "The Beauties": Teaching Aesthetic Theory through a Chekhov Short Story

Thomas Adajian

> What about someone who believes in beautiful things, but doesn't believe in Beauty itself, and isn't able to follow anyone who could lead him to a knowledge of it? Don't you think he is living in a dream rather than a wakened state? Isn't this dreaming: whether asleep or awake, to think that a likeness is not a likeness but rather the thing itself that it is like?
>
> —Plato, *Republic* 6: 476c

> We cannot press upon others by the aid of any reasons or fundamental propositions our judgment that a coat, a house, or a flower is beautiful. We wish to submit the object to our own eyes, as if the satisfaction in it depended on sensation; and yet, if we then call the object beautiful, we believe that we speak with a universal voice, and we claim the assent of everyone.
>
> —Kant, *Critique of Judgment*, sec. 8

Chekhov's "The Beauties" is a delicately modulated tone poem that describes, from the first person, encounters with two beauties. I have taught it, with some success, in an undergraduate philosophy class at a large state university. The class, grandly titled Seminar in Aesthetics, is cross-listed in the university catalog as both a philosophy and an art history class. Most semesters, the class is made up of approximately one-third philosophy students, one-third art history students fulfilling a requirement for their major, and one-third an assortment of studio art students and others who need a philosophy course to graduate. The syllabus varies but always includes about half classical philosophical texts and half contemporary philosophical texts. Plato and Kant are always assigned, along with some subset of the following: Aristotle, Augustine, Hegel, Hume, Plotinus, Schiller, Shaftesbury. The most recent contemporary works used are Thomas Leddy's *The Extraordinary in the Ordinary: The Aesthetics of Everyday Life* and Denis Dutton's *The Art Instinct*.

The hypothesis that drives this pedagogical experiment is that "The Beauties" has significant Platonic and Kantian resonances and that having the students move back and forth between Chekhov's story and Plato's and Kant's texts can shed light on both the story and the philosophies. I make it clear to the class that I lack deep knowledge of Chekhov and of the influences, direct or indirect, that Plato, Kant, or other philosophers might have had on him.

"The Beauties" in Outline

On its face, Chekhov's virtually plotless 3,500-word story concerns two beauties—human and, more specifically, female beauties. In the first of two short sections, the narrator recalls an unexpected encounter he had as a high school boy, in an unnamed village in the steppe, with a beautiful young Armenian girl. Arriving in the village by cart with his grandfather and a driver, the boy waits, bored and listless, in a stifling room, while his gruff grandfather, "indifferent to women and the beauties of nature," discusses grazing, oats, and manure with an Armenian. The Armenian's daughter enters the stuffy room, bringing tea. The boy is thunderstruck by her beauty. There is a meditation on this overwhelming experience. The grandfather finishes his tea and discussions of manure and grazing. Their horses fed, he and the boy leave the village in the cart with their driver. The Armenian beauty is left behind.

The second section describes another remembered chance meeting with a beauty. The narrator recounts a train trip he took some years later, as a university student. The train stops at a station at another town whose identity is unclear ("I believe it was between Byelgorod and Harkov"). The student disembarks with the other passengers. On the railway platform is a young, unnamed Russian woman, whose beauty, though of a very different sort from that of the Armenian girl, affects him (and the other passengers) in the same bewitching, overwhelming way. The student and his fellow passengers reboard the train, which leaves the Russian beauty behind.

Rationale

One of the main goals of my course is to expose students to a more inclusive, abstract, systematic—that is, philosophical—approach to aesthetic matters than many of them have encountered. Art history majors often enter the course with the unexamined conviction that beauty, or the aesthetic in general, has primarily to do with art. They are often, understandably, not aware that this view is philosophically tendentious and that the view that beauty of an artistic sort is conceptually or epistemologically prior to natural or human beauty is one view among many in the history of aesthetics. In particular, students are unlikely to be aware that artistic beauty isn't the focus of two key figures in the history of aesthetics, Plato and Kant. "The Beauties," therefore, concerned as it is with beauty of all kinds, is our first assigned reading. My aim is to put on the table from the start the broad, systematic standpoint on the aesthetic that the course adopts. Beginning the semester with a work of fiction also lets students share an aesthetic experience before we get to the philosophical arguments about the aesthetic that are at the heart of the course.

The philosophies that I explicitly connect with "The Beauties" are Platonism and Kantianism. Plato's *Republic* and *Symposium* are assigned.[1] The connections among his metaphysics, ethics, and aesthetics are stressed. Considerable time is spent on the metaphysics, primarily through the *Republic*'s parables of the Cave, the Divided Line, and the Sun. Several arguments for the Forms are sketched, with emphasis on the One over Many Argument—very roughly, that there must be a unitary something, the Form, present in the great many diverse and yet unified particulars correctly named by general names. Discussion of the material on art in *Republic* books 3, 5, and 10 focuses on what attitude Plato might have had toward "The Beauties," given the moralizing tendencies in his views about art. In discussing the *Symposium*, we focus on the Ascent to Beauty in Diotima's famous speech and also on the connections Plato sees among love, the Form of the Good, and beauty. The assigned reading in Kant is the first part of *The Critique of Judgment*. His theory of the nature of aesthetic judgment is the focus; his views about art also get attention.

My practice has been to assign two short papers. The first, on "The Beauties" and Platonism, is assigned after we conclude our reading of Plato; the second, on "The Beauties" and Kantian aesthetics, is assigned after we conclude our reading of Kant. For each paper, students are asked to read the story from the perspective of the philosopher in question and to identify elements in the story that resonate with that philosopher's views.

Some Platonic Themes

Many and One

Plato, influenced by Cratylus and Heraclitus, puzzles over how things can be both many—variable, changing, impure, subject to decay—and yet nevertheless one. The senses present us with a shifting multitude of appearances. Without some sort of unity or permanence or reality underlying the fluctuating world of the senses, knowledge would be impossible. But we do have knowledge. How? Plato's answer is his theory of Ideas, or Forms—those abstract entities that are real, knowable by reason, unchanging, and perfect and the criteria for naming things in the world of the senses. The Forms are causes; they make the many things in the world of the senses what they are. So the Form of Beauty is the cause of beautiful things. Some beautiful things, like human beings, artworks, and sunsets, are accessed through the senses. Some beautiful things, like mathematical theorems, are not. But all these many beauties are one—that is, they are all, despite their differences, beauties—because they share in, imitate, or participate in the Form of Beauty. The beauties are many, whether sensible or intelligible; the Form of Beauty, beauty itself, which is intelligible but not sensible, is one: it is that in virtue of which the many beautiful things are beautiful.

In Chekhov's "The Beauties," the beauties are of different sorts. The two young women, nominally the subject of the story, are beauties, but the beauty of the Armenian girl, Masha, is "classical and severe" while the Russian woman's beauty is less distant, more sprightly. The "whole secret and magic of her beauty," the narrator says, lay in

> tiny, infinitely elegant movements, in her smile, in the play of her face, in her rapid glances at us, in the combination of the subtle grace of her movements with her youth, her freshness, the purity of her soul that sounded in her laugh and voice, and with the weakness we love so much in children, in birds, in fawns, and in young trees.

Natural beauty is found in the story: "the boy herding the cows, and the surveyor driving in his chaise over the dam, and the gentleman out for a walk, all gaze at the sunset, and every one of them thinks it terribly beautiful." Speaking of Masha's "white neck and her youthful bosom," the narrator uses the language of art: "you fancy the sculptor would need a great creative genius to mold them." Masha's beauty is compared with natural beauty: her features fit together as "the green reeds go with the quiet stream." More strikingly still, uniting the language of art and the language of natural beauty, her features, taken individually and together, are such that "nature has not blundered over the smallest line." Masha, the human beauty, is an artistic and also a natural beauty. Beauties are many: human, natural, artistic. Human beauties are many. From Plato's perspective, it is all-important that these many are one.

The Ascent to Beauty

The appropriate experience of beauty, as described in Diotima's speech in the *Symposium*, involves moral and cognitive ascent. At the lowest level is the love of individual beautiful bodies. Next, one comes to love something more abstract—bodily beauty as present in all instances. From there, one goes on to admire the higher beauty of human souls. The next step is to the admiration of the beauty of good customs and laws, which form beautiful souls. Next in the ascent is the admiration of the various forms of knowledge that engender, nourish, and sustain those beautiful customs and laws. Then, the lover "is turned to the great sea of beauty, and gazing upon this . . . gives birth to many gloriously beautiful ideas" (210d). Finally, the lover comes to the goal of loving, the Form of Beauty, which

> always is, and neither comes to be nor passes away, neither waxes nor wanes . . . [and] is not beautiful this way and ugly that way, nor beautiful at one time and ugly at another, nor beautiful in relation to one thing and ugly in relation to another; nor is it beautiful here but ugly there, as it would be if it were beautiful for some people and ugly for others. . . . In the end [one] comes to know just what it is to be beautiful. (211a–d)

That is what it is to "see the Beautiful itself, absolute, pure, unmixed, not polluted by human flesh or colors or any other great nonsense of mortality" (211e).

The culmination of the ascent is a self-forgetful final vision in which one is in touch with something truly perfect, immortal, and divine. At this point the lover's own incompleteness and mortality cease to matter.

Chekhov's story does not explicitly mention anything this metaphysical. Still, there is a sort of ascent from self-absorption to self-forgetfulness in the narrator's experience of the Armenian girl. After first seeing Masha and being struck by her beauty, the boy feels "hurt and abashed" that she takes no notice of him; she seems wholly separate, "as though a peculiar atmosphere, proud and happy, separated her from me and jealously screened her from my eyes." That self-imposed barrier crumbles, though. "I forgot myself," the narrator says, "and gave myself up entirely to the consciousness of beauty. I thought no more now of the dreary steppe, of the dust, no longer heard the buzzing of the flies, no longer tasted the tea, and felt nothing except that a beautiful girl was standing only the other side of the table." This is of course not a defense of Diotima's vision or Plato's ontology. But when the narrator ponders the feelings that Masha and her beauty call up in him and puzzles over their meaning, the interpretations he entertains begin with self-absorption, pass on to a reflection on the place of beauty in temporal existence (short-lived, accidental), and culminate in his entertaining a viewpoint that is definitely philosophical, viewing Masha's beauty sub specie aeternitatis ("under the aspect of eternity"). The boy begins with pity, first for himself and then for others ("I felt sorry both for her and for myself and for the Little Russian, who mournfully watched her every time she ran through the cloud of chaff to the carts"), alludes to a more abstract and distanced view of the matter ("or whether I vaguely felt that her rare beauty was accidental, unnecessary, and, like everything on earth, of short duration"), and concludes by wondering whether, perhaps, his sadness was "that peculiar feeling which is excited in man by the contemplation of real beauty." There is a parallel ascent from the senses—the heat, smells, sounds, and sights of Masha's village—to the world of intellectual contemplation.

Love and Reproduction

Plato thinks that we love what is really beautiful. There are echoes of this idea in the second half of Chekhov's story. There, the narrator's travelling companion, watching a telegraph operator at the railroad station, who is in turn watching the Russian beauty, remarks that to live out "in the wilds under one roof with that ethereal creature, and not fall in love is beyond the power of man." Love, according to Plato, is in a perpetual state of desire for the beautiful and aims at reproduction—whether it is the reproduction of another person or the reproduction of wisdom and virtue in the soul of a well-loved pupil. The lover at a later stage of the Ascent to Beauty "is turned to the great sea of beauty, and gazing upon this . . . gives birth to many gloriously beautiful ideas." Chekhov's story makes a striking related connection between beauty and reproduction, though of a more phenomenological, less ontological sort: "You gaze" at Masha, the narrator says, "and little by little the desire comes over you to say to Masha something extraordinarily pleasant, sincere, beautiful, as beautiful as she herself was." Masha's beauty stirs longing at first. Then it calls forth a contemplative response and a desire on the part of the contemplator to give birth to beauty.

Art

The attitude of Plato toward art is notoriously ambivalent. In the early books of the *Republic* he argues that only art of certain sorts should be permitted in the ideal city, partly because he thinks that we come to resemble what we contemplate. In *Republic* 10 a less rigid attitude is evident. I encourage the class to consider several Platonic questions: Would the "The Beauties" be forbidden reading in a Platonic republic? Would Plato have held that "The Beauties" is beautiful? What might Plato say about the moral effects of reading "The Beauties"?

Kantian Themes

Some Kantian themes, many of which have Platonic resonances, are present in Chekhov's story. (The amount of Platonism in Kant's aesthetics is disputed—see Fistioc; also Pugh.)

First, Kant says that "the beautiful is that which . . . is represented as the object of a *universal* satisfaction" (sec. 6). Something like universality—consistency across ages and social groups anyway—appears in Chekhov's story: "the boy herding the cows, and the surveyor driving in his chaise over the dam, and the gentleman out for a walk, all gaze at the sunset, and every one of them thinks it terribly beautiful. . . ." Kant's view is not that everybody does in fact find the same things beautiful. Rather, Kant holds, in making a judgment of taste about the beautiful, "we require everyone to like the object"—we "demand" or "lay claim to" the agreement of everyone (sec. 8).[2] So how can the Chekhov passage, which is on its surface merely descriptive, be said to reflect the normativity of a Kantian aesthetic judgment? I think the answer is that the response that the boy, the cowherd, the surveyor, and the gentleman have to the sunset is being commended, if not subtly recommended.

Second, Kant famously held that the judgment of taste is disinterested, that, inasmuch as a judgment is a pure judgment of beauty, the person judging is indifferent to the existence of the thing judged: "Now when the question is whether a thing is beautiful, we do not want to know whether anything depends or can depend on the existence of the thing, either for myself or for anyone else, but how we judge it by mere observation" (sec. 2). Chekhov's narrator says, "[I] forgot myself, and gave myself up entirely to the consciousness of beauty. I thought no more now of the dreary steppe, of the dust, no longer heard the buzzing of the flies, no longer tasted the tea, and felt nothing except that a beautiful girl was standing only the other side of the table." There is something family-related to disinterested contemplation here.

Third, Kant holds that, although the judgment of taste commands the assent of everyone (sec. 32), it is not susceptible of proof (sec. 33): no objective principle of taste is possible (sec. 34). This skepticism about proof (which for Kant is neither equivalent to, nor implies, that the judgment of taste is arbitrary or without justification) seems clearly present in Chekhov's story. "I am ready to swear" the narrator says, that Masha "was a real beauty, but I don't know how to prove it." Again, of the sunset, which "everyone" thinks "terribly beautiful," he remarks that "no one knows or can say in what its beauty lies."

Fourth, Kant holds that there is something self-sustaining and self-perpetuating in the experience of beauty. This is the famous free play of imagination and understanding: "We linger in our contemplation of the beautiful because this contemplation reinforces and reproduces itself" (sec.13). The boy's experience of Masha seems of a piece with this idea:

> I thought no more now of the dreary steppe, of the dust, no longer heard the buzzing of the flies, no longer tasted the tea, and felt nothing except that a beautiful girl was standing only the other side of the table. . . . The three hours of waiting passed unnoticed. It seemed to me that I had not had time to look properly at Masha when Karpo drove up to the river, bathed the horse, and began to put it in the shafts.

Fifth, "aesthetic ideas" for Kant are "presentations of the imagination which prompt much thought, but to which no determinate thought whatsoever, i.e., no determinate concept, can be adequate, so that no language can express it completely and allow us to grasp it." Their function is to "quicken the mind by opening up for it an immense realm of kindred presentations" (sec. 49). The recurrent light imagery in "The Beauties" is relevant here. Three examples will suffice. The boy's instantaneous recognition that Masha is beautiful is described in luminous terms: "I recognized that at the first glance as I should have recognized lightning." In the very next paragraph, it is the sunset that the boy herding the cows, the surveyor, and the gentleman are all said to think "terribly beautiful." In the second section of the story, light is a constant presence. As the train approaches the station in which the student will see the beautiful Russian woman, the sun, which has "not yet quite vanished," tinges the clouds of smoke from the engine. Seeing her, he is "suddenly overwhelmed by the feeling he had experienced in the Armenian village." He ruminates on her beauty and on its effects on the railway guard; then he, his fellow passengers, and the railroad guard reboard the train, which moves away from the station. The sun is referred to again: it has set, and so the station no longer screens it off from the travelers' view. The smoke from the train, "no longer tinged by the sun," now lies in black clouds over the green, velvety young corn. The train car is melancholy; the sky is darkening. The story ends with another light, not as intense but no less real than the sun's: "The familiar figure of the guard came into the carriage, and he began lighting the candles."[3]

There are many additional Kantian and Platonic views that seem to have resonances in the story. To give examples of the former, it would be worth reflecting in a Chekhovian context on Kant's views that "man . . . alone of all the objects in the world [is] susceptible of an Ideal of beauty" (sec. 17), that "to take an immediate interest in the beauty of nature is always a mark of a good soul" (sec. 42), that nature is beautiful because it looks like art (sec. 4), and that all judgments of taste are "singular" (sec. 8).

There are also other Chekhov stories, containing material on natural, artistic, and human beauty, that might fruitfully be discussed in an introductory aesthetics class alongside "The Beauties"—for example, "Gusev," "Work of Art," and "The Steppe."

Many of my students report that they find "The Beauties" to be challenging reading, but many also report that they like the story. Many assert that they appreciate my imaginative or perhaps fanciful attempts to connect it with Platonism and Kantianism, which they find unfamiliar and demanding in a different way. My hope that reading Chekhov's story enhances students' appreciation both of his and of some of Plato's and Kant's ideas about beauty seems so far to have been borne out, at least enough to justify my continuing to refine the experiment.

NOTES

[1] Because it is unlikely that readers will use the same translation or edition of the *Republic* or the *Symposium*, I give the standard Stephanus numbers commonly used in scholarly references to Plato's works. These numbers and letters indicate how the translation corresponds to the page and section on that page of the Greek text.

[2] The judgment of taste does not postulate everyone's agreement, it merely requires it (Kant, sec. 8). Judgments of beauty are necessary, as well: whereas judgments about the agreeable are merely private, judgments about the beautiful are put forward as having general validity (i.e., as being public). This necessity cannot, Kant holds, be inferred from a thorough agreement among judgments about the beauty of a certain object, for "not only would experience hardly furnish a sufficient amount of evidence for this, but a concept of the necessity of these judgments cannot be based on empirical judgments" (Kant, sec. 18).

[3] Plato suggests that the Form of the Good is the Form of the Beautiful (*Symposium* 206a). In the famous Simile of the Sun (*Republic* 508), the Form of the Good is likened to the sun as sovereign over the intelligible and physical worlds: "What gives truth to the things known and the power to know to the knower is the Form of the Good. . . . Both knowledge and truth are beautiful things, but the Good is other and more beautiful than they." If Plato identifies Goodness itself with Beauty itself, and the former is likened to the sun, then perhaps the latter is as well. It is also convenient for present pedagogical purposes that one of the few examples Kant gives of an aesthetic idea is a line of poetry in which the rising of the sun is connected with the springing of hope from virtue (sec. 49).

Chekhov's Art of the Prosaic: Great Ideas and Dramatic Events

Gary Saul Morson

Chekhov puzzles students. His stories seem incredibly simple, and yet they have a profound emotional effect. Often they seem designed to make one point and then wind up suggesting a contradictory one, but without quite canceling the first. It is hard to say just where the shifts occur. What's more, the stories' emotional effect is out of proportion to their subject. How can such trivialities of everyday life move us so much?, students ask.

The plays prove even more mysterious. At first, they are tedious. After all, close to nothing happens. And what are all those discussions about passing time and possible but never performed actions doing there? Why all the pauses? But a second reading, or seeing the plays performed after reading them, discovers a rich sadness, like that evoked by the breaking string at the end of *The Cherry Orchard*. We seem to hear a far-resonant cry of indistinct significance. How does nonaction suggest so much? And why does comedy, verging at times on the slapstick, interrupt the few moments of dramatic action?

Students come to Russian literature presupposing that it will convey big ideas, but Chekhov's stories either neglect ideas entirely or treat them as mere symptoms of something more elusive. The plays, too, upset expectations of what a play should be and what a work of Russian literature should feel like. A student who has read Dostoevsky might expect mounting suspense leading to scandal, murder, and philosophy, but *Uncle Vanya* seems to end where it begins and to avoid philosophy altogether.

To teach Chekhov, one must first get the students to voice these sources of puzzlement, then show why Chekhov works the way he does. Where does the complexity of the stories come from, and what does it mean? What is the point of writing undramatic dramas?

Great Ideas

Chekhov despised the Russian intelligentsia of his day and, most likely, would have disapproved of most scholars who study him now. Whereas we usually assume that any great writer must despise bourgeois values, Chekhov preferred them. Knowing he was defying the opinions of the progressive and well-educated, he believed in self-reliance and self-discipline, preached good hygiene, and counseled moderation. The work ethic that excites the contempt of aristocrats and intellectuals was dear to Chekhov's heart.

In one his most famous letters, he reproached his wayward brother Nikolai in aggressively bourgeois terms. People of real culture, he wrote, must fulfill a number of conditions:

> 1. They respect the human personality and are therefore forebearing, gentle, courteous, and compliant. . . .
>
> 2. They are sympathetic not only to beggars and cats. Their heart aches for things they don't see with the naked eye. . . .
>
> 3. They respect the property of others, and therefore pay their debts.
>
> 4. They are pure of heart and therefore fear lying like fire. They do not lie even in small matters. . . . They don't pose. . . .
>
> 5. . . . They don't play upon the heartstrings in order to excite pity . . . because all this is striving after cheap effect, and is vulgar, stale, and false.
>
> . . . .
>
> 7. If they have talent, they respect it. . . .
>
> 8. They develop an aesthetic taste. They cannot bring themselves to . . . look with unconcern at a crack in the wall with bedbugs in it, breathe foul air, walk across a floor that has been spat on. . . . They try as far as possible to restrain and ennoble the sexual instinct. . . . They don't swill vodka. . . . For they need to have *mens sana in corpore sano* ["a sound mind in a sound body"].
>
> . . . It is not enough to have memorized a monologue from Faust. . . .
>
> What you need is constant work . . . and will power. . . .
>
> (qtd. in Simmons 111–13 [? Mar. 1886])

Pay one's debts? Be orderly and courteous? Exercise willpower instead of playing what Chekhov called "the destined victim of the age" ("Duel" 77)? Isn't all that for the Chamber of Commerce? Aren't great writers supposed to disparage such trivialities?

Above all, Chekhov rejected the belief that theories, especially political theories, could save the world. We need not theory, he felt, but good manners and basic decency. Intellectuals are prone to the opposite belief, because, after all, if theories rule, then theorists rule. Chekhov foresaw that if intellectuals ever gained the power they sought—as they did in 1917—they would be, if anything, more repressive than the regime they replaced. "Under the banner of science, art, and oppressed free-thinking among us in Russia," he wrote in a letter to Aleksei Pleshcheev, "such toads and crocodiles will rule in ways not known even at the time of the Inquisition in Spain" (qtd. in Simmons 165 [27 Aug. 1888]).

In Russia especially, writers were supposed to offer enlightenment, preach the right program, and advocate social justice according to the latest progressive ideas. This Chekhov refused to do. He also refused to cease publishing in the conservative *New Times* (*Новое время*; *Novoe vremia*). He describes one young lady who never read *New Times* but who insisted that he break with it. And such progressive people, he complained, fault their opponents for closed-mindedness (Simmons 168 [letter to Suvorin, 11 Sept. 1888])!

Far from advocating advanced ideas, Chekhov insisted that great art should not offer prescriptions. After all, theories are necessarily simple, whereas human beings are endlessly complex. To describe people as they are, writers require an eye trained to observe fine shades of feeling and a moral sensibility of infinite subtlety. And, to help people, they need not the right opinions but a heart that "aches for things they don't see with the naked eye." The role of art is to teach people such sensitive seeing.

Despite considerable pressure, Chekhov refused to adopt a political tendency (the Russian term *тенденция* was then in vogue). "Do I not protest against lying in the story from beginning to end?" he responded to one such demand. "And in truth is this not [a tendency]?" (qtd. in Simmons 168 [to Pleshcheev, 7–8 Oct. 1888]). For the intelligentsia it was not, as he was well aware. His most famous letter (to Aleksei Pleshcheev) refusing ideology has entered the canon of Russian literature. "I am afraid of those who look for a tendency between the lines and who insist on seeing me as necessarily either a liberal or a conservative," Chekhov explained. "I am not a liberal, not a conservative, not a gradualist, not a monk, not an indifferentist. I should like to be a free artist and nothing more." Singling out two prominent leftist journalists as particularly odious, he offered his credo:

> I hate lying and violence, whatever form they may take. . . . Pharisaism, stupidity, and tyranny reign not only in shopkeepers' homes and lock-ups: I see them in science, in literature, in the younger generation. . . . I look upon trademarks and labels as prejudices. My holy of holies is the human body, health, intelligence, talent, inspiration, love, and the absolute freedom—freedom from force and falsehood, no matter what form the latter two may take.
>
> (Chekhov, *Letters of Anton Chekhov* 81 [4 Oct. 1888])

And yet Chekhov felt the Russian pull to be a teacher of some great idea. If there was Tolstoyism, why not Chekhovism? Receiving an award from the Academy of Sciences in 1888, he lamented to Dmitri Grigorovich, the first important writer to recognize his talent, "I still do not have a firm political, religious and philosophical outlook: I change it monthly, and therefore I'm compelled to limit myself to the description of how heroes love, marry, produce children, die, and how they speak" (qtd. in Simmons 161 [9 Oct. 1888]). It is not hard to detect irony in this description of a "limit," and yet the self-criticism is also partly serious. As always, Chekhov can empathize with positions not his own and suggest contrary ones in a single sentence. His stories are built on such plural empathy.

Plural empathy gives his stories about ideas and idealists a surprising depth—surprising, because when we finish a Chekhov story, we realize that somehow, at a place we can't quite identify, a simple tale has acquired an unlooked-for complexity. I like to think of this sort of surprise as "the Chekhov effect." Chekhov's best-known example of such a surprise is "A Boring Story," a self-mocking title that applies not to the author but to his hero. The story begins with the hero's ironic self-description, offered as if it were the beginning of a story (which of course it is): "There lives in Russia a certain Honored Professor Nikolai Stepanovich, privy councilor and knight, who has received so many decorations, both Russian and foreign, that when he has occasion to wear them all, his student's call him 'the icon stand'" ("Dull Story" 163). This highly successful professor—he refers to himself ironically as "My Excellency"—seemingly wants for nothing yet, as he approaches death, experiences a despair he does not understand. His family disappoints him, and he finds himself escaping to visit his ward, Katya, a woman he remembers as a child. Then, she was enthusiastic about everything, but now she is as unhappy as he. At the story's end, she visits him to beg him for some answer to the relentless depression she feels when contemplating life's pointlessness. He has nothing to say to her, and, as she leaves forever, he can only think, "So you won't be at my funeral?" (218).

Nikolai Stepanovich imagines that he suffers because in his many ideas about science, philosophy, and himself, "there is no common element, nothing that would unify them into a whole. Each thought and feeling exists in isolation . . . even the most skilled analyst would be unable to find what is called a general idea. . . . And without that there is nothing" (216). Chekhov, who sometimes wondered whether to make the same demand of himself, here shows that a "general idea" is not at all what the old man requires.

In a letter about the story, Chekhov suggests what the old professor is missing. His correspondent (Pleshcheev, a radical writer) had complained that readers know so little about the story's other characters. How else could it be, Chekhov replies, when we hear the whole tale from the professor's point of view, and "one of my hero's chief characteristics is that he cares far too little about the inner life of those who surround him. . . . Were he a different sort of man, Liza [his daughter] and Katya might not have come to grief" (*Letters on the Short Story* 16–17). The professor thinks Katya needs a general idea, a philosophical principle he does not have, but she needs him to sense her grief and empathize with her "inner life."

People have the wrong ideas about ideas. They think that to live right, one needs the right abstractions, but much more often, ideas get in the way. In the course of "The Name-Day Party," a husband given to endless political argument exasperates his wife, who goes into premature labor, nearly dies, and loses the child. "Olya!" he sobs as the story ends, "I don't care about property qualifications, or circuit courts . . . or about any particular views. . . . I don't care about anything! Why didn't we take care of our child?" (338). For Chekhov, enlightenment takes us not to but from ideas.

Dramatic Events

The complex of ideas that disturbed Chekhov the most presume that life is truly lived only in moments of great drama. Today, we still cling to the belief that the time when we live most intensely—during tragic love, violent passion, or transports of inspiration—matters most. But in personal life, such a view leads to an underappreciation of the prosaic virtues of daily life: ordinary kindness and small acts of caring for others. We probably do not even remember such actions, because they seem so inconsequential. No one bothers to record them. In politics, the cult of the dramatic leads to the horrible destructiveness of what Russians called "revolutionism" (*революционность*), the love of revolution for its own sake. That belief too is very much with us, from Che Guevara posters to cuisine sold for its revolutionary taste. The term has become part of the advertiser's lexicon. In both everyday life and politics, true goodness is neglected, and the result is waste.

In story after story, Chekhov shows people's lives ruined because of missed opportunity to care and wasted chances to empathize. He shows most evil coming from sheer waste. In *Uncle Vanya*, Astrov criticizes the destruction of the natural environment not when forests are cut down to build something useful—he does not object to that—but when they are destroyed unthinkingly. If we only did not waste our resources and our best impulses, life would be different. Perhaps more than any other writer, Chekhov is the poet of waste.

If life consists primarily of undramatic events, how can an author describe it? When nothing in particular happens, where's the plot? How does the author engage the reader's interest in trivial events—or, rather, nonevents? These questions pertain all the more to drama, because drama, after all, is supposed to be dramatic, in the way that opera is expected to be operatic. One might have imagined that the last form of literature to engage Chekhov would be plays, and yet he has come down to us as the premier dramatist of his time and since. I think he chose to write metadrama, drama about the dramatic. His theatrical innovations reflect this choice. A well-known witticism about a Chekhov play is that nothing happens in *The Three Sisters* except that three sisters do *not* go to Moscow. A few events do happen in his plays, but he tried to dispense even with these—note his often attributed remark about *The Cherry Orchard* that he had finally managed to write a play without a pistol shot.

Literary genres each call for specific types of action and characters at home in performing them. Adventure stories, for example, demand heroes who act in the nick of time. Hamlet cannot be the hero of *Raiders of the Lost Ark*. Epics deal with warriors heroic on a grand scale performing actions significant for a whole people. By contrast, realist fiction focuses on ordinary human beings in everyday settings. Characters wrestle with problems like our own, and actions are plausible, taking place in a world like the one we live in. In the type of realist fiction that I like to call the prosaic tradition, in the novels of Jane Austen, Anthony Trollope, George Eliot, and above all Lev Tolstoy, the ordinary is not just the world in which characters live; it is also the source of value. The most important actions that define a life, and that make people good or bad, are the prosaic ones we perform countless times every day. Do we look at others charitably or uncharitably? Do we overcome natural egoism to understand how we hurt others? How and where do we direct our attention?

In Tolstoy's fiction, dramatic characters like Anna Karenina, who imagines herself the heroine of a tragic romance, occupy the foreground of the work and define the plot, while in the background toil the good, prosaic figures who make all the difference. These unremarkable figures are as easy to overlook as their counterparts in real life. So readers often miss that the real heroine of *Anna Karenina* is Dolly, whose unfaithful husband thinks of her as merely a good mother. The prosaic figures remain hidden in plain view until we learn Tolstoy's lesson about life (see Morson, Anna Karenina 37–40, 94–95). We might call his method of placing what is most important in the background the decoy technique: readers must learn not to equate the noticeable with the important.

Chekhov's stories belong to this prosaic tradition and adapt Tolstoy's decoy technique. It is one of the ways in which Chekhov achieves plural empathy in them. When he turned to the stage, he discovered a way to produce an oxymoronic prosaic drama. *Uncle Vanya*, for example, depends on the decoy technique. In the foreground, the dramatic characters, all intellectuals, shape the plot (or what there is of it). Voinitsky's mother, who is intensely cruel to her son by sheer neglect, seeks all wisdom in radical political pamphlets; the old professor has devoted his life to intellectual abstractions and regards others as his servants; and the melodramatic Voinitsky (Vanya), who wishes he could have become a famous intellectual himself, finally snaps. All the while, we are shown but may not notice the people whose work makes life bearable and even possible: the old nurse, Marina, who feeds the chickens and tends to the peasants, and, above all, Sonya, who is unobtrusively kind. It is Sonya who makes sure that the estate, which supports them all, runs properly.

Sonya is not beautiful; no one pays attention to her, and readers too are likely to give her a secondary status. They also usually overlook the significance of the play's title, which employs the decoy technique. The phrase "Uncle Vanya"—which might be translated as "Uncle Johnnie"—seems to indicate one character but actually indicates two. Overtly, it refers to Ivan Voinitsky, the center of the play's action. But it also alludes to Sonya, the locus of its values. After all, only she can call him "Uncle Vanya," and she does so with deep, touching affection at his most troubled moments. She is the Dolly of the play, and the audience must learn to recognize her prosaic and undramatic heroism.

In Chekhov's plays, the characters in the foreground long to act dramatically, and in most dramas that would be the right thing to wish for. The author would grant their wish, and the characters would be at home in their genre. But they are not at home in Chekhov's prosaic drama. Heroes and heroines of fiction who would be at home in another genre are genre refugees, as I like to call them, finding themselves in a world that does not meet their expectations. Anna Karenina belongs in a romance but lives in a prosaic novel. In *War and Peace*, Prince Andrei aspires to epic heroism but eventually learns that real heroism is not epic but prosaic—embodied not by Napoleon but by his homely sister.

Eliot's *Middlemarch* offers the most explicit use of this technique. Its famous "Prelude" describes Saint Theresa of Avila, who successfully lived an epic life, then asks what would happen to a woman today with the same aspirations? What becomes of these later-born Theresas living in a world like our own? "Many Theresas have been born who found for themselves no epic life wherein there was a constant unfolding of far-resonant action . . . the offspring of a certain spiritual grandeur ill-matched with the meanness of opportunity; perhaps a tragic failure which found no sacred poet and sank its oblivion" (7). That is the story of both Dorothea and Lydgate, idealists ill matched with reality and their genre.

Chekhov's plays do something similar, taking the heroes and heroines we expect from drama and setting them in an undramatic world. As a result, they become genre refugees. Most of his striking innovations—for example, the frequent stage direction "a pause"—derive from this transposition of prosaic fiction into the world of drama. His central theme is theatricality itself, our desire to live dramatically, for effect. High drama is a lie, and, as he wrote to his brother, people of real culture "do not lie even in small matters," "[t]hey don't pose," "[t]hey don't play upon the heartstrings in order to excite pity," "because all this is striving after cheap effect, and is vulgar, stale, and false." People of real culture, in other words, don't act theatrically.

In *Uncle Vanya*, Elena Andreevna expresses the play's core values when she tells Voinitsky that what makes a good life is not what makes a good play:

> ELENA ANDREEVNA. Ivan Petrovich, you are an educated, intelligent man, and I should think you would understand that the world is being destroyed not by crime and fire, but by . . . all these petty squabbles. . . . Your business should be not to grumble, but to reconcile us to one another.
>
> VOINITSKY. First reconcile me to myself! My darling . . .
>
> ([*Major Plays*] 191)

But Voinitsky wants to live as if he were a hero in in a world of "crime and fire," and so his speech is histrionic. He wants to live citationally, as other Chekhov heroes do. In *The Three Sisters*, Solyony, obsessed with acting like the great Romantic poet Lermontov, kills the baron in a duel. In *Uncle Vanya*, the old professor even makes his illnesses allusive: "They say that Turgenev developed angina pectoris from gout. I'm afraid I may have it" ([*Major Plays*] 187). In the play's climax, he calls the family together and asks them "to lend me your ears, as the saying goes [*Laughs*]" (212). Then he cites a line from Gogol's *Inspector General* (*Ревизор*; *Revizor*) in which the mayor summons the officials to a meeting. He is all literary quotation.

Voinitsky is appropriately appalled by the professor's selfish plan to sell the estate, but his response is a mixture of sincere shock and melodramatic role-playing. He responds to the citational proposal with theatrical rhetoric. Elena Andreevna tries to stop him:

> ELENA ANDREEVNA. Ivan Petrovich, I insist that you stop talking! Do you hear?
>
> VOINITSKY. I won't stop talking! [*Barring* SEREBRYAKOV'S *way.*] Wait, I haven't finished! You have ruined my life! I haven't lived! Thanks to you, I have destroyed, annihilated, the best years of my life! You are my worst enemy! . . . My life is over! . . . If I had had a normal life, I might have been a Schopenhauer, a Dostoyevski. . . . (216)

The choice of Dostoevsky—who faced a firing squad, served a term in a Siberian prison camp, and suffered from epilepsy and gambling addiction—to exemplify normal life is decidedly odd, enough so to render this tragic speech suddenly comic. The same unexpected comedy also appears in the moment of highest drama, when Vanya declares, "I know myself what I must do! [*To* SEREBRYAKOV] You will remember me!" (217). It is one thing for an author to engage in foreshadowing, but here it is the character. Vanya runs out, returns firing a pistol, and stages an attempted murder (or attempts to stage an attempted murder):

> SEREBRYAKOV [*runs in, staggering with fright*]. Hold him! Hold him! He's gone mad!
>
> ELENA ANDREEVNA [*trying to take the revolver from him*]. Give it to me! Give it to me, I say!
>
> VOINITSKY. Let me go, Hélène! Let me go! [*Freeing himself, runs in and looks around for* SEREBRYAKOV.] Where is he? Ah, there he is! [*Shoots at him.*] Bang! [*Pause*] Missed him! Missed him! Oh, damn, damn! [*Throws the revolver on the floor and sits down exhausted.*] (218)

How a director presents this scene indicates how well he understands Chekhov. If the scene is performed as written, the audience will first hear the sound of a shot, then hear Voinitsky say, "Bang!" He voices the stage sound of a pistol shot. In most productions the "Bang!" is omitted. But then the comic aspect of the scene is lost. Vanya says, "Bang!," because he is playing a part. Like a child who simultaneously pretends to be a ballplayer and the announcer broadcasting the play-by-play description, he narrates the action as he performs it. If one doesn't laugh, one has missed the point.

Yet people can really be killed that way. Perhaps that is how most murders take place. Perhaps most of the petty squabbles, even without pistols, that spoil lives are cited as well as said. We often exaggerate our feelings of anger, outrage, or insult, as well as love, as if they become more justified by resembling high drama. We let ourselves be carried away as we imitate the emotions we are supposed to feel. The result is cruelty and waste, which we overlook because of the heady feeling of being a theatrical hero or heroine. Sometimes our feelings can be largely sincere but still corrupted by just a shade of citationality.

More than any writer I know, Chekhov is supremely sensitive to theatricality, where we least expect it.

Appendix
Concordance of Translation Variants of Titles Mentioned in This Volume

Entries are alphabetized per the transliteration of the Russian titles. This list is incomplete and targets only those works addressed by contributions to this volume. For a more comprehensive list, see *Cambridge Companion to Chekhov* 239–44.

Transliterated Title
Russian Title
Translations

"Aniuta"
"Анюта"
"Aniuta," "Anyuta"

"Anna na shee"
"Анна на шее"
"Anna on the Neck"

"Arkhierei"
"Архиерей"
"The Bishop"

Chaika
Чайка
The Seagull

"Chelovek v futliare"
"Человек в футляре"
"Man in a Box," "The Man in a Case"

"Chernyi monakh"
"Черный монах"
"The Black Monk"

"Chto chashche vsego vstrechaetsia v romanakh, povestiakh i t.p.?"
"Что чаще всего встречается в романах, повестях и т.п.?"
"Elements Most Often Found in Novels, Short Stories, Etc."

"Dama s sobachkoi"
"Дама с собачкой"
"The Lady with the Dog," "Lady with Lapdog," "The Lady with the Little Dog," "The Lady with the Pet Dog," "The Lady with the Toy Dog"

Diadia Vania
Дядя Ваня
Uncle Vanya

"Doch' Al'biona"
"Дочь Альбиона"
"The Daughter of Albion"

"Dom s mezoninom"
"Дом с мезонином"
"The House with the Mansard," "The House with the Mezzanine"

"Duel' "
"Дуель"
"The Duel"

"Dushechka"
"Душечка"
"The Darling"

"Grisha"
"Гриша"
"Grisha"

"Gusev"
"Гусев"
"Gusev"

"Ionych"
"Ионыч"
"Ionych," "Dr. Startsev"

"Krasavitsy"
"Красавицы"
"Beauties"

"Kryzhovnik"
"Крыжовник"
"Gooseberries"

Leshii
Леший
The Wood Demon

"Medved' "
Медведь
"The Bear"

"Mest'"
"Месть"
"Vengeance"

"Moia zhizn'"
"Моя жизнь"
"My Life"

"Muzhiki"
"Мужики"
"Peasants"

"Nalim"
"Налим"
"The Burbot," "The Fish"

Ostrov Sakhalin
Остров Сахалин
A Journey to Sakhalin, Sakhalin Island

"Palata No. 6"
"Палата No. 6"
"Ward No. 6," "Ward 6"

"Panikhida"
"Панихида"
"Panikhida," "Requiem"

"Pis'mo donskogo pomeshchika Stepana Vladimirovicha N k uchenomu sosedu d-ru Fridrikhu"
"Письмо донского помещика Степана Владимировича Н. к ученому соседу д-ру Фридриху"
"A Letter from the Don Landowner Stepan Vladimirovich N. to His Learned Neighbor Dr. Fridrikh"

"Po delam sluzhby"
"По делам службы"
"On Official Business"

"Poprygun'ia"
"Попрыгунья"
"Butterfly," "The Fidget," "The Grasshopper"

"Potselui"
"Поцелуй"
"The Kiss"

"Predlozhenie"
"Предложение"
"The Proposal"

"Pripadok"
"Припадок"
"Attack of Nerves," "A Nervous Breakdown," "The Seizure"

"Proizvedenie iskusstva"
"Произведение искусства"
"The Objet d'Art," "A Work of Art"

"Rasskaz neizvestnogo cheloveka"
"Рассказ неизвестного человека"
"An Anonymous Story," "The Story of an Unknown Man"

"Roman s kotrabasom"
"Роман с контрабасом"
"Romance with Double Bass"

"Shutochka"
"Шуточка"
"A Joke," "The Little Joke"

"Skripka Rotshil'da"
"Скрипка Ротшильда"
"Rothschild's Fiddle"

"Skuchnaia istoriia"
"Скучная история"
"A Boring Story," "A Dull Story"

"Sluchai iz praktiki"
"Случай из практики"
"A Case History," "A Doctor's Visit," "A Medical Case"

"Smert' chinovnika"
"Смерть чиновника"
"The Death of a Civil Servant," "The Death of a Clerk," "The Death of a Government Clerk"

"Spat' khochetsia"
"Спать хочется"
"I Want to Sleep," "Sleepy," "Sleepy-Eye," "Sleepyhead," "Let Me Sleep"

"Step'"
"Степь"
"The Steppe"

"Student"
"Студент"
"The Student"

"Svirel'"
"Свирель"
"The Reed Pipe"

"Tina"
"Тина"
"Mire"

"Toska"
"Тоска"
"Heartache," "Misery"

Tri sestry
Три сестры
The Three Sisters

"Uchitel' slovesnosti"
"Учитель словесности"
"The Teacher of Literature"

"Ustritsy"
"Устрицы"
"Oysters"

"Utoplenie"
"Утопление"
"Drowning"

"Van'ka" (1886)
"Ванька"
"Vanka"

Vishnevyi sad
Вишневый сад
The Cherry Orchard

"V ovrage"
"В овраге"
"In the Ravine"

"V ssylke"
"В ссылке"
"In Exile"

"Vragi"
"Враги"
"Enemies"

NOTES ON CONTRIBUTORS

Thomas Adajian is associate professor of philosophy and codirector of the Logic and Reasoning Institute at James Madison University. He is the author of "The Definition of Art," in *The Stanford Encyclopedia of Philosophy*; "Defining Art," in *The Continuum Companion to Aesthetics*; and "On the Prototype Theory of Concepts and the Definition of Art."

Carol Apollonio is professor of the practice of Russian at Duke University and a literary translator. She is the author of *Dostoevsky's Secrets: Reading against the Grain* (2009) and essays about Dostoevsky, Chekhov, and translating; editor and translator of *The New Russian Dostoevsky: Readings for the Twenty-First Century* (2010); and coeditor, with Angela Brintlinger, of *Chekhov for the Twenty-First Century* (2012).

Brian James Baer, professor of Russian and translation studies at Kent State University, is the author of *Other Russias: Reading Homosexuality in Post-Soviet Russian Culture* (2009) and the editor of *Contexts, Subtexts, and Pretexts: Literary Translation in Eastern Europe and Russia* (2011), *Russian Writers on Translation: An Anthology* (2013), and *Translation and the Making of Modern Russian Literature* (2015).

Lisa Siefker Bailey is senior lecturer in English at Indiana University–Purdue University, Columbus, where she teaches courses on Shakespeare, drama, literature, composition, and creative writing. She has published articles on pedagogy, is a member of Indiana University's Faculty Colloquium on Excellence in Teaching (FACET), and won the 2015 IUPUC Outstanding Full-Time Faculty Teaching Award.

Jane Costlow is Clark A. Griffith Professor of Environmental Studies at Bates College. Her scholarly work has focused on nineteenth-century Russian literature and visual culture. She is the author of *Heart-Pine Russia: Walking and Writing the Nineteenth-Century Forest* (2013) and the coeditor, with Amy Nelson, of *Other Animals: Beyond the Human in Russian Culture and History* (2010). Her translation of Lydia Zinovieva-Annibal's *The Tragic Menagerie* (1999) received the AATSEEL prize for best translation.

Julie W. de Sherbinin is professor of Russian at Colby College. She was cofounder of the North American Chekhov Society and for many years editor of the society's newsletter. She is the author of *Chekhov and Russian Religious Culture: The Poetics of the Marian Paradigm* (1997) and the coeditor, with Michael C. Finke, of *Chekhov the Immigrant: Translating a Cultural Icon* (2007).

Michael C. Finke is professor and department head of Slavic Languages and Literatures at the University of Illinois, Urbana. He is the coeditor, with Julie de Sherbinin, of *Chekhov the Immigrant: Translating a Cultural Icon* (2007) and the author of *Seeing Chekhov: Life and Art* (2005) and *Metapoesis: The Russian Tradition from Pushkin to Chekhov* (1995).

Stanton B. Garner, Jr., is professor of English and adjunct professor of theater at the University of Tennessee. He is the author of *The Absent Voice: Narrative Comprehension in the Theater* (1989), *Bodied Spaces: Phenomenology and Performance in*

Contemporary Drama (1994), and *Trevor Griffiths: Politics, Drama, History* (1999) and the coeditor, with J. Ellen Gainor and Martin Puchner, of the *Norton Anthology of Drama* (2nd ed., 2013). He is currently writing a book on kinesthetic empathy in the theater.

John Griswold is assistant professor of fiction in the MFA program at McNeese State University. He is the author of a collection of essays, *Pirates You Don't Know: Adventures in the Examined Life* (2014); a novel, *A Democracy of Ghosts* (2009); and the narrative nonfiction *Herrin: The Brief History of an Infamous American City* (2009). He is an editor for Crux: The Georgia Series for literary nonfiction.

Michael Holquist is professor emeritus of comparative literature at Yale University and a senior fellow at the Heyman Center for the Humanities at Columbia University. He is a past president of the MLA and author of *Dostoevsky and the Novel* (1977); *Mikhail Bakhtin*, with Katerina Clark (1984); and *Dialogism: Bakhtin and his World* (1990). He has also edited or translated several volumes of the works of Mikhail Bakhtin.

Benjamin Knelman is a former student of Gabriella Safran at Stanford University, holding a BA in Russian language, culture, and history as well as in economics; interdisciplinary honors in environmental science, technology, and policy; an MA in Russian, Eastern European, and Eurasian studies; and an MS in engineering. He is founder and CEO of Juntos Finanzas.

Olga Levitan is a teaching fellow in the Department of Theatre Studies at Hebrew University, Jerusalem, and a lecturer at the David Yellin Academic College of Education, where she has taught, among other courses: Poetics and Analysis of the Modern Drama, Methods of the Theatre Research, Russian Avantgarde Direction, and Chekhov and the Art of Direction. She has published on Russian, Israeli, and Yiddish theater. She is a coeditor of the forthcoming book *Multicultural Theatre in Israel*.

John MacKay is professor of Slavic languages and literatures and chair of Film Studies at Yale University. He teaches a wide variety of culture and literature courses in and beyond film studies. He is the author of *Inscription and Modernity: From Wordsworth to Mandelstam* (2006), *True Songs of Freedom:* Uncle Tom's Cabin *in Russian Culture and Society* (2013), and *Dziga Vertov: Life and Work* (forthcoming).

Gary Saul Morson is Lawrence B. Dumas Professor of the Arts and Humanities and professor of Slavic languages and literatures at Northwestern University. He is the author of *Prosaics and Other Provocations: Empathy, Open Time, and the Novel* (2013); *The Long and the Short of It: From Aphorism to Novel* (2012); *The Words of Others: From Quotations to Culture* (2011); and Anna Karenina *in Our Time: Seeing More Wisely* (2007).

Lyudmila Parts is associate professor in the Department of Languages, Literatures, and Cultures at McGill University. She is the author of *The Chekhovian Intertext: Dialogue with a Classic* (2008) and the editor of *The Twentieth-Century Russian Short Story: A Critical Companion* (2009).

Annamaria Pileggi is professor of the practice in the Department of Performing Arts at Washington University, St. Louis, and a professional actor and director. A five-time recipient of the university's College of Arts and Sciences Faculty Award recognizing excellence in teaching, she teaches these courses: Acting, Movement for the Actor, Musical Theatre, and Theatre for Social Change.

Cathy Popkin is Jesse and George Siegel Professor in the Humanities, Department of Slavic Languages, Columbia University. She is the editor of a new Norton Critical Edition of Chekhov's stories (2014) and coeditor of *Teaching Nineteenth-Century Russian Literature: Essays in Honor of Robert L. Belknap* (2014). Since her monograph *The Pragmatics of Insignificance: Chekhov, Zoshchenko, Gogol* (1993), she has published a range of articles on Chekhov and the medical sciences.

Valleri J. Robinson is associate professor of theater history and criticism at the University of Illinois, Urbana. She is the author of *Russian Culture and Theatrical Performance in America, 1891–1933* (2011) and various articles and reviews. She received a Fulbright award to work with the Kolyada Theater in Ekaterinburg in 2014 and has worked as a dramaturg with theater companies and playwrights throughout the United States.

Rita Safariants is visiting assistant professor of Russian studies at Vassar College. She is the author of essays on Russian literature, cinema, and popular culture and is completing a book on popular music and late-Soviet cinema.

Gabriella Safran is professor of Slavic Languages and Literatures at Stanford University. She has written on Russian, Polish, Yiddish, and French literatures and cultures; her most recent book is *Wandering Soul: The Dybbuk's Creator, S. An-sky* (2010). She teaches and writes on Russian literature, Yiddish literature, folklore, and folkloristics.

Maia Solovieva is a lecturer in the Department of Russian Language, Literature, and Culture at Oberlin College. She specializes in upper-level Russian-language instruction with an emphasis on cross-cultural perspectives in language pedagogy. She has taught a first-year seminar Conversations with Chekhov, utilizing Chekhov's prose as a point of departure for discussions about Russian culture in literary and historical contexts.

Dmitry Tartakovsky is a library specialist at Grainger Engineering Library at the University of Illinois, Urbana. As a visiting research associate at the Slavic Reference Service at the university, he was involved in creating the Chekhov Libguide. He holds a PhD in history and has served as a Balkans analyst for Army Special Forces at Fort Bragg and as a political attaché with the United States Embassy in Chisinau, Moldova.

Conevery Bolton Valencius, associate professor of history at the University of Massachusetts, Boston, is the author of *The Lost History of the New Madrid Earthquakes* (2013) and the prize-winning study *"The Health of the Country": How American Settlers Understood Themselves and Their Land* (2002), as well as articles on environmental history, women's history, and scientific exploration of the United States West.

SURVEY PARTICIPANTS

Carol Apollonio, *Duke University*
Brian James Baer, *Kent State University*
Lisa Siefker Bailey, *Indiana University–Purdue University, Columbus*
Robert Craig Baum, *River Valley Community College, NH, and European Graduate School*
Elizabeth Beaujour, *Hunter College*
Doug Buchanan, *Dawson College*
Julie Cassiday, *Williams College*
Julie de Sherbinin, *Colby College*
Yelena Francis, *Bennett College*
Slav N. Gratchev, *Purdue University*
Warren G. Green, *Dominican University, IL*
Ann C. Hall, *Ohio Dominican University*
William Hutchings, *University of Alabama, Birmingham*
Michael R. Katz, *Middlebury College*
Sabina Knight, *Smith College*
James McGinnis, *James Madison University*
Jason Merrill, *Michigan State University*
Susan Mooney, *University of South Florida, Tampa*
Daniel Morris, *Purdue University*
Scott Proudfit, *Elon University*
Irina Renfro, *California Baptist University*
Grant Shen, *National University of Singapore*
Janet Smarr, *University of California, San Diego*
Maia Solovieva, *Oberlin College*
Andrea F. Trocha–Van Nort, *United States Air Force Academy*
Hugo Walter, *Berkeley College*

WORKS CITED

Abram, David. *The Spell of the Sensuous: Perception and Language in a More-than-Human World*. New York: Vintage, 1997. Print.

Akunin, Boris. "Ia nikogda ne sochinial shpionskikh romanov v zhanre 'Spokoino, Dunkel'" ["Я никогда не сочинял шпионских романов в жанре 'Спокойно, Дункель'"; "I Never Wrote Spy Novels in the Genre of 'Easy, Pal'"]. *Izvestiia* [*Известия*; "News"] 23 Dec. 2004. Web. 11 Feb. 2013.

———. *The Seagull*. Trans. Michael Katz. *New England Review* 3 (2006): 115–59. Print.

Alberti, Joe. *Acting: The Gister Method*. New York: Pearson Educ., 2013. Print.

Allen, David. *Performing Chekhov*. London: Routledge, 1999. Print.

Andrew, Dudley. *What Cinema Is! Bazin's* Quest *and Its Charge*. Malden: Wiley-Blackwell, 2010. Print.

Angelo, Thomas A., and K. Patricia Cross. *Classroom Assessment Techniques: A Handbook for College Teachers*. 2nd ed. San Francisco: Jossey-Bass, 1993. Print.

Anton Chekhov. Ed. and introd. Harold Bloom. Philadelphia: Chelsea, 1999. Print. Modern Critical Views.

A. P. Chekhov: Dokumenty: Fotografii [*А. П. Чехов: Документы: Фотографии*; "A. P. Chekhov: Documents: Photographs"]. Ed. I. Varentsova and G. Shcheboleva. Moscow: Sovetskaia Rossiia, 1984. Print.

A. P. Chekhov: Entsiklopediia [*А. П. Чехов: Энциклопедия*; "A. P. Chekhov: Encyclopedia"]. Ed. Vl. B. Kataev. Moscow: Prosveshchenie, 2011. Print.

Apollonio, Carol. "Gained in Translation: Chekhov's 'Lady.'" Apollonio and Brintlinger 281–98.

Apollonio, Carol, and Angela Brintlinger, eds. *Chekhov for the Twenty-First Century*. Bloomington: Slavica, 2012. Print.

Appelbaum, Anne. *Gulag: A History*. New York: Anchor, 2005. Print.

Appiah, Kwame Anthony. "Thick Translation." *Translation Studies Reader*. Ed. Lawrence Venuti. New York: Routledge, 2000. 417–29. Print.

Aristotle. *Poetics*. Trans. Ingram Bywater. *The Basic Works of Aristotle*. Ed. Richard McKeon. New York: Modern Lib., 2001. 1453–87. Print.

August. Dir. Anthony Hopkins. Perf. Hopkins, Leslie Phillips, Kate Burton, Gawn Grainger, and Rhian Morgan. Granada, 1996. MGM Home Entertainment. 2011. DVD.

Baechtel, Mark. *Shaping the Story: A Step-by-Step Guide to Writing Short Fiction*. New York: Longman, 2004. Print.

Baker, Annie. "Part 38: Annie Baker." Interview by Adam Szymkowicz. *I Interview Playwrights*. Szymkowicz, 19 Aug. 2009. Web. 10 May 2012.

Bakhtin, Mikhail. "Forms of Time and of the Chronotope in the Novel." *The Dialogic Imagination: Four Essays by M. M. Bakhtin*. Ed. Michael Holquist. Trans. Caryl Emerson and Holquist. Austin: U of Texas P, 1981. 84–258. Print.

Balázs, Béla. *Early Film Theory*. Trans. Rodney Livingston. Introd. Erica Carter. New York: Berghahn, 2010. Print.

Ball, David. *Backwards and Forwards: A Technical Manual for Reading Plays*. Carbondale: Southern Illinois UP, 1983. Print.

Balukhaty, Sergei, ed. The Seagull *Produced by Stanislavsky*. Trans. David Magarshack. London: Dobson; New York: Theatre Arts, 1952. Print.

Barker, Chris. *The SAGE Dictionary of Cultural Studies*. London: Sage, 2004. Print.

Barnes, David S. *The Great Stink of Paris and the Nineteenth-Century Struggle against Filth and Germs*. Baltimore: Johns Hopkins UP, 2007. Print.

Barrett, Frank A. "August Hirsch: As Critic of, and Contributor to, Geographical Medicine and Medical Geography." Rupke 98–117.

———. "Daniel Drake's Medical Geography." *Social Science and Medicine* 4.6 (1996): 791–800. Print.

———. *Disease and Geography: The History of an Idea*. Toronto: Atkinson Coll., York U, 2000. Print.

Barth, John. "Incremental Perturbation: How to Know Whether You've Got a Plot or Not." *Creating Fiction: Instruction and Insights from the Teachers of Associated Writing Programs*. Ed. Julie Chekoway. Cincinnati: Story, 2001. 126–34. Print.

Barthes, Roland. "An Introduction to the Structural Analysis of Narrative." Trans. Lionel Duisit. *New Literary History* 6.2 (1975): 237–72. *JSTOR*. Web. 13 Feb. 2010.

———. "The Reality Effect." *The Rustle of Language*. Trans. Richard Howard. New York: Farrar, 1986. 141–48. Print.

Bartlett, Rosamund. *Chekhov: Scenes from a Life*. London: Simon, 2005. Print.

Basina, Nataliia, and Zoia Khravchuk. "Poslednii avtobus Iosifa Kheifitsa" ["Последний автобус Иосифа Хейфица"; "The Last Bus of Iosif Kheifits"]. *Rossiiskaia Gazeta* [*Российская газета*; "Russian Gazette"] 16 Dec. 2005. Rossiiskaia Gazeta, n.d. Web. 9 Jan. 2015.

Basinskii, Pavel. "Svoi shestok, Chuchelo 'Chaiki'" ["Свой шесток, Чучело 'Чайки'"; "A Perch of One's Own, the Stuffed *Seagull*]. *Literaturnaia gazeta* [*Литературная газета*; "Literary Gazette"] 26 Apr. 2000. Literaturnaia Gazeta, n.d. Web. 11 Feb. 2013.

Baudrillard, Jean. *Simulacra and Simulation*. Trans. S. F. Glaser. Ann Arbor: U of Michigan P, 1994. Print.

Benedetti, J. *Stanislavski: His Life and Art*. London: Methuen, 1999. Print.

Benjamin, Walter. "On the Concept of History." Trans. Dennis Redmond. *Walter Benjamin Archive*. Marxists Internet Archive, n.d. Web. 26 Sept. 2015.

Benveniste, Emile. "Subjectivity in Language." *Problems in General Linguistics*. Trans. Mary Elizabeth Meek. Coral Gables: U of Miami P, 1971. 223–30. Print.

Bergson, Henri. *Creative Evolution*. Trans. Arthur Mitchell. Mineola: Dover, 1998. Print.

Berkeley, Anthony. *The Poisoned Chocolates Case*. New York: Dell, 1980. Print.

"Bernard Malamud: Biography." *Masterpieces of Amercan Literature*. Ed. Steven G. Kellman. *eNotes*. eNotes, n.d. Web. 10 May 2013.

Beumers, Birgit. "*Uncle Vanya* [dir. Konchalovsky]." *Directory of World Cinema: Russia*. Ed. Beumers. Bristol: Intellect, 2011. 182–84. Print.

The Birth of Modern Theatre: Chekhov's Uncle Vanya *in Performance*. Princeton: Films for the Humanities, 1988. Videocassette.

Bitsilli, Peter, M. *Chekhov's Art: A Stylistic Analysis*. Trans. Toby Clyman and Edwina Cruise. Ann Arbor: Ardis, 1983. Print.

Bocking, Stephen. "Science and Spaces in the Northern Environment." *Environmental History* 12.4 (2007): 867–94. Print.

Bonhomme, Brian. *Russian Exploration, from Siberia to Space: A History*. Jefferson: McFarland, 2012. Print.

Bransford, John D., Ann L. Brown, and Rodney R. Cocking, eds. *How People Learn: Brain, Mind, Experience, and School*. Washington: Natl. Acad., 2000. Natl. Acad., n.d. Web. 26 Nov. 2012.

Brunello, Piero, and Lena Lenček, eds. *How to Write like Chekhov: Advice and Inspiration, Straight from His Own Letters and Work*. Trans. Lenček. Philadelphia: Perseus, 2008. Print.

Brustein, Robert. "More Masterpieces." *PAJ: A Journal of Performance and Art* 30.3 (2008): 1–7. *Project Muse*. Web. 6 Dec. 2012.

Buell, Laurence. *The Environmental Imagination: Thoreau, Nature Writing, and the Formation of American Culture*. Cambridge: Harvard UP, 1996. Print.

Bunin, Ivan. *About Chekhov: The Unfinished Symphony*. Trans. Thomas Marullo. Evanston: Northwestern UP, 2007. Print.

———. *O Chekhove: Nezakonchennaia rukopis'* [*О Чехове: Незаконченная рукопись*; "About Chekhov: An Unfinished Manuscript"]. New York: Chekhov, 1955. Print.

Burroway, Janet, Elizabeth Stuckey-French, and Ned Stuckey-French. *Writing Fiction: A Guide to Narrative Craft*. 8th ed. New York: Longman, 2010. Print.

Burry, Alexander. "From Prison to Paradise: Michael Blakemore's Transposition of *Uncle Vanya*." *Literature/Film Quarterly* 38.2 (2010): 84–97. Print.

The Cambridge Companion to Chekhov. Ed. Vera Gottlieb and Paul Allain. Cambridge: Cambridge UP, 2000. Print.

Carnicke, Sharon. "Translating Chekhov's Plays without Russian; or, The Nasty Habit of Adaptation." *Chekhov the Immigrant* 89–100.

Carver, Raymond. *No Heroics Please*. New York: Vintage, 1992. Print.

———. *Where I'm Calling From*. New York: Vintage, 1989. Print.

Cattaneo, Anne. "Dramaturgy: An Overview." Jonas, Proehl, and Lupu 3–15.

Charcot, Jean-Martin. *Charcot, the Clinician: The Tuesday Lessons*. Trans. Christopher G. Gotz. New York: Raven, 1987. Print.

Chekhov, Anton P. *Anton Chekhov's Life and Thought: Selected Letters and Commentary*. Ed. Simon Karlinsky. Trans. Michael Henry Heim. 1975. Evanston: Northwestern UP, 1997. Print.

———. *Anton Chekhov's Selected Stories: Texts of the Stories: Comparison of Translations: Life and Letters: Criticism*. Ed. Cathy Popkin. New York: Norton, 2014. Print. Norton Critical Ed.

———. *Anton Chekhov's Short Stories*. Ed. Ralph E. Matlaw. New York: Norton, 1979. Print.

———. "The Beauties." Trans. Constance Garnett. *"The Schoolmistress" and Other Stories*. Eldritch Press, n.d. Web. 9 Jan. 2015.

——— [Tchekhoff, Anton]. *"The Black Monk" and Other Stories*. Trans. R. E. C. Long. New York: Stokes, 1916. Print.

———. "A Boring Story." Chekhov, *Selected Stories* [Pevear and Volokhonsky] 55–107.

———. "The Butterfly." *"Ward Number Six" and Other Stories*. Trans. Ronald Hingley. Oxford: Oxford UP, 1992. 1–22. Print.

———. *The Complete Plays*. Trans. Laurence Senelick. New York: Norton, 2006. Print.

———. *The Complete Short Novels*. Trans. Richard Pevear and Larissa Volokhonsky. New York: Vintage, 2004. Print.

———. "The Duel." Chekhov, *"Ward Six"* 61–161.

———. "A Dull Story." Chekhov, *"Ward Six"* 163–218.

———. *The Early Stories, 1883–1888*. Trans. Patrick Miles and Harvey Pitcher. New York: Collier, 1982. Print.

———. *The Essential Plays*. Trans. Michael Henry Heim. New York: Modern Lib., 2003. Print.

———. "The Fidget." Chekhov, *Selected Stories* [Pevear and Volokhonsky] 137–60.

———. "The Fish." *Classic Reader*. Classic Reader, n.d. Web. 15 Aug. 2014.

———. *Forty Stories*. Trans. Robert Payne. New York: Vintage, 1991. Print.

———. *Four Plays and Three Jokes*. Trans. and ed. Sharon Carnicke. Indianapolis: Hackett, 2009. Print.

———. "The Grasshopper." Trans. Ivy Litvinov. Chekhov, *Anton Chekhov's Short Stories* 69–90.

———. "The Grasshopper." *"The Grasshopper" and Other Stories*. Trans. A. E. Chamot. New York: Books for Libs., 1926. 17–52. Print.

———. "The Grasshopper." Chekhov, *"Lady with Lapdog"* 105–30.

———. "The Grasshopper." *"The Wife" and Other Stories*. Trans. Constance Garnett. New York: Ecco, 1985. 89–127. Print.

———. "Gusev." Chekhov, *Selected Stories* [Pevear and Volokhonsky] 109–21.

———. "In Exile." Trans. Constance Garnett. Chekhov, *Anton Chekhov's Short Stories* 90–97.

———. "In the Ravine." Chekhov, *Selected Stories* [Pevear and Volokhonsky] 383–420.

———. "I Want to Sleep." *Oocities*. Oocities, n.d. Web. 12 July 2014. <http://www.oocities.org/athens/delphi/6422/sleep.html>.

———. *A Journey to Sakhalin*. Trans. Brian Reeve. Cambridge: Faulkner, 1993. Print.

———. "The Kiss." Chekhov, *Selected Stories* [Dunnigan] 95–114.

———. "A Lady with a Dog." *"The Russian Master" and Other Stories*. Trans. Ronald Hingley. Oxford: Oxford UP, 1988. 7–21. Print.

———. *"Lady with Lapdog" and Other Stories*. Trans. David Magarshack. London: Penguin, 1964. Print.

———. "The Lady with the Dog." Trans. Ivy Litvinov. Chekhov, *Anton Chekhov's Short Stories* 221–35.

———. "The Lady with the Dog." *"The Lady with the Dog" and Other Stories*. Trans. Constance Garnett. New York: Ecco, 1984. 3–28. Print.

———. "The Lady with the Little Dog." *"About Love" and Other Stories*. Trans. Rosamund Bartlett. Oxford: Oxford UP, 2004. 167–83. Print.

———. "The Lady with the Little Dog." Trans. Jessie Coulson. *Selected Stories*. London: Oxford UP, 1963. 271–92. Print.

———. "The Lady with the Little Dog." *Short Stories*. Trans. Elisaveta Fen. London: Folio Soc., 1974. 223–41. Print.

———. "The Lady with the Little Dog." Chekhov, *Selected Stories* [Pevear and Volokhonsky] 361–76.

———. "The Lady with the Little Dog." *"The Lady with the Little Dog" and Other Stories*. Trans. Ronald Wilks. London: Penguin, 2002. 223–40. Print.

———. "The Lady with the Pet Dog." *Forty Stories*. Trans. Robert Payne. New York: Vintage, 1991. 284–303. Print. Vintage Classics.

———. "The Lady with the Pet Dog." Trans. Avrahm Yarmolinsky. *The Portable Chekhov*. New York: Book Soc., 1950. 412–33. Print.

———. "The Lady with the Toy Dog." *"My Life" and Other Stories*. Trans. S. S. Koteliansky and Gilbert Cannan. Freeport: Books for Libs., 1971. 206–31. Print.

———. "Let Me Sleep." Chekhov, *Early Stories* 191–96.

———. *Letters of Anton Chekhov*. Ed. Avrahm Yarmolinsky. New York: Viking, 1972. Print.

———. *Letters on the Short Story, the Drama, and Other Literary Topics*. Ed. L. Friedland. London: Vision, 1965. Print.

———. *The Major Plays*. Trans. Ann Dunnigan. New York: Signet, 1982. Print.

———. "The Man in a Case." Chekhov, *Selected Stories* [Pevear and Volokhonsky] 299–310.

———. "The Name-Day Party." Chekhov, *"Ward Six"* 307–38.

———. *Note-book of Anton Chekhov*. Trans. S. S. Koteliansky and Leonard Woolf. Folcroft: Folcroft Lib., 1973. Print.

———. "On Love." Chekhov, *Forty Stories* 273–83.

———. *The Oxford Chekhov*. 9 vols. Trans. and ed. Ronald Hingley. London: Oxford UP, 1965–80. Print.

———. "Oysters." Trans. Constance Garnett. Chekhov, *Anton Chekhov's Short Stories* 2–5.

———. *Pis'ma v dvenadtsati tomakh* [*Письма в двенадцати томах*; "Letters in Twelve Volumes"]. 12 vols. Ed. N. F. Bel'chikov et al. Moscow: Nauka, 1974–83. Print. Vols. 19–30, but numbered 1 to 12, of *Polnoe sobranie sochinenii i pisem v tridtsati tomakh* [*Полное собрание сочинений и писем в тридцати томах*; "Complete Collection of Works and Letters in Thirty Volumes"].

———. "Rothschild's Fiddle." Chekhov, *Selected Stories* [Pevear and Volokhonsky] 253–62.

———. *Sakhalin Island*. Surrey: Alma Classics, 2013. Print.

———. *The Selected Letters of Anton Chekhov*. Ed. Lillian Hellman. Trans. S. K. Lederer. New York: Hill, 1965. Print.

———. *Selected Stories*. Trans. Ann Dunnigan. New York: New Amer. Lib. of World Lit., 1960. Print.

———. *Selected Stories of Anton Chekhov*. Trans. Richard Pevear and Larissa Volokhonsky. New York: Bantam, 2000. Print.

———. "Skripka Rotshil'da" ["Скрипка Ротшильда"; "Rothschild's Fiddle"]. Chekhov, *Sochineniia* 8: 297–305.

———. "Sleepy." Trans. Constance Garnett. 1922. *Read Print*. Read Print, n.d. Web. 18 Feb. 2014.

———. "Sleepy," Chekhov, *Selected Stories* [Pevear and Volokhonsky] 49–54.

———. "Sleepy-Eye." *Cosmopolitan Magazine* 41 (1906): 151–56. Electronic Text Center, U of Virginia Lib., n.d. Web. 13 Mar. 2013.

———. "Sleepyhead." Chekhov, *Forty Stories* 131–38.

———. *Sochineniia v vosemnadtsati tomakh*. [*Сочинения в восемнадцати томах*; "Works in Eighteen Volumes"]. 18 vols. Ed. N. F. Bel'chikov et al. Moscow: Nauka, 1974–83. Print. Vols. 1–18. of *Polnoe sobranie sochinenii i pisem v tridtsati tomakh* [*Полное собрание сочинений и писем в тридцати томах*; "Complete Collection of Works and Letters in Thirty Volumes"].

———. "The Steppe." Chekhov, *Complete Short Novels* 1–113.

———. "The Student." Chekhov, *Selected Stories* [Pevear and Volokhonsky] 263–66.

———. *The Three Sisters*. Trans. Vlada Chernomordik. Adapt. David Mamet. New York: French, 1990. Print.

———. *Uncle Vanya*. Trans. Vlada Chernomordik. Adapt. David Mamet. New York: Grove, 1988. Print.

———. *Uncle Vanya*. Chekhov, *Major Plays* 171–231.

———. *The Undiscovered Chekhov: Thirty-eight New Stories*. Trans. Peter Constantine. New York: Seven Stories, 1998. Print.

———. "Ward No. 6." Chekhov, *Selected Stories* [Pevear and Volokhonsky] 171–221.

———. *"Ward Six" and Other Stories*. Trans. Ann Dunnigan. New York: Signet, 1965. Print.

Chekhov, Anton, Maria Fornes, et al. *Orchards: Seven Stories by Anton Chekhov and Seven Plays They Have Inspired*. New York: Knopf, 1986. Print.

Chekhov, Mikhail. *Anton Chekhov: A Brother's Memoir*. Trans. Eugene Alper. New York: Palgrave, 2010. Print.

Chekhov: A Collection of Critical Essays. Ed. Robert L. Jackson. Englewood Cliffs: Prentice, 1967. Print.

A Chekhov Companion. Ed. Toby W. Clyman. Westport: Greenwood, 1985. Print.

Chekhov: New Perspectives. Ed. René Wellek and Nonna D. Wellek. Englewood Cliffs: Prentice, 1984. Print.

Chekhov's Doctors: A Collection of Chekhov's Medical Tales. Ed. Jack Coulehan. Fwd. Robert Coles. Kent: Kent State UP, 2003. Print.

Chekhov's Great Plays: A Critical Anthology. Ed. and introd. Jean-Pierre Barricelli. New York: New York UP, 1981. Print.

"Chekhov's Gun." *Wikipedia*. Web. 15 June 2013.

"Chekhov Stories." *Sparknotes*. Sparknotes, n.d. Web. 20 July 2014.

Chekhov the Immigrant: Translating a Cultural Icon. Ed. Michael C. Finke and Julie de Sherbinin. Bloomington: Slavica, 2007. Print.

Christie, Agatha. *Black Coffee: A Mystery Play in Three Acts*. New York: French, 1961. Print.

Chudakov, Aleksander. "Chaika" ["Чайка"; "*The Seagull*"]. Chekhov, *Sochineniia* 12: 379–86.

———. *Chekhov's Poetics*. Trans. Edwina Cruise and Donald Dragt. Ann Arbor: Ardis, 1983. Print.

Cold Souls. Dir. Sophie Barthes. Perf. Paul Giamatti, Dina Korzun, Emily Watson, and David Strathairn. Samuel Goldwyn, 2009. 20th Century Fox, 2010. DVD.

Coles, Robert, and Michael Finke. "A Conversation with Robert Coles." *Chekhov the Immigrant* 271–84.

Constantine, Peter. Introduction. Chekhov, *Undiscovered Chekhov* ix–xxiii.

Costlow, Jane. *Heart-Pine Russia*. Ithaca: Cornell UP, 2013. Print.

Country Life. Dir. Michael Blakemore. Perf. Sam Neil, Gretta Scacchi, John Hargreaves, and Kerry Fox. 1994. Miramax Home Entertainment, 2012. DVD.

Dama s sobachkoi [*Дама с собочкой*; "Lady with a Little Dog"]. Dir. Iosif Kheifits. Lenfil'm, 1959.

Damrosch, David. *How To Read World Literature*. Oxford: Wiley, 2009. Print.

Dark Eyes. Dir. Nikita Mikhailov. Excelsior Film-TV, 1987. Film.

Dear Writer, Dear Actress: The Love Letters of Anton Chekhov and Olga Knipper. Ed. and trans. Jean Benedetti. Hopewell: Ecco, 1997. Print.

Delbanco, Nicholas. *The Sincerest Form: Writing Fiction by Imitation*. New York: McGraw, 2004. Print.

Deleuze, Gilles. *Cinema 2: The Time-Image*. Trans. Hugh Tomlinson and Robert Galeta. Minneapolis: U of Minnesota P, 1989. Print.

de Sherbinin, Julie. "Chekhov and Christianity: The Critical Evolution." *Chekhov Then and Now: The Reception of Chekhov in World Culture*. Ed. Douglas Clayton. New York: Lang, 1997. 285–94. Print.

———. *Chekhov and Russian Religious Culture: The Poetics of the Marian Paradigm*. Evanston: Northwestern UP, 1997. Print.

———. "The Poetics of Middle Ground: Revisiting 'The Lady with the Little Dog.'" *Anton Pavlovich Chekhov: Poetics—Hermeneutics—Thematics*. Ed. J. Douglas Clayton. Ottawa: Slavic Research Group, 2006. 179–81. Print.

Diadia Vania [*Дядя Ваня*; *Uncle Vanya*]. Dir. Andrei Konchalovsky. Perf. Sergei Bondarchuk, Irina Kupchenko, Irina Miroshnichenko, and Innokenti Smoktunovsky. Mosfilm, 1971. Krupni Plan, 2006. DVD.

Diadia Vania [*Дядя Ваня*; *Uncle Vanya*]. Dir. Georgi Tovstonogov. Perf. Oleg Basilashvili, Yevgeni Lebedev, Natalya Danilova, Kirill Lavrov, and Tatyana Bedova. 1986. Gosteleradiofond, 1999. VHS.

Dobroliubov, Nikolai. "Luch sveta v temnom tsarstve" ["Луч света в темном царстве"; "Ray of Light in the Kingdom of Darkness"]. *Sobranie sochinenii* [*Собрание сочинений*; "Collected Works"]. Vol. 6. Moscow: Khudozhestvennaia literatura, 1963. 289–363. Print.

Dorn, Michael L. "(In)Temperate Zones: Daniel Drake's Medico-moral Geographies of Urban Life in the Trans-Appalachian American West." *Journal of the History of Medicine* 55 (2000): 256–91. Print.

Dostoevsky, Fyodor. *Notes from the House of the Dead*. Trans. Boris Jakim. Grand Rapids: Eerdmans, 2013. Print.

Drake, Daniel. *A Systematic Treatise, Historical, Etiological, and Practical, on the Principal Diseases of the Interior Valley of North America, As They Appear in the Caucasian, African, Indian, and Esquimaux Varieties of Its Population*. 1850. Ed. S. Hanbury Smith and Francis G. Smith. Philadelphia: Lippincott, Grambo, 1854. Print. 2nd ser.

Dutton, Denis. *The Art Instinct*. New York: Bloomsbury, 2008. Print.

Edwards, Christine. *The Stanislavsky Heritage: Its Contribution to the Russian and American Theatre*. New York: New York UP, 1965. Print.

Efros, Anatoly. *The Joy of Rehearsal: Reflections on Interpretations and Practice*. Trans. James Thomas. New York: Lang, 2006. Print.

Elbow, Peter. *Writing without Teachers*. London: Oxford UP, 1973. Print.

Eliot, George. *Middlemarch*. New York: Modern Lib., 1984. Print.

Emerson, Caryl. "The Tolstoy Connection in Bakhtin." *Rethinking Bakhtin: Extensions and Challenges*. Ed. Gary Saul Morson and Emerson. Evanston: Northwestern UP, 1989. 149–70. Print.

Emerson, Ralph Waldo. "Nature." *Project Gutenberg*. 17 July 2009. Web. 22 Dec. 2012.

Epstein, Julia. "Historiography, Diagnosis, and Poetics." *Literature and Medicine* 11 (1992): 23–44. *Project MUSE*. Web. 18 Jan. 2015.

Fife, Jane Mattison. "Using *Facebook* to Teach Rhetorical Analysis." *Pedagogy: Critical Approaches to Teaching Literature, Language, Composition, and Culture* 10.3 (2010): 555–62. *Project MUSE*. Web. 26 Nov. 2012.

Filippov, Aleksei. "Doktor Dorn idet po sledu: Trepleva ubivaiut vse" ["Доктор Дорн идет по следу: Треплева убивают все"; "Doctor Dorn Is Following the Tracks: They All Kill Treplev"]. *Izvestiia* (Rossiia) [*Известия* (Россия); "The News" (Russia)]. Izvestiia, 28 Apr. 2001. Web. 11 Feb. 2013.

Finke, Michael. "Anton Pavlovich Chekhov (17 January 1860–2 July 1904)." *Russian Literature in the Age of Realism*. Ed. Alyssa Dinega Gillespie. Detroit: Gale, 2003. 54–79. Print. Vol. 277 of *Dictionary of Literary Biography*.

———. "Heal Thyself, Hide Thyself: Why Did Dr. Chekhov Ignore His TB?" *Chekhov the Immigrant* 285–97.

———. "Of Interpretation and Stolen Kisses: From Poetics to Metapoetics in Chekhov's 'The Kiss.'" Apollonio and Brintlinger 127–47.

———. *Seeing Chekhov: Life and Art*. Ithaca: Cornell UP, 2005. Print.

Fistioc, Mihaela. *The Beautiful Shape of the Good: Platonic and Pythagorean Themes in Kant's* Critique of the Power of Judgment. London: Routledge, 2002. Print.

"Forum on Translation." Moderated by Carol Apollonio Flath and Julie de Sherbinin. *Chekhov the Immigrant* 29–66.

Freeze, ChaeRan Y. *Jewish Marriage and Divorce in Imperial Russia*. Hanover: Brandeis UP, 2002. Print.

French, Philip. "Chekhov on Screen." *Cambridge Companion* 149–61.

Frieden, Nancy. *Russian Physicians in an Era of Reform and Revolution, 1856–1905*. Princeton: Princeton UP, 1981. Print.

Frierson, Cathy. *Peasant Icons: Representations of Rural People in Late-Nineteenth-Century Russia*. Oxford UP, 1993. Print.

Fuchs, Elinor. "Visit to a Small Planet: Some Questions to Ask a Play." *Theatre* 34.2 (2004): 4–9. Print.

Furstenberg, Gilberte. "Reading between the Cultural Lines." *Reading between the Lines: Perspectives on Foreign Language Literacy*. Ed. Peter C. Patriks. New Haven: Yale UP, 2003. 74–98. Print.

Garrard, Greg. *Ecocriticism: The New Critical Idiom*. New York: Routledge, 1997. Print.

Gentes, Andrew A. "No Kind of Liberal: Alexander II and the Sakhalin Penal Colony." *Jarbücher für Geschichte Osteuropas. Neue Folge* 54.3 (2006): 321–44. *JSTOR*. Web. 14 Aug. 2014.

Gerhart, Genevra. *The Russian's World: Life and Language*. 4th ed. Bloomington: Slavica, 2012. Print.

Gillés, Daniel. *Chekhov: Observer without Illusion*. Trans. Charles Lam Markmann. New York: Funk, 1968. Print.

Gilman, Richard. *Chekhov's Plays: An Opening into Eternity*. New Haven: Yale UP, 1995. Print.

Gitovich, N. I., ed. *A. P. Chekhov v vospominaniakh sovremennikov* [*А. П. Чехов в воспоминаниях современников*; "A. P. Chekhov in the Memoirs of Contemporaries"]. Moscow: Khudozhestvennaia Literatura, 1986. Print.

Gladstone, Bill. *Bernard Malamud's Collected Stories*. Gladstone, 27 Oct. 2011. Web. 10 May 2013.

Golomb, Harai. *A New Poetics of Chekhov's Plays: Presence through Absence*. Brighton: Sussex Academic, 2014. Print.

Gorky, Maksim. *Literary Portraits*. Trans. Ivy Litvinov. Moscow: Foreign Langs., 1956. Print.

Gotlieb, Vera. *Chekhov in Performance in Russia and Soviet Russia*. Cambridge: Chadwyck, 1984. Print.

Hahn, Beverly. *Chekhov: A Study of the Major Stories and Plays*. Cambridge: Cambridge UP, 1977. Print.

Hale, Allean. "Introduction: Two Masters, One Play." T. Williams ix–xx.

Hall, Edward. *The Hidden Dimension*. Garden City: Doubleday, 1966. Print.

———. *The Silent Language*. Garden City: Doubleday, 1959. Print.

Harrigan, Stephen Lawrence. "The Case History of Chekhov, Freud, and Conan Doyle." Diss. Yale U, 1991. Ann Arbor: UMI, 1994. Print.

Hawkins, Anne Hunsaker, and Marilyn Chandler McEntyre, eds. *Teaching Literature and Medicine*. New York: MLA, 2000. Print.

Heim, Michael Henry. "Translating Chekhov's Plays: A Collaboration between Translator, Director, and Actors." *Chekhov the Immigrant* 83–88.

Hensher, Philip. "Incomparable Naturalism." *Atlantic Monthly* Jan. 2002: 126–31. Print.

Hingley, Ronald. *A New Life of Anton Chekhov*. London: Oxford UP, 1976. Print.

Hirsch, August. *Handbook of Geographical and Historical Pathology*. Trans. Charles Creighton. 3 vols. London: New Sydenham Soc., 1883–86. Print.

Hobgood, Burnet M. "Stanislavski's Preface to *An Actor Prepares* and the Persona of Tortsov." *Theatre Journal* 43.2 (1991): 219–28. *JSTOR*. Web. 12 June 2012.

Holquist, Michael. *Dostoevsky and the Novel*. Evanston: Northwestern UP, 1986. Print.

Hyllegard, Karen H., et al. "An Exploratory Study of College Students' Fanning Behavior on *Facebook*." *College Student Journal* 45.3 (2011): 601–16. *Project Innovation*. Project Innovation, n.d. Web. 26 Nov. 2012.

Ignatieva, Maria. "The Flight of the Dead Bird: Chekhov's *The Seagull* and Williams's *The Notebook of Trigorin*." *Adapting Chekhov: The Text and Its Mutations*. Ed. Douglas Clayton and Yana Meerzon. New York: Routledge, 2013. 57–67. Print.

Ivanov, Andrey. "The Far East: Sakhalin." *The Physical Geography of Northern Eurasia*. Ed. Maria Shahgedanova. Oxford: Oxford UP, 2002. 428–31. Print.

Jackson, Robert Louis. "Chekhov's 'Rothschild's Fiddle': 'By the Rivers of Babylon' in Eastern Orthodox Liturgy." *Chekhov the Immigrant* 201–06.

———. "'If I Forget Thee, O Jerusalem': An Essay on Chekhov's 'Rothschild's Fiddle.'" Senderovich and Sendich 35–49.

———. "Kontsovka rasskaza 'Toska': Ironiia ili pafos?" ["Концовка рассказа 'Тоска': Ирония или пафос?"; "The Ending of the Story 'Grief': Irony or Pathos?"]. *Russian Literature* 40.3 (1996): 355–61. Print.

Jonas, Susan, Geoff Proehl, and Michael Lupu, eds. *Dramaturgy in the American Theatre: A Source Book*. Orlando: Harcourt, 1997. Print.

Jones, David Richard. *Great Directors at Work*. Berkeley: U of California P, 1986. Print.

Jones, Ryan Tucker. "Running into Whales: The History of the North Pacific from below the Waves." *American Historical Review* 118.1 (2013): 349–77. Print.

Josephson, Paul, Nicolai Dronin, Ruben Mnatsakanian, Aleh Cherp, Dmitry Efremenko, and Vladislav Larin. *An Environmental History of Russia*. Cambridge: Cambridge UP, 2013. Print.

Kant, Immanuel. *Critique of Judgment*. Trans J. H. Bernard. 1914. Mineola: Dover, 2005. Print.

Karlinsky, Simon. Introduction. *Letters of Anton Chekhov*. Trans. Michael Henry Heim and Simon Karlinsky. New York: Harper, 1973. 1–32. Print.

Kataev, Vladimir. *If Only We Could Know! An Interpretation of Chekhov*. Trans. Harvey Pitcher. Chicago: Dee, 2002. Print.

Katz, Leon. "The Compleat Dramaturg." Jonas, Proehl, and Lupu 115–20.

Kennan, George. *Siberia and the Exile System*. 1891. Chicago: U of Chicago P, 1958. Print.

Kheifits, Iosif Efimovich. *Poidem v kino!* [*Пойдем в кино!*; "Let's Go to the Cinema!"]. St. Petersburg: Iskusstvo, 1996. Print.

Kiceluk, Stephanie. "The Patient as Sign and Story: Disease Pictures, Life Histories, and the First Psychoanalytic Case History." *Journal of Clinical Psychoanalysis* 1 (1992): 336–67. Print.

Kirsch, Adam. "Chekhov in American." *Atlantic Online*. Atlantic Monthly Group, 1 July 1997. Web. 13 July 2013.

Knapp, Liza. "Fear and Pity in 'Ward Six': Chekhovian Catharsis." *Reading Chekhov's Text*. Ed. Robert L. Jackson. Evanston: Northwestern UP, 1993. 145–54. Print.

Knutson, Elizabeth M. "Teaching Whole Texts: Literature and Foreign Language Reading Instruction." *French Review* 67.1 (1993): 12–26. JSTOR. Web. 26 Nov. 2012.

Kostova-Panajotova, Magdalena. "'Chaika' Borisa Akunina kak zerkalo 'Chaiki' Chekhova" ["'Чайка' Бориса Акунина как зеркало 'Чайки' Чехова"; "*Seagull* of Boris Akunin as Mirror of Chekhov's *Seagull*"]. *Deti Ra* [*Дети Ра*; "The Children of Ra"] 19.13 (2005): n. pag. Deti Ra, n.d. Web. 11 Feb. 2013.

Krasilnikova, Elena. "Intertekstual'nye sviazi p'es B. Akunina i A. P. Chekhova 'Chaika'" ["Интертекстуальные связи пьес Б. Акунина и А. П. Чехова 'Чайка'"; "Intertextual Connections of the Plays of B. Akunin and A. P. Chekhov, *Seagull*]. Diss. 2008. Tula State Pedagogical U, 10 Feb. 2001. Web. 11 Feb. 2013. <www.dslib.net/russkij-jazyk/intertekstualnye-sviazi-pes-b-akunina-i-a-p-chekhova-chajka.htm>.

Kugel, Aleksandr R. (Homo novus). "Chaika" ["Чайка"; "*Seagull*"]. *Peterburgskaia gazeta* [*Петербургская газета*; "Petersburg Gazette"] 19 Oct. 1896: 3. Print.

Kurylo, C. C. "Chekhov and Katherine Mansfield." Diss. U of North Carolina, Chapel Hill, 1974. Print.

Lantz, K. A. *Anton Chekhov: A Reference Guide to Literature*. Boston: Hall, 1985. Print.

Lapushin, Radislav. *Dew on the Grass: The Poetics of Inbetweenness in Chekhov*. New York: Lang, 2010. Print.

———. "Potselui" ["Поцелуй"; "The Kiss"]. *A. P. Chekhov: Entsiklopediia* 152–55.

Leddy, Thomas. *The Extraordinary in the Ordinary: The Aesthetics of Everyday Life*. Peterborough: Broadview, 2012. Print.

Leighton, Lauren. *A Bibliography of Anton Chekhov in English*. Lewiston: Mellen, 2005. Print.

Levertov, Denise. "Chekhov on the West Heath." McConkey 137–49.

Levine, Norman D. *Malaria in the Interior Valley of North America: A Selection from* A Systematic Treatise . . . *by Daniel Drake*. Urbana: U of Illinois P, 1964. Print. Facsim. Rpts. in the History of Science 3.

Leyda, Jay. *Kino: A History of the Russian and Soviet Film*. 3rd ed. Princeton: Princeton UP, 1983. Print.

Like Life: The Making of Vanya on Forty-Second Street. Criterion Collection, 2012. DVD.

Lippard, Lucy. "All over the Place." *The Lure of the Local: Sense of Place in a Multi-centered Society*. New York: New, 1998. 4–20. Print.

London, Todd. *Andre Gregory Sees the Light*. Theater Communications Group, n.d. Web. 20 Feb. 2014.

Lyotard, Jean-François. *The Postmodern Condition: A Report on Knowledge*. Trans. Geoff Bennington and Brian Massumi. Minneapolis: U of Minnesota P, 1984. Print.

MacIntyre, Alisdair. "The Virtues, the Unity of a Human Life, and the Concept of a Tradition." *After Virtue: A Study in Moral Theory*. Notre Dame: U of Notre Dame P, 1984. 2nd ed. 204–25. Print.

Magarshack, David. *Stanislavsky: A Life*. London: Faber, 1986. Print.

Malcolm, Janet. *Reading Chekhov: A Critical Journey*. New York: Random, 2002. Print.

Mansfield, Katherine. *Stories*. New York: Vintage, 1991. Print.

Markandaya, Kamala. *Nectar in a Sieve*. New York: Signet, 2002. Print.

Markovin, A. P. "Historical Sketch of the Development of Soviet Medical Geography." *Soviet Geography: Review and Translation* 3.8 (1962): 1–12. Print.

———. *Razvitie meditsinskoi geografii v Rossii* [*Развитие медицинской географии в Россиu*; "Development of Medical Geography in Russia"]. Saint Petersburg: Nauka, 1993. Print.

Marks, Steven G. *How Russia Shaped the Modern World*. Princeton: Princeton UP, 2003. Print.

May, Rachel. *The Translator in the Text: On Reading Russian Literature in English*. Evanston: Northwestern UP, 1994. Print.

McConkey, James, ed. *Chekhov and Our Age: Responses to Chekhov by American Writers and Scholars*. Ithaca: Cornell U Center for Intl. Studies, 1978. Print.

McLean, Hugh. "Chekhov, Anton Pavlovich, 1860–1904." *Handbook of Russian Literature*. Ed. Victor Terras. New Haven: Yale UP, 1985. 79–81. Print.

Meister, Charles. *Chekhov Bibliography: Works in English by and about Anton Chekhov: American, British, and Canadian Performances*. Jefferson: McFarland, 1985. Print.

Messud, Claire. "Chekhov and Aspiring Writers." *Chekhov the Immigrant* 169–75.

Metz, Christian. "On the Impression of Reality in the Cinema." *Film Language: A Semiotics of the Cinema*. Trans. Michael Taylor. Chicago: U of Chicago P, 1991. 3–15. Print.

Milner–Gulland, Robin. *The Russians: People of Europe*. Oxford: Blackwell, 1997. Print.

Mirsky, D. S. *A History of Russian Literature from Its Beginnings to 1900*. Ed. Francis J. Whitfield. New York: Vintage, 1958. Print.

Mitchell, John D. *Staging Chekhov:* Cherry Orchard. New York: Inst. for Advanced Studies in the Theatre Arts, 1991. Print.

Mitman, Gregg, and Ronald L. Numbers. "From Miasma to Asthma: The Changing Fortunes of Medical Geography in America." *History and Philosophy of the Life Sciences* 25 (2003): 391–412. *JSTOR*. Web. 14 Aug. 2014.

Morson, Gary Saul. Anna Karenina *in Our Time: Seeking More Wisely*. New Haven: Yale UP, 2007. Print.

———. *Narrative and Freedom: The Shadows of Time*. New Haven: Yale UP, 1994. Print.

The Moscow Art Theatre: Letters. Ed. and trans. Jean Benedetti. New York: Routledge, 1991. Print.

Mulvey, Laura. *Death 24x a Second: Stillness and the Moving Image*. London: Reaktion, 2006. Print.

Nabokov, Vladimir. "Anton Chekhov." *Lectures on Russian Literature*. New York: Harcourt, 1981. 245–96. Print.

———. *Strong Opinions*. New York: McGraw, 1973. Print.

Nemirovich-Danchenko, Vladimir I. "Iz proshlogo" ["Из прошлого"; "From the Past"]. *Chekhov i teatr* [*Чехов и театр*; "Chekhov and Theater"]. Ed. Evgenii D. Surkov. Moscow: Iskusstvo, 1961. 296–308. Print.

Nilsson, Nils Ake. *Studies in Čechov's Narrative Technique*. Stockholm: Almqvist, 1968. Print.

O'Connor, Flannery. *The Habit of Being: Letters of Flannery O'Connor*. Ed. Sally Fitzgerald. New York: Farrar, 1988. Print.

O'Connor, Frank. "The Slave's Son." *The Lonely Voice: A Study of the Short Story*. Cleveland: World, 1962. 78–98. Print.

O'Connor, Katherine Tiernan. "Chekhov's Death: His Textual Past Recaptured." *Studies in Poetics*. Ed. Elena Semeka-Pankratov. Columbus: Slavica, 1995. 39–50. Print.

Pallot, Judith. "Russia's Penal Peripheries: Space, Place, and Penalty in Soviet and post-Soviet Russia." *Transactions of the Institute of British Geographers* ns 30 (2005): 98–112. *JSTOR*. Web. 14 Aug. 2014.

Parts, Lyudmila. *The Chekhovian Intertext: Dialogue with a Classic*. Columbus: Ohio State UP, 2008. Print.

Pasternatskii, I. "Istero-epilepsiia" ["Истеро-эпилепсия"; "Hystero-Epilepsy"]. *Vrach* [Врач; "Doctor"] 3 (1881): 49–50. Print.

Paul, Bimal Kanti. "Approaches to Medical Geography: An Historical Perspective." *Social Science and Medicine* 20.4 (1985): 399–409. Print.

Peace, Richard. *Chekhov: A Study of the Major Plays*. New Haven: Yale UP, 1983. Print.

Piglia, Ricardo. "Theses on the Short Story." *New Left Review* 70 (2011): 63–66. Print.

Pitcher, Harvey. *The Chekhov Play: A New Interpretation*. New York: Barnes, 1973. Print.

———. *Chekhov's Leading Lady: A Portrait of the Actress Olga Knipper*. New York: Watts, 1980. Print.

Plato. *Complete Works*. Ed. John M. Cooper. Indianapolis: Hackett, 1997. Print.

———. *Republic*. Trans. G. M. A. Grube. Rev. trans. C. D. C. Reeve. Plato, *Complete Works* 971–1223.

———. *Symposium*. Trans Alexander Nehamas and Paul Woodruff. Plato, *Complete Works* 457–505.

Poggioli, Renato. "Storytelling in a Double Key." Chekhov, *Anton Chekhov's Short Stories* 307–28.

Popkin, Cathy. "Chekhov as Ethnographer: Epistemological Crisis on Sakhalin Island." *Slavic Review* 51.1 (1992): 36–51. *JSTOR*. Web. 14 Aug. 2014.

———. "Hysterical Episodes: Case Histories and Silent Subjects." *Self and Story in Russian History*. Ed. Laura Engelstein and Stephanie Sandler. Ithaca: Cornell UP, 2000. 189–216. Print.

Porter, Roy. *The Greatest Benefit to Mankind: A Medical History of Humanity*. New York: Norton, 1998. Print.

Postlewait, Thomas. *The Cambridge Introduction to Theatre Historiography*. Cambridge: Cambridge UP, 2009. Print.

Program notes. *The Anton Chekhov Collection*. BBC Worldwide Ltd. Programs, 2008. DVD.

Prose, Francine. "Francine Prose: By the Book." *New York Times*. New York Times, 3 Jan. 2013. Web. 3 Jan. 2013.

———. "Learning from Chekhov." *Chekhov the Immigrant* 177–88.

Pshenitsyn, Sergei. "Cultural Models and the Meaning of a Translated Work." *Translation and Meaning*. Ed. Marcel Thebin and Barbara Lewandowska-Tomoszczyk. Maastricht: Maastricht School of Translation and Interpreting, 2001. 357–64. Print.

Pugh, David. *The Dialectic of Love*. Montreal: McGill-Queen's UP, 1997. Print.

Ramage, John D., John C. Bean, and June Johnson. *The Allyn and Bacon Guide to Writing*. 6th ed. Boston: Longman, 2012. Print.

Rayfield, Donald. *Anton Chekhov: A Life*. New York: Henry Holt, 1998. Print.

———. *Understanding Chekhov: A Critical Study of Chekhov's Prose and Drama*. Madison: U of Wisconsin P, 1999. Print.

Reid, Jean. "'We Don't Twitter, We Facebook': An Alternative Pedagogical Space That Enables Critical Practice in Relation to Writing." *English Teaching: Practice and Critique* 10.1 (2011): 58–80. *ProQuest*. Web. 26 Nov. 2012.

Remizova, Maria. "Chuchelo Chekhova" ["Чучело Чехова"; "Chekhov's Stuffed Bird"]. *Nezavisimaia gazeta* [*Независимая газета*; "Independent Press"]. Nezavisimaia Gazeta, 28 Apr. 2000. Web. 11 Feb. 2013.

Rohter, Larry. "Translation as Literary Ambassador." *New York Times*. New York Times, 7 Dec. 2010. Web. 15 Dec. 2012.

Romance with a Double Bass. Dir. Kai Hansen. 1911. Milestone Cinamatheque, 2009. DVD.

Romance with a Double Bass. Dir. Robert Young. Anton Films, 1974. Film.

Ross, Zackary. "Opening *The Notebook of Trigorin*: Tennessee Williams's Adaptation of Chekhov's *The Seagull*." *Comparative Drama* 45.3 (2011): 245–70. Print.

Rossolimo, G. I. "Vospominaniia o Chekhove" ["Воспоминания о Чехове"; "Recollections of Chekhov"]. Gitovich 428–38.

Rueckert, William. "Literature and Ecology: An Experiment in Ecocriticism." *The Ecocriticism Reader: Landmarks in Literary Ecology*. Ed. Cheryll Glotfelt and Harold Fromm. Athens: U of Georgia P, 1996. 105–23. Print.

Rupke, Nicolaas A., ed. *Medical Geography in Historical Perspective*. London: Wellcome Trust Centre for the History of Medicine, 2000. Print.

Sanders, Julie. *Adaptation and Appropriation*. London: Routledge, 2007. Print.

Say, Jean-Baptiste, and Frédéric Bastiat. *Traktat politicheskoi ekonomii* [*Трактат политической экономии*; "Treatise on Political Economy"]. Moscow: O. I. Lashkevich, 1896. Print.

Schmidt, Paul, trans. *The Plays Of Anton Chekhov*. New York: Harper, 1997. Print.

The Seagull. By Anton Chekhov. Trans. and adapt. Stark Young. Dir. Nikos Psacharopoulos and John J. Desmond. New York: Image Entertainment, Broadway Theatre Archive, 2002(?). DVD.

Senderovich, Savely. "Anton Chekhov and St. George the Dragonslayer: An Introduction to the Theme." Senderovich and Sendich 167–87.

———. *Chekhov—s glazu na glaz: Istoriia odnoi oderzhimosti A. P. Chekhova: Opyt fenomenologii tvorchestva* [*Чехов—с глазу на глаз: История одной одержимости А. П. Чехова: Опыт феноменологии творчества*; "Chekhov—Eye to Eye: The History of an Obsession: An Essay in the Phenomenology of Creation"]. Saint Petersburg: Bulanin, 1994. Print.

———. "*The Cherry Orchard*: Čechov's Last Testament." *Russian Literature* 35 (1994): 223–42. Print.

———. "Towards Chekhov's Deeper Reaches." Senderovich and Sendich 1–8.

Senderovich, Savely, and Munir Sendich. *Anton Chekhov Rediscovered: A Collection of New Studies with a Comprehensive Bibliography*. East Lansing: Russian Lang. Journal, 1987. Print.

Senelick, Laurence. *Anton Chekhov*. London: Macmillan, 1985. Print. Macmillan Modern Dramatists.

———. *The Chekhov Theatre: A Century of the Plays in Performance*. Cambridge: Cambridge UP, 1997. Print.

———. "Seeing Chekhov Whole." *Chekhov the Immigrant* 65–78.

Shalamov, Varlam Tikhonovich. *Kolyma Tales*. Trans. John Glad. New York: Norton, 1980. Print.

Shaw, J. Thomas. *The Transliteration of Modern Russian for English-Language Publications*. Madison: U of Wisconsin P, 1967. Print.

Shepard, Paul. *Nature and Madness*. Athens: U of Georgia P, 1982. Print.

Shereshevskii, A. M. "The Development of the Psychiatric Periodic Press in Russia between the Late Eighteenth and Early Twentieth Centuries." *Journal of Russian and East European Psychiatry* 27 (1994–95): 155–69. Print.

Shermer, Michael. *How We Believe*. 2nd ed. New York: Henry Holt, 2003. Print.

Shumway, Nicolas. "Searching for Averroes: Reflections on Why It Is Desirable and Impossible to Teach Culture in Foreign Language Courses." *Redefining the Boundaries of Language Study*. Ed. Claire D. Kramsch. Boston: Heinle, 1995. 251–60. Print.

Silko, Leslie Marmon. *Ceremony*. New York: Penguin, 2006. Print.

Simmons, Ernest J. *Chekhov: A Biography*. Boston: Atlantic Monthly, 1962. Print.

Skaftymov, A. P. "Principles of Structure in Chekhov's Plays." *Chekhov: A Collection* 69–88.

Slonim, Marc. *Russian Theater from the Empire to the Soviets*. Cleveland: World, 1961. Print.

Smirnova, A. P. "Chekhov i kino" ["Чехов и кино"; "Chekhov and Cinema"]. *A. P. Chekhov: Entsiklopediia* 608–20.

Smith, Anthony. "Nation and Ethnoscape." *Myths and Memories of Nations*. London: Oxford UP, 1999. 149–59. Print.

Solzhenitsyn, Aleksandr Isaevich. *The Gulag Archipelago, 1918–1956: An Experiment in Literary Investigation*. 3 vols. Trans. Thomas P. Whitney. New York: Harper, 1974–79. Print.

———. *One Day in the Life of Ivan Denisovich*. Trans. Ralph Parker. New York: Dutton, 1963. Print.

Special Focus Issue: Chekhov and Film. Spec. issue of *North American Chekhov Society Bulletin* 8.3 (1999): 1–12. Print.

Stam, Robert. "Introduction: The Theory and Practice of Adaptation." *Literature and Film: A Guide to the Theory and Practice of Adaptation*. Ed. Stam and Alessandra Raengo. Malden: Blackwell, 2005. 1–52. Print.

Standards for Foreign Language Learning: Preparing for the Twenty-First Century. ACTFL, n.d. Web. 8 Jan. 2015.

Stanislavsky, Konstantin. *An Actor Prepares*. Trans. Elizabeth Reynolds Hapgood. New York: Theatre Arts, 1936. Print.

———. "A. P. Chekhov at the Arts Theater." Turkov 89–131.

———. "A. P. Chekhov v Khudozhestvennom teatre (Vospominaniia)" ["А. П. Чехов в Художественном театре (Воспоминания)"; "A. P. Chekhov in the Art Theater: Recollections"]. Gitovich 373–416.

———. "From *The Actor*: Work on Oneself." Trans. Jean Benedetti. Introd. Sharon Marie Carnicke. *TDR* 37.1 (1993): 38–42. *JSTOR*. Web. 7 Dec. 2012.

———. *My Life in Art*. Trans. and ed. Jean Benedetti. London: Routledge, 2008. Print.

———. *My Life in Art*. Trans. J. J. Robins. New York: Theatre Art, 1952. Print.

Stanislawski, Michael. "Russia." *The YIVO Encyclopedia of Jews in Eastern Europe*. YIVO Inst. for Jewish Research, n.d. Web. 3 June 2014. <http://www.yivoencyclopedia.org/article.aspx/Russia/Russian_Empire>.

States, Bert O. *Great Reckonings in Little Rooms: On the Phenomenology of Theater*. Berkeley: U of California P, 1985. Print.

Stein, Gertrude. *The Autobiography of Alice B. Toklas*. New York: Random, 2000. E-book.

Stepanov, Andrei D. *Problemy kommunikatsii u Chekhova* [*Проблемы коммуникации у Чехова*; "Problems of Communication in Chekhov"]. Moscow: Iazyki Slavianskoi Kul'tury, 2005. Print.

Stewart, Maaja A. "Scepticism and Belief in Chekhov and Anderson." *Studies in Short Fiction* 9 (1972): 29–40. Print.

Stroeva, Mariia N. "Chekhovskie spektakli MKhT" ["Чеховские спектакли МХТ"; "Chekhov Productions of the MAT"]. *K. S. Stanislavskii: Materialy: Pis'ma:*

Issledovaniia [*К. С. Станиславский: Материалы: Письма: Исследования*; "K. S. Stanislavsky: Materials, Letters, Studies]. Ed. I. E. Grabaria et al. Moscow: Akademii Nauk, 1955. 613–70. Print.

Stull, William L. "Raymond Carver." *Dictionary of Literary Biography Yearbook: 1988*. Ed. J. M. Brook. Detroit: Gale Research, 1989. 199–213. Print.

Styan, J. L. *Chekhov in Performance: A Commentary on the Major Plays*. Cambridge: Cambridge UP, 1971. Print.

Taylor, Robert, et al. "Student Learning through Social Media." *Journal of Sociological Research* 3.2 (2012): 29–35. Macrothink Inst., n.d. Web. 26 Nov. 2012.

Thacker, Robert. *Alice Munro: Writing Her Lives*. Toronto: McClelland, 2005. Print.

Tolstoy, Leo. "The Death of Ivan Ilych." Trans. Aylmer Maude. *"The Death of Ivan Ilych" and Other Stories*. New York: New Amer. Lib., 1960. 95–156. Print.

———. "How Much Land Does a Man Need?" *The Portable Tolstoy*. Ed. John Bayley. New York: Viking, 1978. 506–22. Print.

———. *What Is Art?* Trans. Aylmer Maude. New York Public Lib., 8 Feb. 2008. Web. 22 Dec. 2012.

Turgenev, Ivan. *Sketches from a Hunter's Album*. Trans. Richard Freeborn. London: Penguin, 1990. Print.

Turkov, Andrei, ed. and introd. *Anton Chekhov and His Times*. Trans. Cynthia Carlile and Sharon McKee. Fayetteville: U of Arkansas P, 1995. Print.

Uncle Vanya. By Anton Chekhov. Dir. Stuart Burge. Perf. Laurence Olivier, Michael Redgrave, Rosemary Harris, Joan Plowright, Max Adrian, and Sybil Thorndike. British Home Entertainment, 1963. Videocasette.

Uncle Vanya. By Anton Chekhov. Dir. John Goetz and Franchot Tone. Perf. Tone, George Voskovec, Dolores Dorn, and Peggy McCay. 1957. VCI Entertainment, 2010. DVD.

Uncle Vanya. By Anton Chekhov. Dir. Christopher Morahan. Perf. Anthony Hopkins, Freddie Jones, Jenifer Armitage, Ann Bell, and Roland Culver. BBC, 1970. BBC Video, 2008. DVD. Anton Chekhov Collection.

Uncle Vanya. By Anton Chekhov. Dir. Gregory Mosher. Perf. Ian Holm, David Warner, Mary Elizabeth Mastrantonio, and Rebecca Pidgeon. BBC, 1991. BBC Video, 2008. DVD. Anton Chekhov Collection.

Urban, Peter. *Anton Čechov: Sein Leben in Bildern*. Zurich: Diogenes, 1987. Print.

Valencius, Conevery Bolton. "Chekhov's *Sakhalin Island* as Medical Geography." *Chekhov the Immigrant* 299–314.

———. *"The Health of the Country": How American Settlers Understood Themselves and Their Land*. New York: Basic, 2002. Print.

———. "Histories of Medical Geography." Rupke 3–30.

Valency, Maurice. The Breaking String: The Plays of Anton Chekhov. New York: Oxford UP, 1966. Print.

Vanya on Forty-Second Street. Dir. Louis Malle. Perf. Wallace Shawn, Julianne Moore, Phoebe Brand, Lynn Cohen, George Gaynes, Jerry Mayer, Larry Pine, and Brooke Smith. Sony Pictures Classics, 1994. Film.

Vernet, Marc. *Figures de l'absence: De l'invisible au cinema*. Paris: Cahiers du cinéma, 1988. Print.

Vineberg, Steven. "*Vanya on Forty-Second Street*: An American *Vanya*." *The Criterion Collection*. Criterion Collection, n.d. 9 Mar. 2012. Web. 20 Feb. 2014.

Wasson, Sam. "Filming *Osmosis*: A Conversation with Declan Quinn." *The Criterion Collection*. Criterion Collection, 9 Mar. 2012. Web. 20 Feb. 2014.

Weiner, Douglas R. *A Little Corner of Freedom: Russian Nature Protection from Stalin to Gorbachev*. Berkeley: U of California P, 1999. Print.

———. *Models of Nature: Ecology, Conservation, and Cultural Revolution in Soviet Russia*. Rev. ed. Pittsburgh: U of Pittsburgh P, 2000. Print.

Welty, Eudora. "Reality in Chekhov's Stories." *The Eye of the Story: Selected Essays and Reviews*. New York: Random, 1978. 61–81. Print.

Whyman, Rose. *Anton Chekhov*. London: Routledge, 2011. Print. Routledge Modern and Contemporary Dramatists.

Wierzbicka, Anna. *Semantics, Culture, and Cognition: Universal Human Concepts in Culture-Specific Configurations*. Oxford: Oxford UP, 1992. Print.

Williams, Robert C. "The Russian Soul: A Study in European Thought and Non-European Nationalism." *Journal of the History of Ideas* 31 (1970): 573–88. Print.

Williams, Tennessee. *The Notebook of Trigorin: A Free Adaptation of Anton Chekhov's* The Seagull. New York: Dramatists Play Service, 1997. Print. Based on trans. of Ann Dunnigan.

Williams, William Carlos. *Paterson*. New York: New Directions, 1995. Print.

Winner, Thomas. *Chekhov and His Prose*. New York: Holt, Rinehart, 1966. Print.

Woolf, Virginia. "The Russian Point of View." *Collected Essays*. London: Hogarth, 1966. 238–46. Print.

Youngblood, Denise J. *The Magic Mirror: Moviemaking in Russia, 1908–1918*. Madison: U of Wisconsin P, 1999. Print.

INDEX OF WORKS BY CHEKHOV

INDEX OF NAMES